OREALLA

Other novels by Roy Heath:

The Murderer
From the Heat of the Day
One Generation
Genetha
Kwaku

OREALLA

a novel by
ROY HEATH

ALLISON & BUSBY
LONDON

First published 1984
by Allison and Busby Limited
6a Noel Street, London W1V 3RB

British Library Cataloguing in Publication Data
Heath, Roy A.K.
  Orealla.
  I. Title
  813 **(F)**   PR9320.9.H4

  ISBN 0-85031-528-X

Set in 10/11pt Baskerville by Ann Buchan Typesetters
and printed in Great Britain by
Billings and Sons Ltd, Worcester.

To all the de Weevers

1

BEN HAD known Tina as a schoolgirl and used to talk to her over the paling fence during recreation when she was supervising the younger children in the playground. Sometimes her back would be towards him while she pretended to be interested in what the little ones were doing. But he would stare at her until she turned around, slowly, as if he held her on a string.

One day she did not come to school and Ben kept watching the school gate, dragging out the grooming of one of the horses for which he was responsible. In the afternoon just after school began, a lady called out from the gate of the yard he was working in, and a single look was enough to tell him she was Tina's mother.

"I want to talk to you," she told him, not waiting for him to return her call.

He went up to her on the bridge, trying to hide his nervousness, although he had done her daughter no harm. She looked him straight in the eye and started talking. Tina was her only daughter and was in love with him. Had he ever touched her? No, he had only spoken to her over the paling, and after all she was still at school.

"Oh, these days!" she said, waving her hand. "She feel flattered that a grown man like you show a interest in her. I could tell the first day you talk to her, the first day; from the way she start ironing her school uniform. You ever touch her?"

"No," Ben answered, surprised at his mild-mannered way with the lady. He knew then that he wanted to marry Tina, though he had vowed never to marry, because he was the sort who was liable to wake up one morning and decide he did not like his job and clear off in the direction of the trade wind. "No, I never touched her, lady . . . . Why isn't she at school today?"

"You noticed?" she said with a suffering look. "She not well."

"What's wrong with her?"

"She say she got her period. Is true. 'But is not the first time and it never stop you from going to school,' I tell her. She din' answer 'cause she's not the lying kind. Straight as a locust tree. Well, if you din' touch her, why she iron her uniform twice?"

Ben mastered his growing irritation, since he did not want her to forbid Tina to see him. He ended by promising Tina's mother not to touch her daughter; and from that day she started giving him food

5

whenever she cooked something special. She brought it herself in an enamel saucepan with a tight-fitting lid and stayed, to admire the horses she said, but in fact to let him know that she saw him as a protector of her only child and under the obligation to keep his promise.

"I'd make any sacrifice for Tina," she told him one day. "Any sacrifice." She would make any sacrifice to keep him from touching her daughter.

He was tempted to take her at her word, but he had lived long enough to know how devious Georgetown women could be. If he lifted up her skirt she would be able to return to Tina in triumph and say, "You see! Now you can't meet him no more." Besides, what was he to make of her not wanting him to *touch* Tina? Suppose she was jealous of her? If that was it, he had to be even more careful. With women it was always *possibilities*. Only a fool would pretend to understand what was behind their words.

She never tired of repeating the same thing when she came with her two-layered saucepan with rice in one bowl and fish or beef in the other: "I'd make *any* sacrifice for Tina." Even after Tina had been taken on at the Public Hospital as an apprentice nurse, her mother kept talking of this sacrifice.

Ben asked her one day if she would permit Tina to go to the vaudeville with him.

"Why not? No one's got anything to hide."

That night he went to their house, a neat cottage with yellow shutters and a garden.

"She's nearly ready," her mother said as she opened the door.

He was suprised to see Tina's mother all dolled up in beads and a black dress as though she were in mourning; and when Tina came out some minutes later there was little to choose between them. These were not people with a single going-out dress carefully put away on a clothes-hanger that allowed you to recognize them from afar, he reflected.

"Well, let's go then," said the mother.

"I . . . I . . . " Ben stuttered, only now grasping the situation.

"Ma's coming too," Tina said with an expression that made it plain she had nothing to do with the arrangement.

"I see," her mother put in. "Well, if you don't want me to . . . . "

Neither Tina nor Ben did anything to help her and they stood in silence, avoiding one another's eyes.

6

"Well, go on," Tina's mother said finally. "Go on and enjoy yourselves."

"But you're dressed and everything," Tina said, genuinely concerned.

"Why not come then?" Ben said. "And some time next week I can take Tina out alone."

It was the first time he detected an expression of annoyance, even hatred in her eyes. But she covered up almost at once.

"Next time you'll go out alone," she agreed. "After all, who wants a old woman going out with them?"

More than once he tried to take Tina's hand during the show, but she would not let him; and even when he looked at her pointedly she gazed straight ahead. Thus they sat from beginning to end, her mother and he on either side of her; and when the last number was over and the audience in the pit started throwing money on to the stage he had to exercise the utmost control and resist the impulse to jump up and leave the hall.

They left with the crowd, which thinned out as people went off down the side streets or stopped by the nut-sellers' stalls, lit by pale lamps that puffed their flames in the direction of the blustering wind. Around them people were calling to one another and an outburst of laughter was followed by the sound of running and then another peal of laughter as one youth caught up with another.

"How you young people enjoy yourselves!" Tina's mother said. "When I was your age I had to be home by six. And as for vaudevilles . . . . "

Tina took his hand under cover of the dark and Ben's knees nearly gave way with relief.

"How long you been working with horses?" her mother enquired, aware of what was going on between them.

"Since I was a boy," he answered. "My father had horses."

"Horses," she muttered. "Tina's uncle was in the horse guards. He rode a horse as if he was born on one. He only retired two years, in 1925."

Ben pressed the back of his hand against Tina's thigh and felt the border of her drawers beneath her thin dress and petticoat. Passing a line of East Indian beggars asleep on the pavement, they were obliged to separate and come together further on. He and Tina took each other's hands again and he started thinking of his father who, according to Ben's grandmother, went to Venezuela, where he learned to paint dark-skinned Harlequins with menacing smiles.

"I study to help her," Tina's mother said, "but she din' want any help."

"Who're you talking about, Ma?" Tina asked.

"About you."

"Did you like the show?" Ben enquired.

"I liked it, Ben. It's years since I've been to one. When you get married to Tina the two of you won't go off to shows like tonight and hold hands in the dark."

Tina let go of his hand.

"I've got a mind to how people're living," her mother continued. "If they're living good, I'm glad."

Tina began trembling, and only then did Ben understand that their outing was not as straightforward a matter as he imagined.

"I can't lie, Ben," the mother continued after a long pause. "I came from a back yard, unlike my husband. And the last thing I want to see is for Tina to end up in a back yard."

"Ma!" Tina protested in her gentle tone.

"I can't understand," her mother went on, "how a man who does talk like you can spend all his time with horses."

"That's not what you said yesterday, Ma," Tina cut her short.

"Yesterday . . . . I've never held his work against him before tonight. But the sight of all those loafers coming out of the show with not a cent to their name made me think."

Tina was as simple as she was complicated, and that was why Ben did not flee. He was convinced, somehow, that if he stopped seeing Tina it would be her mother who would seek him out and tell him to come back. Despite her objections to the difference in age between her daughter and him, despite his lowly work, Ben knew that she thought highly of him. Yet she was running the risk of driving him away with her observations.

They went by a hall from which the feeble sound of singing came. There could not have been more than three or four in the congregation. Finally they stopped in front of Tina's house. Her mother looked up at it as if it belonged to someone else, while Tina and Ben stared at each other in the dark.

"Tomorrow," he said in a louder voice than he had intended, "I'll bring a letter asking for Tina's hand in marriage."

The mother stared at him. Then, having got over her surprise, she grasped his hand with both of hers.

8

"I knew you were an honourable man, Ben," she said fervently. "Forgive me. Forgive me! It was when I did see all those young people with nothing in their heads except music that I had bad thoughts."

"I —" Ben tried to speak.

"No!" she exclaimed. "Tina can tell you what I'm really like. *I* apologize. Come tomorrow. Tomorrow." She ran up the stairs and closed the door behind her, leaving the two young people at the foot of the stairs.

"I understand," Ben told Tina. "Don't tell me anything."

She let him paw her, leaving him dumbfounded at her trust. He had made a resolution not to marry, yet he was on the threshold of marriage. A slight girl with eyes as still as a forest pool had bewitched him into promising to write for her hand in the formal manner which the most straitlaced people were in the habit of using. An absurd thought passed through his mind: suppose he became deaf and lost her!

"Suppose I became sick?" he asked her.

"Everybody does get sick," she said.

He stroked her neck in the most tender gesture he had ever made and she responded by taking his hand and leading him under her house, where they kissed long and passionately among the piles of discarded furniture. They talked in a way that would have been unthinkable the day before, when her mother might have come downstairs on the flimsiest of excuses and ordered Tina upstairs to do something or other. A tree next door made a creaking sound as it rubbed against a fence post, and at that late hour they could hear the footfalls of passers-by dying away on the road where the lamplight was broken by the shadows of trees and paling fences. Briefly someone walked across the room above their heads.

"It's Ma," Tina said.

When she left him she went up the back stairs instead of the front, perhaps to avoid being seen by neighbours. Ben carefully lifted the latch on the gate and left the yard, feeling that he had been singled out to be the caretaker of a precious possession.

On his way home he considered the things he remembered her mother saying. He must not get the idea that she was courting him: what she was doing was for Tina's sake, because she thought her daughter could not take care of herself. Did he like Tina's father? A shadowy figure who hardly ever spoke, he was never to be seen without his panama hat, under which he looked handsome and authoritative. Without it he was prey to the conviction that people found him ridiculous.

The women with whom Ben had been associated until then knew all about him, about the way he earned most of his money, not by caring for horses but by stealing from people's houses and selling what he stole. Of course a lot of people knew you could not live on the wages the owners of horses paid, but those who liked you either pretended ignorance of what you earned or put the matter out of their minds. "Ben is good with horses." Not: "How does he live doing that job?" Those who did not care for him, on the other hand, would make sure the woman he was friendly with knew that it was impossible to keep body and soul together on a groom's wages. Although Ben knew how Tina's family kept to themselves and were protected from gossip, he dreaded being informed that their association must end because of what one of her parents had been told.

The more he reflected on the relationship between Tina and himself, the more reasons he found for his attachment. She was born in the house she and her parents occupied, while he had lived in various villages in Berbice and the Courantyne, ending up in Skeldon with his grandmother before he came to Georgetown. It seemed to him extraordinary that anyone could have enjoyed such stability. The painted shutters that opened upwards as in a salute were old and solid; even the debris under the house was the waste of permanence, of years of occupation, like the cast-off garments of an ageing generation which litter the bottom of trunks. *"Now and ever shall be . . . ."* He had never known anything like it, the fascination this woman exercised over him, the power of louvred shutters opening upwards, of cats asleep in the shadow of a porch, of words in a certain order, of tastes that reach deep into the memory, of a friend walking on the other side of the road, of masked faces. She wore a black dress to protect her innocence from his lechery, because God would not have him touch her, a mesmeric flower not yet ready to be crushed.

2

MABEL WAS a few months younger than Tina and used to attend the same school. Having stood on the sidelines while Ben was courting, she only showed an interest in him after he got married. She told him how she used to watch him talking to Tina over the paling, half-hidden behind a wooden pillar. Not once had he caught her, nor suspected from a glance or gesture that she was interested. It was a few weeks after his marriage that she walked boldly into the yard and made her way between the flanks of the horses, something few women would have done.

"So you married her," she said to him without so much as an introduction.

"Who're you?" Ben asked, pretending he had never set eyes on her.

"I used to go to the same school as Tina, next door."

"What's your name?"

"Why you want to know my name for?"

"You're fresh for someone not long out of school," he told her. "You know what happens to fresh girls?"

"I'm seventeen . . . . You don't believe me? I was born in 1909. I know you're married and living with her and her parents."

She did not come back until one morning months later when she rushed in all breathless from the road to shelter from the rain.

"You ever come away from them horses?" she asked.

"Why you ask? I bet your heart's beating hard from running."

He took her hand and placed it against his chest. "You see, you can't feel a thing," he said. "No heartbeat. But yours must be pounding."

Then he led her hand slowly towards her chest and placed it on her left breast, so that only his fingertips spread out beyond hers and sank into the soft roundness beneath the cotton dress.

"I don't mix with girls who've only just left school," he said provocatively. "They're afraid of everything and then go home and tell their mothers . . . . "

Mabel ran out of the yard into the drizzle as if he had struck her.

A week later he saw her pass in the company of an aged-looking woman who, as he was to learn later, was her mother; but she did not even look in. He had forgotten about her when one afternoon — soon after Tina's mother had brought his food — Mabel entered the yard,

11

swaying her hips like a professional dancer.

"You're still alive," he joked.

"You so damned conceited!" she said angrily. "Every time I come and want to talk to you nice, you does go on as though the women in the colony kissing your yachting shoes." She made as if to turn.

"All right," he said. "I like you, even if I tease you all the time. If I didn't like you, you'd know and not come back."

He must have found the right words, for she held his gaze.

"I come to invite you. My mother going out tonight and I frighten to stay home all by myself."

"Where're you living?"

"Upper Princess Street. I goin' be standing at the gate, so you can't miss me."

"Suppose it's raining?" Ben asked.

"I goin' be standing there," she repeated.

"Even if it's raining hard?"

"You goin' find me standing there."

"What time?"

"Come after half-past eight."

So he went, and there was no messing around. Like those married women who allow themselves to be seduced the first or the second time because their husbands are waiting for them at home, Mabel's attitude was, "We've got a short time, so let's use it."

She was not a virgin and, judging by her gestures and words, Ben thought he could not teach her much. No. She was a woman among women, as calculating as Tina was straight. When Tina said, "It's blue," it was blue, not pink or green. For Mabel words had many meanings and were weak or strong according to the occasion. If she said, "I saw Ethel," it could mean: "I want to see Ethel," or, "I thought I saw Ethel," or even, "I saw Ethel's cousin's sister-in-law."

When Mabel's mother came to know of her daughter's association with Ben she warned her about his ruthless character; but the more she carried on, the more Mabel cleaved to him, vowing during their acts of intimacy that she would kill Tina and move into her house.

At first Ben found it difficult to remain with her for more than half an hour without quarrelling; but gradually he came to know what kind of remark caused her to lapse into mute resentment and to understand her unwavering hatred of Tina, her peculiar sensitivity about her mother and her loyalty to her brother,

12

an ambitious boxer of small ability.

One day, finding Ben with one arm bandaged Mabel undid the cloth to examine the skin underneath, which was covered with weals from the wrist to the elbow. For three days he drank the bush tea she prescribed, an infusion of moka-moka and sapodilla leaves, while abstaining from alcohol. On awaking on the fourth morning he did not even realize that the weals had disappeared until he began washing. Then it occurred to him that there was no itching to be relieved by the cold water coursing down from his head and shoulders. He waited impatiently for Mabel that day and on hearing her voice went to meet her at the gate.

"So I healed you, Ben!" she said.

"How did you know?"

"It does always work; it's no surprise . . . . I healed you, so what you're going to give me?" She burst out laughing, with a youthful, uncontrollable laughter.

"Listen to me," he said angrily, "you're talking to a grown man. You either behave or get out of the yard."

"I'll behave, Ben," she said with mock submissiveness. "But what you goin' give me?" Her expression had changed swiftly to one of utter seriousness, as if she had said something threatening.

"I'll give you a slap unless you start behaving like a normal person. Are you tetched or something?"

"Tetched? You think I'm tetched? . . . You going to tell me what you'll give me or not?"

He was perplexed by her unpredictable conduct and disappointed that what he had expected to be a meeting at which he would express his gratitude openly, without risking the accusation of making fun of her, was turning into one of their senseless rows.

"So you not giving me anything," she persisted.

"I told you what I'd give you if you don't look out."

"Good. I gone then. But you already give me something."

He grabbed her arm. "You stop talking to me in that tone of voice or don't come and see me again."

To his astonishment she started laughing again, a put-on laugh that did not suit her; and when he moved away she followed him with her eyes, deliberately prolonging her provocative laughter.

"You don' have to see me again," she said softly. "But I'm getting your child . . . . Don' touch me! I might catch whatever you got."

She turned and left the yard defiantly. Stunned by the news, he sat down on the tree stump used as a bench. In the morning he had been certain that Mabel was more securely under his spell than ever, for she had healed his arm. In her woman's wrong-headed way she could not think otherwise, he reckoned. Now this! Like lightning from a clear sky, Mabel had given him the news that was bound to have a profound effect on his relations with Tina and her parents, with herself, her mother and brother. He had managed until then to avoid them, except for two or three meetings at her mother's house on the occasion of some celebration. Above all, above all he had to tell Tina before anyone else knew.

That evening he sat with Tina on the front stairs and got her to talk about the hospital. While she spoke of the new wing and the visiting Guyanese doctor who practised abroad and severely criticized the offhand way things were done in the wards, Ben was thinking of an opportune moment to make his confession. He kept on pumping Tina with questions, judging that he was not yet ready, that *she* was not ready.

"Why you asking me all those questions?" she said. "You never ask me so many questions before."

"I asked you all those questions because I've got something to tell you. Your school friend Mabel is getting a child for me."

He knew she would not shout or strike him, but her long, cold silence made him wish he had not set eyes on Mabel. He cursed their first evening of intimacy, when they had had her mother's house to themselves and Mabel had finally declared that it was time to put out the plants for the night. What was once a memory that quickened the blood now drained him of any tenderness for her.

"What you're going to do?" Tina asked at length.

"Well . . . nothing. I don't *want* to be with her. It happened . . . . "

"I don' want to know. I don' want to know about you and her. Just don' say anything to Ma. It's a *long time* to go yet."

The words "a long time" were not lost on him. Like her mother, Tina avoided embarrassing suggestions by using words in an oblique way.

They sat for a good half-hour side by side without speaking, long after her mother had locked up and the night had become as still as the countryside. He knew she wanted him to speak but that she would be offended by anything he said.

"I got to go to work early tomorrow," she told him in the end.

14

"What if I can't get children?"

"I don't mind, Tina. I didn't marry you for children."

"I never looked at another man. Don't I do everything you ask? What you want another woman for?"

"Tina," he said, not resisting a tender gesture towards her, "I do what you want too. Did I ever go out when you wanted me to stay home?"

"I did ask you to stay home *one time*, and that was the day after our wedding." She embraced him, sensing that they were on the point of quarrelling. "If you was married to one of those women who does follow their men about and don' let them out of their sight . . . . "

He made love to her under the house to appease her, to cure this malady that had sprung up between them so suddenly. Then they went walking along the empty streets, in spite of her early morning shift and her need for nine hours' sleep. They walked past the fireworks factory, down Saffon Street and into the southern suburbs across the narrow-gauge lines of the sugar estate, on to Houston, where they turned back and made for home. Through the huge wheel of a koker could be seen a moon hanging over the river like a tailless kite, blotched with shadows.

"You think you can settle everything by making love," she told him, breaking the silence.

Neither of them wanted to go to bed: he, because he had not made up his mind whether he should give Mabel up, and Tina because she was waiting for him to say something decisive on the subject.

"What the two of you does talk about?" she asked, resisting his attempt to embrace her under the street lamp.

"We talk about her brother when we talk. Most of the time we quarrel because we don't suit each other."

He had no idea why he told her that, even though it was true. He had intended simply saying, "We talk about her brother." But once in a while that happened to him: words pressed themselves to the fore, demanding to be heard, like some wilful child.

The night was more silent than ever as they turned into the yard. The dance hall opposite, noisy and ablaze with light from its hundred windows when a fête was at its height, now stood mute and aloof above the two low cottages that flanked it.

"You're vexed like anything," he said.

"I want to know if you toying with me, that's all."

She showed no sign of sleepiness, but he persuaded her to go to bed.

15

They must have been the last to retire in that long street.

On learning of his relations with Mabel, Tina's mother went to see her and demanded that she give Ben up. Mabel listened to her in silence, and with a show of respect. Then, after Tina's mother had talked her heart out, telling her that an attractive young woman like herself should not waste time on an ugly man ten years her senior, Mabel announced that she was expecting his child. Tina's mother would have cursed her but for her upbringing; instead, she said she was going to get her husband to settle the matter, because Tina was not one of those range-yard women who knocked about and ended up with someone who took pleasure in beating her publicly. Mabel knew the remark was meant for her, yet, true to her style, did just the opposite of what was expected of her. She said nothing.

Tina's father, a very proper man, was in the habit of putting on his cut-away coat at sunset and sitting on his back porch, out of sight, and smoking until it was time for bed. He cultivated one enduring passion, the expectation of the arrival of the ice-ship from Canada, which he would go down to the wharf to watch being unloaded. The world could tear itself apart, provided the ice-ship was left to transport its translucent cargo, unload it on the wharf, then leave in the wake of a high-pitched whistle to cross the Caribbean with a promise of return. It was no surprise that his wife's attempt to involve him in Ben's private life came to nothing. In fact Tina's mother probably had no serious intention of involving him, for she admired Ben, whatever her professed opinions regarding his relations with Mabel. She admired any man who was tall and had a straight back and did not speak creolese as the usual currency of conversation.

3

LIFE WENT on in more or less the same way, and Mabel bore Ben three children, a boy and two girls. When Tina became accustomed to seeing him as a man who behaved like most other men in town, devoting some of his nights to another woman and dividing his income in two, Ben thought it was time to confess to his old career as a professional thief. But he kept putting it off, telling himself that confessions were best made in the dry season. In the end he kept his past to himself, preferring to take no risk with his future in the company of a woman who had turned out to be an antidote to his criminal inclinations and a rock upon which he could build an uncertain future.

One night on leaving the rum-shop he was overwhelmed by a feeling of elation, for no reason at all. The sight of the royal palms with their swelling trunks astounded him, as though he had been abroad for years or had been living in a perpetual dream. He called to mind the dictator about whom he had read, who began to have all the mad people shot because he had been told in a dream that they were his most dangerous enemies, and suddenly was thrilled with the fascination of evil things and the deeds of evil people, of men who send women they idolize to whore in order to humiliate them, of women who abandon their children on account of a vision of a church on a hill; of teachers who grow to love the wild cane and the weals that sprout on soft palms in the aftermath of an orgy of punishment. Held in suspension between the poles of two women with entirely different dispositions, he managed to be a model citizen for the time it took to create three children; but the evil that fascinated within now seemed to ooze from him in the form of terrible images of torment and cadences of mute despair. It was intolerable to have to go home and listen to bland conversation or to go to Mabel's and risk meeting her mother there, her mother who must have had dealings with an obeah man to give birth in her late forties when most women had long lost the capacity to cream, even when roused.

He had to do some evil deed, just one, as an epitaph to his old criminal life, before the women appeared from nowhere to domesticate him like a sheep or a hog or a dog wrenched from its freedom on the streets and the alleyways and a life regulated by the munificence of cook-shop proprietors and the coming of long rains. The evil he was most familiar with was theft, simply because it was against the law. He was marked as the dead are, with a blue triangle on the cheek.

He walked up North Road along the Lamaha Canal, briskly, like a man with a firm destination. On arriving at an unlit house almost obscured by an almond tree, he crossed the bridge and opened the gate, expecting to be met by a fit of barking from a watchdog. Experience had taught him that hesitation was dangerous, because of the eyes watching from darkened windows and the shadows of

17

bottom-houses. He hid behind the front staircase, which branched off midway, like a massive fork. Turning around he surveyed the straight concrete pillars, the long back stairs and the flooring above, which was almost certainly polished to a shine. He was sure he had lost the art of walking on such elegant boards, to whose care a special servant girl was usually devoted. He took off his shoes and left them at the foot of the back stairs, which he would climb to penetrate into the mansion.

The house facing the foot of the back stairs was lit, which pleased him. Anyone at one of the windows could be seen by him, in which case he would have time to flee. But he changed his mind and decided to attempt to enter the house from that side, in spite of the light falling on the wall and Demerara windows.

Climbing on to the sturdy wallaba paling fence, he tried one window; and when it failed to open he walked along the horizontal support until he was under the next window. His attempts to lift the window-flap upwards were no more successful than with the last, and as he eased himself into a squatting position on the narrow cross-piece he saw someone approach the lighted window of the adjoining house. Balancing on his perch, Ben held his breath until the figure moved away after emitting a puff of cigarette smoke. His instincts saw the occurrence as a bad omen, but, seized by the need, the urgency to assert himself, he moved along to the next window, the flap of which easily came away. The only difficulty that remained was judging whether the broad ledge would support his weight. At the first attempt to pull it downwards, the ledge began to creak; and just as Ben decided to try entering the house by way of the back stairs, an electric torch was shone in his face.

"All right, come down on this side of the paling," a voice told him.

And so began two nightmarish days during which Ben was visited in a police cell by several men who had taken it into their heads that he had had some motive beside theft for wishing to break into the North Road mansion.

"You've got a bad record," said the sergeant, a big-chested man with a face resembling those avuncular heads that decorate the "In Memoriam" pages of the two national newspapers. "You want us to send you up to the Mazaruni? Eh? Hard labour in the bush? That's what you want?"

"I was out walking," Ben replied. "I only wanted to peep into a

18

rich man's house. Did you find any jemmy? Any house-breaking tools at all? . . . If—"

"How you talk so good? That's what I want to know. Where you *learn* to talk like that?"

"At school," Ben said.

"Ah ah!" he said firmly. "Is not school that does teach you to talk like that. I been to school till I was sixteen and I don' talk like that."

He was angered by Ben's silence.

"We *know* you, you crook!" the man thundered. "We know you. You and your horses. Now why you didn' become a policeman, join the horse guards if you like horses so? Tch! You got something to hide, man. You're dabbling in politics, and you better tell me rather than one of the white inspectors out for promotion. They don' question, they does interrogate. If they suspect you're in politics or belong to one of those unions, it's the Mazaruni and hard labour. So you're going to tell me?"

"I told you, I just wanted to look into a rich man's house."

"Tch!" the sergeant exclaimed, waving his hand in exasperation. "With your record of thieving you're walking along a paling to look into somebody house? In the dark? You take me for a fool?"

"Why're you taking so much trouble over me, eh?" Ben asked.

For an answer the sergeant pounded the table at which Ben was sitting and got up.

"It's the Mazaruni for you . . . and don' say a black man like you didn't warn you. When one of them brown-skin arse-lickers take over from me he'll hand you over to some white man who left school at fourteen and does walk about with a rosewood stick under his armpit to give him confidence. And he'll *do* for you; and you'll tell him more than you tell me. You'll tell him what he wants you to tell him, O God, because he'll put the fear of the Lord up your arse and you'll confess to what you did do and to what you didn' do and you'll hop around like a God-bird on a window-sill. We try to help you people, but you don' understand until it happen to somebody you know. Tch!"

He left, slamming the door, which was then locked with a succession of keys.

Early next morning he came back in the company of one of those brown-skinned brethren he had been talking about, a short, fat man who declined to sit in the chair offered him.

The stranger looked past Ben, an almost impossible feat in the tiny

19

cell. Keeping his hands behind his back he let the sergeant speak without intervening, although the visit had been arranged in *his* interest.

"You have a visitor," the sergeant said. "And think yourself lucky you're not before the magistrate. Now, the gentleman heard about the way you talk and about your experience with horses. Do you understand?"

Ben had stood up as the stranger and the sergeant entered the cell. "Yes."

"No, you don't speak until he invites you," the sergeant ordered.

For a long while the stranger kept slapping one hand in the other. "Have you ever driven a cab?" he then asked, still looking past Ben as if he didn't exist.

"Once or twice."

"What does that mean?"

"I haven't driven often, but on occasion. I —"

"So you know what it's about," the man interrupted. "I want someone who knows about the care of horses and is able to turn his hands to any repair, guttering and . . . and so on. He must be able to keep the harness in good order, work closely with the servant who is in charge of the kitchen and the house generally. Would you like the job?"

"Yes," Ben answered without hesitation, assuming that charges would be dropped if he took it.

"Why should I give it to you?" the stranger demanded, suddenly fixing Ben with a stare. "Why should I entrust my horse and the security of my house to a criminal who lies about his activities and is in the habit of walking along fences like a friendless cat?"

Ben was at a loss for words, not caring to be humiliated in front of the sergeant, who had not once taken his eyes off him.

"Are you offering me a job?" he asked, summoning up as much dignity as he dared.

The stranger looked past Ben once more, and apparently he had decided. It seemed that he was as anxious to have Ben as Ben was to work for him. When he did address Ben again his expression was one of contempt as though he were avenging himself on him for some wrong.

"The job requires you to live in, in case of an emergency — illness for instance. My wife has been known to take in at the dead of night. Are you prepared to live in?"

20

"I've got a wife . . . . "

"Well, that's it," the man said, waving to the sergeant. "You can charge him, as far as I'm concerned."

"I accept," Ben said hurriedly. "May I ask where you live?"

" 'May I ask'?" the stranger said, "May I ask indeed." He grinned, mocking Ben with a stare. " 'May I ask' from a fence walker. Well, I never! Anyway the sergeant will tell you how to find my house. One other thing: don't meddle in politics or anything like that. I don't myself, and that's sufficient reason why you shouldn't . . . . Sergeant!"

The sergeant opened the cell door and saw the stranger out.

Immediately Ben thought of Tina, that she had no idea where he was. He thought of the new complications living away from home would bring to their lives, of the way he would go down in her parents' estimation. And it was only after turning the matter over and over in his mind that he realized how none of his thoughts had been for Mabel and the children.

The sound of keys in the door caused him to take his place behind the table, involuntarily, as though ashamed to be caught standing in the middle of the cell.

"Right!" the sergeant bellowed. "Now show some gratitude. The slightest complaint from him and you'll be charged. Whether it's tomorrow or ten years from now. Right! I've informed your wife. She'll be up after she's finished at the hospital."

"Why can't I go home if I'm to start work for this man? I don't want my wife to come here."

"Suits me. You'd better go up to the hospital after you've been discharged. That'll take a good half-hour . . . . Let me give you a piece of advice. What the hell does it matter to me? You're not liked. You know that, don't you? I don't give a damn, but there's something in your manner people resent."

"I can't help that. Is it you who got me the job?"

"Don't bother about that. I'll tell you this: the house is big, a mansion; and he's a big man in the Civil Service responsible for the destruction of old currency notes. He once had two carriages and many servants, but that's some time ago. Right! You'll be brought your release papers and the things we did take from you."

He shook his head and laughed softly. "These brown-skin people! These red men!"

From one of the cells came the sound of coughing. Ben recalled how

21

the police photographer had taken eight photographs of him the morning after he had been arrested, four in profile and four full-face. The first exploding flare pained his eyes, but the photographer kept on and on, manhandling him whenever he had to change position. He was well known as an ardent church-goer, and admired for his lusty singing from a back pew, where his low status as a police employee had assigned him until his death or the trumpet call on doomsday when humans were promised equality in the sight of God. Ben felt he could not wait that long.

At the hospital Tina came over at once when she saw him. No, she was going to do three extra hours and could not come home right away. But she would stand and talk.

"You know it was lies," Ben told her.

"They didn't say you were at the station until this morning. Ma and me went tramping all about the town searching for you. We went to Mabel first, and Ma was sure you were there hiding behind the screen. I was afraid of what Mabel would do to her if she went and looked. But you know Ma. She looked behind the screen and under the bed and Mabel stand aside with her hands folded . . . . They give you enough to eat? What they give you?"

"Peas and rice. It was only two days."

"Why you didn't tell me you steal from people's houses before, Ben? Ma tell me not to tell Pa, 'cause he would die of shame. But you know Ma: 'Your father would die of shame.' This time Pa couldn't care if you or anyone else end up on the gallows. He's like that, he can't help it. But Ma kept on saying, 'He'd die of shame.' . . . I wouldn't like to cross that Mabel. She didn't say one single word o' protest when Ma searched the room. All under the bed and under the house. She had to bend down 'cause the house is so low near the ground. She bent down and couldn't see good and I was praying she'd come away. Mabel din' say a single word, but her eyes, my God! When we were walking home Ma kept saying, 'He's under the house, I'm sure!' This time you were at the station."

"Listen, M . . . Tina. Listen. I've got something to tell you."

He told her about the new job and she listened without interrupting. Then, when he had finished she said, "Is better than being in jail . . . . But if ever I leave you I won't come back."

"If you don't want me to take the job just say so and it's no to the man. I wouldn't hesitate. Once you don't like it that's enough."

22

"You love me?" she asked.

"What I just said proves I do, doesn't it?"

"Yes, yes. You're a good man and I'm going to save you, Ben. I'll wipe away all that mud from your soul. But you musn' think bad of Ma. She's far, far superior to me and Pa . . . . All I need to know is that you love me and I'll make any sacrifice to save you."

She pointed him the way out of the vast complex of buildings, and on finding himself in East Street he went over to the coconut-water seller. He had just sold a coconut to a young couple who each drank in turn from the fractured husk. Ben took the young coconut from the vendor's outstretched hand and applied it to his mouth, and when he had drained it threw the husk on to the pile of discarded shells, which rose from the edge of a puddle where the foliage of a wayside tree was reflected.

4

BEN WAS required to call him Master; no doubt to emphasize the humiliation of his position. The master's name was Schwartz, but Ben was not allowed to address him as such. He addressed Ben by his name. Within a week of becoming his cabman several people made it their business to tell Ben about his employer's disposition and background. The chief informants were Fatpork, a tenant in one of the rooms under the house, and Edna the maid.

Fatpork used to be one of the family's hangers-on, who came and went at will, ate upstairs and frequently took their daughter for walks when she was a little girl. According to Edna, his peculiar status in the household was due to a long-standing protection afforded him by Mr Schwartz's father when he was alive. The obligation was maintained even after the master married and had great difficulty in allaying the mistress's fears about a stranger appearing in her home at all hours of the day. In the end she came to like him so well that when her husband stayed out late at night she made Fatpork remain with her until he came back. The couple's friends accepted him as soon as they were certain that Mrs Schwartz no longer resented his presence; and Fatpork's inoffensiveness, naïvely displayed in everything he did and said, ensured for him the tolerance of most visitors to the Regent

Street house. Yet, aware of his status as hanger-on, they never invited him to their homes.

Fatpork's privileged position was brought to an abrupt end when he was found to be diseased. At the first enquiry as to the nature of his ailment he declared his intention of going away "to the islands". When he came back three years later he found the family's fortunes in decline and rented one of the rooms which were once servants' quarters. The second room the master let to a family of religious fanatics, while the third was reserved for the coachman, who, apart from Edna the maid, was the only employee Mr Schwartz could afford. The family, ignorant of much that went on in the vast working people's world around them, had no idea that Fatpork was syphilitic. But with time his former status was forgotten, and they even ceased greeting him. Even their daughter, whose companion and storyteller he had been, barely acknowledged his existence with a nod and, as he often complained to Edna, had not even sent him a crumb of her wedding cake. It was Fatpork himself who told Ben all this, ending his story by saying that he forgave "the little one". "Children change, you know," he added.

But the story about the Schwartzes' marriage and the mistress's brother Ben heard from Edna. The family's fortunes began to decline when the master gave his wife's brother money to avoid an embezzlement charge and suspension from the Civil Service.

However, Edna's fancy took flight when she spoke of their employers' courtship and marriage, so that it was difficult to separate truth from fiction. She told Ben that the mistress was once engaged to a very handsome man whose business interests were as obscure as his past. He claimed to have come from Panama, but rumour had it that he was a small-islander who arrived in the colony penniless, without even a change of clothing. According to wagging tongues he was taken in by a woman who found him drinking alone in a wharf-side dive. On learning that he had not eaten for three whole days, she invited him to an eating-place where he fainted at the smell of cooked food. It was she who managed to slip him in among the guests at a Christmas party in the house where she worked as a maid; and there he met the mistress, then only twenty. She was accompanied by an aunt-chaperone. The small-islander lost no time in seducing the aunt, an ugly spinster in her forties, an ardent churchgoer and completely devoted to her niece. In no doubt as to her feelings for him he disclosed his plan to be introduced to the mistress's household; and

24

the aunt, anxious that he should settle in the colony, helped him to secure invitations to the houses of the mistress's relations. On the second occasion when he and the mistress found themselves in the same room, she was unable to keep her eyes off him; he finally spoke to her and she was so dumbfounded she found it difficult to open her mouth or respond to his advances. Thus their courtship began, under the supervision of a chaperone with a vested interest in encouraging indiscretions in her love-stricken ward.

Eventually the suitor asked for the mistress's hand in marriage, thereby prompting her father to make the usual enquiries, which disclosed that his future son-in-law entertained an ambiguous relationship with a woman from the dock area, who was fond of taking him to the country to parade among her relations. And, to the dismay of the mistress and her aunt, the house was barred to the suitor, as were the drawing-rooms of the well-to-do and all those who until then had been liberal with their hospitality.

Yes, it was then that the master came on the scene, when the mistress had already been softened up by the small-islander. His prospects in the Civil Service and his lack of imagination were, in the eyes of her parents, an attraction, after their experience with the smooth-tongued suitor who had taken in their daughter. She was given to him like the sacrificial goat at a Kali Mai Pujah ceremony, in atonement for the disaster that might have befallen them.

Mr Schwartz colonized his wife and provided a constitution that regulated her conduct and the quality of tribute she was to pay him, before submitting her to a régime of a most benign variety. He subdued her with promises of emeralds, a glittering carriage, furniture of mahogany and huber-balli, and voyages to the islands during the indolent weeks. But to her disappointment she was to learn that his undistinguished appearance concealed a personality no more prepossessing and that his career prospered even less than his extravagant promises.

All this, known to every Tom, Dick and Harry, increased Ben's respect for the mistress, whom he had liked from the moment he set eyes on her, not least for her dignity, which was evident even when she was silent. Her twin sister was just the opposite, Edna assured Ben, a veritable gad-about who courted scandal and gave the family such a bad name that her parents sent her to New York, where all well-to-do exiles are banished. But, unable to scandalize New York, she settled for marriage and a quiet life. However, her nostalgia for Georgetown grew with the years and she invited her twin — the mistress — to visit her one Christmas, to save her from dying of boredom and loneliness among the exiles who unfolded their tapestry of memories at the slightest prompting and spoke of going home with tears in their eyes. The sister was one of the vanguard of the diaspora which had begun after the First World War and was impelled, people said, by a sad south wind that defied the trade winds from the north-east. Like her, the mistress would have been carried away too, had she not been moored to the wharf of marriage.

An odd story about the mistress began to circulate after her return from the States. *She* had not come back, it was said, but her twin sister, who had been persuaded to take her place as Schwartz's wife. Edna, who had not been with the family long, noticed nothing herself, except that the mistress's wardrobe was completely different from the one she knew. Edna did not believe the rumours since the two sisters were so different in temperament. Any change would have been plain for all to see. Besides, the master's behaviour towards his wife had not altered. But the story persisted, despite its inconsistencies.

"People believe it 'cause they like the mistress and wish she did really leave him," Edna said. "But if it wasn't the mistress, how is it her best friend was still her best friend when she come back? Tell me that! You mean your husband and your best friend wouldn't notice you not the same person?"

Edna thought that the mistress's brother — the same one the master saved from prison — had a hand in spreading and keeping alive the rumour. It was from the time of her return that he was allowed to visit the family again.

"He spread the story to spite the master. Is so our people stay: they don' got no unity. But what you expect of a man who say he don' believe in God? You don' say things like that. If you stupid enough to think them, you keep them to yourself."

If Ben admired the mistress, he detested the master as much for his arrogance as because of the continual blackmail with which he kept him in line. Should Ben misbehave he would be handed over to the police to face the charge from which the master had saved him.

Ben decided to give satisfaction in his duties, while biding his time. Somehow he had to find a way out of the trap in which he found himself, at the same time contriving the means to set himself up in a business after he gained his freedom. He was in no doubt that his bouts of thieving could not be explained simply by a need to come by

26

enough money to maintain a family. It had more to do with his pride as a man, which could not be satisfied by tending horses belonging to someone else. He had never once stolen in his childhood or youth, even in the days when, without a cent to his name, he used to spend long evenings outside the dance halls listening to the music of flaring trombones.

His humiliating position in the Schwartz household hardly left him the time to visit Tina and Mabel. And when he was free — usually after eight o'clock at night if the master and mistress were not going out — he preferred to walk the streets rather than face the scorn of his women.

One night he stopped to watch an aboriginal Indian, a genuine raw bush-man who must have been completely out of his depth in town. He said he was a Macusi, a tribe Ben had never heard of, believing that all Indians were Arawaks. He met him standing at a street corner in North Road, watching a man offering birdcages for sale. All Ben knew about aboriginal Indians at that time was that they drank paiwari, the cassava beer. When he was at school a man once showed him and a friend a photograph of an Arawak woman naked, her legs sprawled apart. The man did not want any money from them, only the satisfaction of showing them the picture. And here was this Indian now watching a bird-seller whistling to his birds. Ben went with him to the aboriginal Indian agency where Water Street and Lombard Street meet, to fetch his things before bringing him home to the master's house.

Since his school days, Ben had been picking up pale, bloodless characters as friends, squeezing them for blood and then finding to his dismay that he liked them as they were, in spite of his desperation for a friendship with a man's man who loved boasting about his conquests and possessed his own insatiable appetite for knowledge and for pushing a pen.

"How're you called Carl and you're a Macusi? That's not a Macusi name."

Carl didn't answer. Ben watched him unfold his hammock and in no time sling it across the room over his bed.

These bucks don't talk, Ben reflected. *They would lie all day and not say a word; and you would think they disliked you. Sometimes it is true they hate you, but then they would not come and live with you.*

After Carl had been in his room a few days, Ben asked him if he

27

wanted to stay and he said yes. He liked sitting on the back stairs watching Ben's employer's stables at the back of the yard and watching Ben come down the stairs with the mistress's four-year-old nephew in front of him holding the whip; he liked watching Ben groom the horse before he put the harness on it, hitch it to the carriage and then drive it out front so as to be ready for his employer at ten minutes to eight, at ten minutes to eight whether rain was falling or Ben was sick.

"Do you expect me to walk to work?" the master asked, the morning Ben dragged himself up the back stairs to tell him he was too sick to go out.

Ben took the harness from the nails when he was not even fit to carry the whip, and carried it downstairs, then to the stable at the back of the yard. And while he was resting on the straw, wondering how he would put the saddle on the horse and hitch it to the carriage, he heard the master's voice from the house. *He was right*, Ben thought, *if you are not dead you can work*.

One morning Ben asked his employer if he could not find work for Carl, who was living next door, he said — he did not tell him Carl was staying in his room and not paying rent. The master refused point blank.

"You mean the buck-man? You want to give me a bad name? We had one at the Treasury doing some messenger job or other, and as soon as someone shouted at him he did a moonlight flit. I don't know how you find time to cultivate these strays. You're not in trouble again?"

He could never forget how he had saved Ben when he was arrested and made him a servant, and when he discovered that Ben used to catch his hand writing articles for the *Argosy* newspaper he imposed extra work on him out of spite. Ben recalled the rage on his face when he asked, "You wrote this? You? Where did you learn to write like this?" And from then on Ben had to do all sorts of menial jobs and clean the stables in the afternoon as well, when all cab-drivers rested.

Ben was in with Edna the cook who, although she had a man, respected him. She consented to giving him a little food for Carl; and in the end Ben had him eating at the table in the kitchen with him because Edna would have it. The mistress would never know, finding it degrading to enter the kitchen with its smoke grime from the wood fires and the coal-pots. She and her husband saw it as a hole down which they risked falling into the even more frightening world below

28

where Ben and their tenants lived, where their servants used to live before the rooms were rented out to pay for the carriage and entertaining their friends.

Sometimes Carl remained half the day in Edna's company, with his feet perched on the cross-bar of the chair. She had been with the family for years and was prepared to say he was her mother's godson if the master or mistress happened to come in unexpectedly. Once when Edna was about to throw away an old piece of furniture Carl rescued the top of it and made a handsome birdcage with a sawn-off section, and from then on he spent hours designing and constructing bird-cages of all shapes and sizes, which he sold at street corners for half the price a townsman would have asked. But Edna got tired of chasing him from the kitchen, which became cluttered with his fantasies and left-over pieces of cedar and pine. Once she hid the glue he had concocted from a mixture of resin and gum and only restored it after his promise never to work in the kitchen again. She relented, however, and it was she who invited him back upstairs when she missed his company and his implacable silences.

If Carl's earnings were little more than enough to buy the wood he used, Ben was not in the least concerned, since Carl and Edna were the only company he had between the visits from Tina and Mabel. Carl and Ben began going out at night after eight o'clock, unless the master had to pay someone a visit. Then Ben's day might finish at eleven, or even midnight. But mostly they went out after eight, to visit Tina or to roam the town.

One night Ben took him riding on the tram. That was Ben's secret passion, riding on the new tramway, not knowing whom he would meet, listening to the clatter-clatter of the wheels, waiting for town to merge into country. Ruimveldt, Meadow Bank, Houston, McDoom, Jonestown, Eccles, Bagotstown, Peter's Hall. Carl said it was like the bush out there, with the candleflies blinking over the cane field. He wanted to walk back and Ben asked if he was right in the head. *He* liked moving about on wheels, passing places at speed and looking down at the road, not feeling his feet on it.

In a street behind the Public Road they found a little shop, where Ben bought Carl two Tennent's beers.

"You know if Edna does do it?" Carl asked after the second beer.

"Yes, but with her man. Nothing doing for you."

"She man does allow she to go and come like that? He don' care?"

"Eh, heh," Ben said. "I see. Is not like that in the bush, eh? Well,

29

ten to one it's she who's bringing in the money."

Ben felt sorry for him, but thought it was better to wait until he met some woman who would allow him to fondle her for nothing, rather than pay one of those whores who could finish you for life with a five-minute embrace.

"Wait, ne. Till you meet someone," Ben told him.

"But I goin' away next month," Carl said.

Ben was stunned by the disclosure, for in the couple of months Carl had been with him he had grown to love him as a brother. He stayed looking across the room, pretending that Carl had said the most ordinary thing in the world. Then Ben tried to look like him, as though there was no suffering in the world or joy either.

After that night, Carl used to go riding the trams with the coppers Ben gave him, in the hope of meeting a woman who understood what he was out for. That was what Carl hated about Georgetown, the way the women looked away when he stared at them, when every bruck-foot Johnny had a woman to frolic with. He had become obsessed with Edna, thinking she had no man because she lorded it over the kitchen and you could see down to her crutch between her bubbies when she bent down. And he hated this, too, this gulf between wanting and satisfaction that townspeople had no difficulty in bridging.

Ben and Carl talked at length for the first time when they were at Tina's place one night. She just had enough time to cook for them before she went off on duty, when Carl enquired how it was Ben had no children and Ben told him that he did, two girls and a boy and that the woman who had them for him was not his wife.

"But Tina?" Carl asked, for she had evidently made a big impression on him.

"The wife's barren. It's like pissing in the sand at Soesdyke."

Carl was pensive for a while as he picked his teeth. In the beginning Ben had considered him to be ugly, with his flat face and vacant look. The Arawaks were darker and taller — not that Ben knew much about them, except for what he saw at the Indian reception centre.

Carl started telling Ben about his life, how his mother's clan had to disperse when they were being wiped out by influenza; he was then six. His family travelled along the Courantyne river until they came to Orealla where there was an Arawak settlement and the Indians were protected. A rancher took his mother in as a servant because his father was not allowed to settle any land and could find no work. But by the time he did find work on a timber grant his mother was pregnant by

30

the rancher, who told his father he would keep her in the house because she was a good woman and did not sulk like the women from Skeldon and Springlands and Crabwood Creek. His father took the five children to Crabwood Creek, all the way up that treacherous Courantyne River. And in the midst of a storm that blew up he said to them, "Somebody dead." It was true, because weeks later news reached them in Crabwood Creek that the rancher had fallen down dead during a storm. Many months after that, Carl's mother came back to live with them, bringing the child with her.

While he was talking, he was crushing chicken bones to get at the marrow. The spoon and knife always remained unused next to his plate since it was beneath him to use them. According to him, his food would not digest if he did.

Carl then talked of his brother who came to town two years previously and wasted his money buying friends in the cook-shops. Back in Orealla he hankered after Georgetown, which he, Carl, hated with every fibre in his body.

"If I come back here, is to visit you and you wife. Especially you wife."

Carl went off to Orealla one morning as Ben was waiting on his perch for the master to appear at ten to eight. He bent down and shook Carl's hand, to his great surprise, and Carl left with the morning sun on his back without even saying how he was going or with whom. Ben was certain he would not say a word on the trip.

When Ben drove off with the master, he felt like going another way and turned down Hadfield Street.

"Where the devil're you going? You've never taken this route before!" the master shouted at him.

Ben grunted to himself, feeling that there was no better way of starting the day. As he got out in front of the Public Buildings he realized why the master was so angry. He would have to walk round to the front of the building to the gate he was accustomed to using, a good fifty yards further.

Glaring at Ben he said, "Don't forget to clear that gutter on the roof. Test it when you've finished, to see if water can get down."

Ben reflected that he and the master had more than their fair share of hatred; they were brothers in hatred, and one of them had to be master. But he was only having those violent thoughts because Carl had gone to Orealla and left a void in his room. And all he had taken

31

were a hammock and a birdcage.

The master got out of the carriage that evening pompously, with deliberate gestures, an unfailing sign that something was wrong.

"I am not going out tonight," he told Ben, "so you're free after eight o'clock. . . . By the way, about your friend Carl. You didn't believe I didn't know he was living in your room, did you? I know everything that goes on in this house."

Buttoning up his jacket he turned on Ben, knowing he had violent thoughts about him. And in those minutes of confusion, Ben, feeling humiliated because he had no answer, feeling ridiculous, worse than a mangy dog, thought up a new name for his employer: Grunt-Hoo. It was the name of a pig in a story Edna once told him.

Late afternoon: a cyclist riding past slowly, an umbrella raised over her head to protect her from the sun; a young dandy with a parting in his hair, waiting outside the house; the painted swing-doors of the barber-shop opposite; and breaking into these sights Grunt-Hoo's eyes with that cold stare of dead fish. Ben reflected that his sister was the dupe of jewellers, who would sell her anything, and his brother was the creature of women who could do him anything . . . . He took in the carriage and set about cleaning out the stables, or rather made a show of cleaning them out. Then after a quick shower with Edna's connivance he went out into the night with his polished shoes and the slow forgetting of his daily humiliation at having to work for a man who had a hold over him.

5

THE RAIN always arrived with a rustling of leaves and scurrying of feet from the road. There was no light in the back yard and no street beyond the stables, so Ben had to imagine what it was like from the patter on the stairs and the smell of damp and the sudden chill creeping through the window, and the feeling of indescribable contentment when it came. But he only enjoyed rain when he was in his room at night time, alone. There are those who are bored when alone; so they put on their clothes and run to see an aunt or a friend or an uncle or a godchild. In those days he could sit on a chair and look at the wall and think and think. Somtimes he thought so hard — in fact it was not thinking at all; it was more like losing his way — he ended up in all sorts of places. One night he went to Ethiopia; and another time he found himself next door. But mostly he thought of women: fat ones, fine ones, tall ones, short ones, domineering and docile ones. Some men liked only a certain kind of woman — tall, short, big-battied and so on. He was not discriminating. But he noticed one thing: only a certain type of woman liked him, the solicitous kind. They wanted to *do* for him.

"Who's that?" Ben called out.

"Is Carl," the voice came through the rain, not loud, but distinct.

Ben rushed to the door, unbelieving. There was Carl standing in front of him, his long, blue-black hair plastered down with the rain.

"Where's your hammock?"

"I don' got it," he answered.

He had fled Georgetown and now, according to him, he had been arrested in Springlands for smuggling. Only day-before-yesterday he had escaped from the sergeant's house, having stolen his own money the sergeant had confiscated.

"You've eaten anything?"

Carl shook his head.

"All right, we're going to Mabel to eat."

Ben lent him an old pair of trousers and one of the cotton shirts he rarely had occasion to wear. Edna had gone home long before, so he hung out Carl's wet clothes on the window-sill. His wet shoes Ben placed in a corner of the room, knowing they would be mouldy by the time they were fit for wearing again. But Carl was never comfortable in them and he set out barefoot.

Leaving through the front gate was out of the question, for the master and mistress had not gone to bed. Ben took a hammer from his tool-box and knocked out a paling-stave in the fence that divided the stables from the alleyway. When he had replaced the hammer he and Carl left by the alleyway, sheltering under the umbrella kept in the carriage for passengers to use during the rainy weather. They were silent all the way to Howes Street where Mabel lived in the yard with the sign saying "WinDows of aLL KinDs cheaP" in mixed capital and common letters. The silence on Carl's part, Ben thought, indicated complete trust in Ben's willingness to accept him; and on Ben's side it was because he did not understand Carl, who had never written in the four months he had been away, because writing was unnecessary. If he had wanted anything he would have written, "I

33

want such and such a thing," for that was how aboriginals were.

They stood on the edge of the yard, wondering how to avoid the mud lake, not knowing how to find the coconut-husk islands in the dark.

"Mabel!" Ben shouted. "Come out!"

A woman's voice shouted out in turn, "Mabel! Is for you. It sound like you man."

Mabel appeared with an umbrella. "Is why you stan' in the road for? Come, ne?"

"We can't find the coconuts."

She came out and led them back to her room along the coconut-husk path.

"I say stay in bed!" she screamed at the children, who were behind the screen in the room.

"I want to talk to Pa!"

Ben recognized Bamford's voice. He was the eldest and boldest.

"All right, I'm coming."

He went behind the screen and lay down on the floor while the three children crawled over him, emptied his pockets, poked their fingers up his nostrils, bit his ears, rode him like a horse and whipped him. At his church-wife's house it was all silence and orderliness, with doilies prettifying the dressing-table and photographs aligned on the walls, pictures of her relations who bore expressions of abiding calm.

"Lef' you father alone!" Mabel called out, and Ben understood that the words were meant for him.

He laid the children on the floor one by one and brought calm to the room with a gift of one cent to each of them.

"You got food?" he asked Mabel, on coming out.

"Why you din' bring something?" she asked. She was already tying a scarf round her head.

He gave her two bit coins, deciding there and then that he would supplement his earnings by using the carriage for hire once or twice a day after he dropped the master off at work. It would be risky and he would have to operate away from the centre of town.

Mabel went out in the rain, surly. When she was like that Ben avoided her. Besides, from her watery eye he could see she had her period. That grey flesh and wet eyeball never lied.

Ben and Carl sat listening to the murmuring lamp, each wondering what the other was thinking. Ben was thinking nothing except that the next day he would take Carl to eat at Tina's house, unless she went

34

on duty before he could get away. Then he would be obliged to go back to Mabel and pretend he was pleased with her. He reflected that Carl was like a drug to him. He liked people and liked to show his power over them by helping them, but he knew it was different in Carl's case. *And when you think how people despise bucks! They like them, but they despise them for living in the bush and wearing nothing but a small cloth, and for speaking an obscene language and for being free.*

They sat listening to the hypnotic buzzing of the lamp, with a blanket of wood and corrugated iron round them. And Ben was thinking of the horse in the stable, shitting heaps because of the rain and because it has not been out all day, expecting Ben to go and pat its neck before he retired for the night, when all the time he was here listening to a lamp making sounds like a woman calling from across the road, "*Psst!*"

Mabel brought back cooked food.

"You see Carl come back," Ben said to her.

"I can see Carl come back."

"But you not to say anything. He's in trouble."

"What trouble?" she demanded.

"Smuggling trouble."

She sat down with them and ate, while she looked Carl over as if he were a stranger.

"He can work?" she asked at length.

"I'll find him work."

"As long as you find him work."

"Why?" Ben asked.

" 'Cause he kian' stay coop up in a room all day like fat duck in a cage, that's why."

Ben grunted because he was certain the reason she gave was not the one she really meant. *I think I'll come tomorrow and beat her,* he reflected. *The trouble is the children make so much noise when I beat her; yet they make no noise when I beat one of them.* When she was in the mood, she would sit in his lap and kiss him and make him feel like king of Howes Street. "Go to bed!" she would say to the children. And if one of them protested that it was too early she would shout and they would all rush to get undressed and lie down. And she would go behind the screen and bed them down and come out with her drawers off. He could tell by the way the dress clung to her backside. Then she would sit on his lap and kiss him and start getting worked up until he put his hand on her dootal and felt it all wet; and only then she would calm down. One night one of the girls came out rubbing her eyes and found her mother kneeling on the floor with him up her. But Mabel did not budge and just carried on looking at the floor in her kneeling position until she started coming and he could tell that her eyelids were fluttering as if she was having fits.

"You like her?" Ben asked Carl, knowing that neither of the two was willing to start a conversation.

"I eat her food. How I not goin' like her?"

Mabel gave Carl a withering look, but pulled herself together almost at once and sat down opposite him. She rarely talked in the presence of strangers, though Ben could see she might burst out at any moment, feeling superior to Carl who, when all was said and done, was only a "buck-man" and had never worn out a pair of shoes in his life.

Praying she would not do anything foolish, Ben enquired about her brother, a professional boxer.

"He all right," was the only answer he got for his pains.

Her brother had become her protector since her father went to the Rapununi, and he and her mother had taken it into their heads to keep an eye on Mabel in relays. Whenever Ben came to see her and the children he was as likely as not to meet one of them there, taking root in a corner or holding forth on a subject about which they knew nothing.

"He tell you about me, I suppose," Mabel said to Carl, suddenly springing to life. "He tell you how I follow him about like a dog after he get married? And how I make three children for him without him even courting me? He tell you? Well, he lying!"

"I told him nothing!" Ben protested angrily. "Carl doesn't even know the town properly and you're burdening him with our private business. *You're* telling him, not me."

"If he in' tell you, he going to tell you," she went on, "'cause he's a man. My brother been with only one woman an' if you hear him talk you'd think he throw down every woman in town. So men stay! It's in your blood. Well, Ben telling lies. I din' run after him. He *entice* me. While he been courting Tina through the paling he used to talk loud so I could hear. . . ."

"O Lord, woman, what's wrong with you? Carl doesn't understand that kind of story. And in any case you're not telling the truth."

"He used to talk to her and look at me," she continued, "'cause he greedy an' can't be satisfy with one woman."

36

Ben let her talk, knowing the alternative was an almighty row in which the neighbours would join and end up abusing him for having accepted his employer's condition to live in.

"You should've hear the lies he used to tell Tina 'cause no man did ever look at her until then and she din' understand how men does tell lies like they does shave an' can do it with their eyes closed. He only married Tina 'cause she got a father behind her; but me . . . he don' care if I end up with ten children so long as I keep my figure and he can bully my mother. O Saviour! Sometimes I sit in that rocking-chair listening for a noise on the bridge, thinking he was coming to show himself to the children at least. And all I got for company is my three children and the dogs barking outside and the neighbours talking through the partition."

"Why you don't go next door then?" Ben asked her. "You're the only one in the yard who keeps herself to herself."

"The last time you come and find me next door," she replied hotly, "you beat me. You tell your friend Carl how you does beat me? He does beat me from the back of the room to the front and when all my energy drain away with the blows and the shouting he does want to lie down 'pon me . . . ."

"Enough!" Ben shouted at her.

"So you shouting at me in front of your friend?" she said softly. "Just 'cause I inform him you been telling lies; but he know now, and all your shouting can't take back my words . . . . Anyway is why you bring him back here? Why you din' take him to see your wife? She got house an' a job; she does walk like a lady and got money to buy clothes. But she in' got child, eh? You shamed of my room, but you still bring your friend here. Remember that beggar man you pick up in the rum shop? You bring him here first, *then* you take him to see Tina, where it so neat he had to sit 'pon the edge of the chair and din' move his big toe for the two hours he been there. You did tell me so yourself. But when he was in my untidy room, with clothes lying all 'bout the place, he did hawk and spit through the window all the time 'cause I living in one room. And you din' tell him nothing 'cause you din' feel no shame. Round there at the neat house you would've drag him out in the yard if he did so much as sneeze. Yes, Carl, is so he stay! He got one kind of behaviour for his common-law wife and another for his church-wife, who got his gold ring and the blessings of her parents."

She was angry, and so was Ben; and the charged atmosphere had the effect of deepening the silence in the room. The bird in the cage over the door was fluttering about nervously, alarmed by the peremptory way he ordered her to be silent. All of a sudden he noticed that the sounds from the adjoining room had ceased altogether and he came to the conclusion that the neighbours had been listening to the mother of his children holding forth.

The peach-coloured light from the humming lamp, nothing more than an oasis in the dark, appeared to be the only thing alive in the room, where three children slept and three adults were cowering behind their reflections. Mabel always contrived to make him feel like a fugitive from Tina's cottage, half-submerged under its régime of unobtrusive orderliness.

Carl sat staring at his empty plate impassively, wondering why Mabel had not yet cleared it away, making comparisons between intransigent town women and the compliant aboriginal women from the bush, who allowed porknockers and other intruders into their world to take obscene photographs of them dressed in nothing but a blank expression and a string of beads. If only he knew how Mabel was dependent on Ben, on her brother, on her mother and on all her relations! Without them she would wilt and die. Yet she had something forbidding and mysterious about her, like those tambourine players who follow the dead.

Ben kept wondering whether she was not laughing behind the veil of her professed anger, and her words were not meant exclusively for Carl.

Hours later, after she had calmed down, Ben asked her to escort them through the labyrinthine yard, more untidy than her room, to the narrow street whose stony surface ensured that it was used only by pedestrians. Stirred by a vague anxiety, he asked Carl to wait for him at the street corner and on being left alone with Mabel challenged her about her conduct. "I want to know why you carried on like that in front of Carl," he asked her.

"I mus' explain why I carry on in front of Carl, but when your mother-in-law come here and treat my room as if she own it *you* don' got to explain anything. She din' even say anything to the children, although Bamford keep saying, 'Ma, who the lady is?' I not apologizing for nothing! You come here with this Carl only to vex me. You know I don' like him, but it in' stop you from bringing him to vex me."

"Just a minute," Ben said to her, "let me ask you something: you're right in your head?"

"I right in my head, yes; but that in' goin' stop me from doing for those two women if they come to this room again. You tell Tina I say: 'Remember school.' She'll know what I talking 'bout. I smash her slate when she was eleven, so she know me good. But is something else I talking 'bout, and she understand. All you men don' know women 'cause you come out o' we guts. You can't know the person that make you. But Tina know me and if she wasn' frightened of me she wouldn' have come with her mother to look for you under my bed. She would've come alone. Next time she mus' come alone, Ben."

"Sometimes I wonder if you're right in your head," was all he could say, surprised at the virulence of her tone. She was gasping as if she had been running, and she stared at him brazenly, reminding him of the first time she came to speak to him among the horses.

"Sometimes I wonder . . . " he repeated. "I don't know. Whatever I do for you won't make any difference. It's your character."

"And Tina don' have character? What she got, then?"

"Tina . . . " he began.

"Don' talk to me 'bout Tina!" she screamed.

Ben turned away abruptly and left her standing at the entrance to the yard. And as he went off in the dark she shouted after him:

"Don' forget, Ben! Tell her: 'Remember school!' *And* tell her to come *alone* next time. She's old enough to walk alone."

Once more he recalled his resolve to go and beat her, because she was no Tina with whom he had a different relationship and did not need to play boss.

Ben joined Carl, who was waiting for him further up the street in the vicinity of the larger houses from whose yards came the scent of flowers and ripe fruit.

6

ONE EVENING the master sent for Ben. He was worried. It could only be about Carl, Ben thought. "I know everything that goes on in this house," the master had told him.

Far from delaying with the carriage, Ben unhitched the horse, got its molasses ready and then went to bathe at the stand-pipe in the yard. The bats were out again, raiding the fruit trees. They slept all

39

day and lived by night in the manner of whores.

Carl was sleeping on the floor when Ben got back, and that was no good sign, he reflected; only old people and the sick and those who have lost interest in life sleep all the time.

On the way up the back stairs Ben nearly fell over Fatpork, who was sitting in the dark.

"Eh-eh, Fatpork, what're you doing in the dark?"

"Well, as you know, I am not permitted to sit out in front where the street lamp is. And I obligated to obey. After all, he's the landlord."

"He wouldn't see you if you sit on the Frankers' steps."

"I'm not a man to take risks," he snapped.

Fatpork was in a bad mood, so Ben left him without more.

He opened the bolt of the half-door that gave access to the back porch, which was encumbered with the saddle, bit, two whips, traces and the rest of the harness. Then, turning the brass doorknob, he entered the kitchen, which still smelt of cooking although Edna had gone home hours earlier. He had painted it for her, bit by bit, so as not to spoil her cooking. But it was grey again from the wood-smoke and the underlying grime of thirty years since the house was built.

In the corner of the dining-room was an ice-box from America that the mistress's sister had sent for her. The oblong mahogany dining-table, with its shadow-streaked grain and carved base representing the legs of a big cat, was uncovered and empty — but the next day Edna would strew it with pepper-bottles, salt-cellars, plates for the master and mistress and for unexpected guests, and with earthenware jugs of ginger-beer and green bottles of sorrel and mauby and all manner of containers for eatables and drinkables and the accoutrements of good living.

The drawing-room was lit by two oil-lamps, but the gallery where the master and mistress were sitting benefited from the street lighting as well as the fierce light of a gas lamp.

"Why're you skulking about the house?" the master flung at Ben even before he was sure who it was.

"I'm not skulking. You told me to come, so I've come."

"Hm . . . ! You disobey me, you steal from me, you run me down to the neighbours and encourage the tenants to hold back their rent. I don't know why I bother to put up with you."

Ben stood looking at him without uttering a word.

"So you don't deny it, then," he continued.

"I won't defend myself when I haven't done any of these things."

"You see that?" the master said to his wife. "Everybody knows he steals, but he denies it."

"Come to the point, Tom," she said in a flat tone of voice.

"You disobey me, though," the master went on. "I've got you on that one . . . . You know why you're here?"

"No," Ben answered.

"Lord, give me patience!" the master said angrily. "You're the kind of person one can't pin down. I'll tell you and sure enough you'll have some excuse. Have you *ever* admitted anything in your life? Have you ever admitted to lying just *once*, one single time? Have you?"

"Do come to the point, Tom," the mistress said in the same tired voice.

"Don't you have that Amerindian fellow living in your room?" he asked.

"He's visiting, sir."

"O mother of God, it's not possible! He's been here a month and he's visiting! He slinks out of the yard disguised in your old felt hat and jacket and he's visiting! He's the first one to the latrine in the morning and the last at the stand-pipe in the night and he's visiting! He's . . . he's . . . . No. I must control myself because you're no ordinary kind of villain."

"Please, *do* come to the point, Thomas," the mistress said, this time with a wicked smile.

"Get that buck-man out of my house or pay rent for him, you —"

"How much, sir?"

"So you admit your friend's not visiting then!" the master said, flashing a finger at Ben.

"No, sir. He is a visitor, but if you want me to charge a visitor and a relation rent, I'll do so."

"A relation? What relation?" the master asked, trying to make out he was laughing.

"He's my first cousin, sir. . . on my father's side."

"You're a black man and he's a buck-man and you're cousins!"

"Yes, sir, my father had buck blood."

Even the mistress looked surprised.

"So your father had buck blood," the master declared. "Do you understand why I call you a liar? Now get out of my sight! And every Friday morning I want fifty cents in rent for your cousin and guest or you're out on your ears."

"Did you say Friday?" Ben asked.

41

"I damn well did!"

"Morning or afternoon?"

"You see when I collect rent. Why do you ask?"

"I have no idea when you collect rent, sir."

"In the afternoon, you twisted cretin!"

"Very well, sir."

"Oh, Ben," the mistress called as he was about to go. "Can you get me some citronella oil from the dispenser? Not from the man up the road. The last time I had a bottle of something from him it was green instead of red. You can get the money from Edna."

"All right, Mistress. Anything else?"

"No, thanks, Ben."

And as he made his way through the drawing-room he heard her say to the master, "I've never been so badly bitten by sandflies as I was today at the Sea-Wall."

Once in the kitchen Ben stopped, reflecting that this was a turning point in his life. Unable to afford fifty cents a week, he would have to put the plan he had conceived into operation from the day he went back to work. He would use his horse and cab for hire and run the risk of being prosecuted for plying without a licence and of having to weather the storm if the master found out.

On reaching the back porch he began to think about the house; that he associated the gallery with the mistress, the kitchen with Edna, the back porch with himself, the drawing-room with nobody because people only used it for passing through. Except visitors, of course, who admired the letter-wood Indian bows hung up on the wall and the jaguar skin on the floor, and did not realize that ghosts might as well live there because nobody sat in it or lingered in it to look through the window. He associated the master with the bedrooms upstairs when Ben had never been and only saw through the window from the ladder when he went up to clear the gutter of leaves or do some little repair. Somebody once told him that a girl used to live up in one of the rooms, but nobody ever saw her. She had gone away when she was eleven to some kind of school. He was not even sure how many bedrooms there were up there, because the gutters on the south side and the west never needed doing in the time he had been there. Getting none of the rain, the metal took long to corrode, even after the paint flaked off.

Ben was seething inside because half his wages would have to go to the master and yet at the same time he was reflecting on associations

42

between rooms and persons in a house that was not his own, but belonged to someone who was flying on a collison course with him. The master had called him a thief and a liar in front of a woman, as if . . . as if he were a nothing. Yet this was the man he lived *through*, who preoccupied his thoughts.

By now the bats were really at it, taking over where the birds left off.

Ben woke Carl up and told him he was free to show himself and that one day, to celebrate his freedom, they would waylay Grunt-Hoo and flay him or take him out on the groin by force and throw him into the ocean in which your body did not come up after three days as in the river because the sharks did for you.

They went out to a parlour in Rosemary Lane where you could drink in the back-shop, even though the proprietor had no licence to sell liquor and a police sergeant living next door was always on the look-out to crush any small man who broke the law. Carl was grinning all over his face. Ben had not told him that he was to pay rent for him. He was celebrating his freedom with a long, uninterrupted grin, thinking Ben had worked some kind of magic on his employer and that that was the way town-people managed things, complaining one day and achieving their end the next.

Carl began talking, volubly. He had made yet another unsuccessful attempt to start something with a woman, following the advice someone had given him, namely to flatter the woman he was after.

"I say: 'Darlin', you got nice eyes.' This time she eyes look like crab, you know. I say: 'Darlin', you got a sweet, sweet mouth.' This time she lips so thin they like two string join together. She so ugly I couldn't look at she without thinkin' 'bout yowaree. And she say: 'Buckman, if you tellin' me all these things to get me to loose the strings in me drawers, you wastin' you time 'cause I got man already, and though he deaf an' dumb he got a big prick between he legs; not like all-you from the bush.' "

In the corner, four very young men — boys almost — were playing cards with a pack that was so old and dirty that the cards made a sound on hitting the table. The owner was standing over one of them while his little grandson kept crawling round his legs and occasionally annoying the card-players. Ben knew a postman who nearly died of despair because his area included Rosemary Lane and he did not know who lived in which room in three yards with the same lot number and a hundred people inhabiting them. He looked around the

43

place, wondering why he liked drinking there with the continual threat of a raid at any time; then suddenly he knew he liked it for the same reason he liked Carl, because he was strange and different — or the same reason he used to like giving beggars money when he was young.

Ben's thoughts had migrated while Carl was overturning his bucket of words on him, just as Ben was beginning to believe his friend had gone nearly dumb from being cooped up in his little room for weeks, except for a few furtive outings, dressed in his old jacket.

There was the hooting of a ship from the river. It must have been moving out on high tide with a pilot on board to take it across the bar. Ben could imagine him climbing down the side of the ship on a rope ladder and coming back to shore on the harbour-master's launch. The pilot would probably have hated to be a cabman like him, just as Ben could not stand the water.

"Let's go and see Mabel," he said to Carl. "I've got to give her some money before I spend it."

"Le' we go an' see Tina, ne?"

"All right; we'll go and see Mabel first and Tina afterwards."

They got up and left the card-players to their game, ruining their eyes in the light of a kerosene lamp.

"We gone," Ben said.

"Cool," the proprietor replied, picking up his grandson from the floor.

7

THERE WAS laughing and talking coming from Mabel's room. Ben suddenly felt jealous. Who the devil was she laughing and talking with, and at a time when he was breaking his head trying to think where he could get money to feed her and the children? He pretended that there was nothing unusual in the goings-on, and as Carl and he entered the yard he began to sing softly. With the next outburst of laughter Ben started singing even more loudly.

The door to the room was wide open and the first person he caught sight of was a stranger, a man in his middle twenties who behaved as if he was living there. Ben knew there had to be an explanation for what

44

was going on, but at the same time he was seized by a kind of rage which, if it could be converted into words, would say, "I pay the rent for this room; this is my woman and the children living here are my children. If you want to laugh here, whoever you might be, you have to ask my permission."

Mabel must have sensed that they were just out of sight, next to the stairs, for she came to the door.

"Is wha' you lookin' so sour for? You don't own me," she said.

Before he could reply she stamped her feet, laughed out loud and put her arms round him.

"Is Seetram! Wha' wrong with you?"

It was her brother, and no doubt his woman was with him.

"You must be a master of disguise," Ben said, putting out his right hand to Seetram while grabbing his woman's arm with his left across the narrow room. "Come up, ne, Carl?" he called out.

Carl appeared in the doorway, but would not enter the room.

"He don' like me," Mabel said to the two visitors.

They seemed to take her remark seriously, for they looked Carl over and gave him no encouragement.

"The children sleeping?" Ben enquired.

"They in bed, but I don' know 'bout sleepin," Seetram's woman friend said.

"Carl, sit down, man," Ben told him. "It's my brother-in-law and Claris. When he vaselines his head to look like film star even his sister doesn't recognize him."

Seetram and his lady friend laughed.

"When's your next fight?" Ben asked.

"When that swindling promoter can raise the money for the purse. By January, I think."

Carl was squatting in the corner of the room and you would hardly think they had been celebrating his freedom a few minutes earlier and that he had been grinning from ear to ear and talking about a woman.

Mabel came in from the back of the room with two plates of fried plantains and fish and gave one each to Carl and Ben.

"They eat a'ready," she said, referring to the two guests.

Every time Seetram won a fight he used to make the rounds of his family, bringing food and money for the children. The last time Ben had taken him aside and told him, "It doesn't do your sister and me any good throwing your money around, 'cause when you go we aren't any better off." Seetram said he understood, but here he was, doing it

45

all the same. Furthermore, Ben knew that he was in for a round-by-round, blow-by-blow run-down of his last fight.

It was not long in coming. The moment Claris said, "As long as he keep winning I in' mind if he carry on," he jumped in.

"The losing days over, gone for good."

He got to his feet, made a few flourishes with his fist to keep out an imaginary adversary. "Fighting Farley come out o' his corner an' throw a left to me head, but I duck an' counter-punch. He ride it an' then throw a combination to me body. I counter-punch again, 'cause that's what my manager say to me before the fight: 'Don' mix it, jus' counter-punch and when he start tiring then you take the fight to him.' "

With each description of a punch Seetram went through the motion of hitting his opponent or evading the punch thrown at him, while Claris and Mabel watched goggle-eyed. Encouraged by the reaction from the women, Seetram was speaking faster and bobbing and weaving around the room, treating it like a ring where he spilled his sweat. Ben thought: *With him around there's no point floating an idea or making a worthwhile observation because he's as dense as Edna's vegetable soup.*

"We got to go, man," Ben announced, interrupting just as Seetram was on top of his opponent. "Carl and I going somewhere we promised to go before we came."

Ben slipped Mabel the money he had brought and was already standing up when Carl said, "Le' we stay a lil bit, ne?"

Flabbergasted at his intervention Ben sat down again. Carl of all people, he thought, who could not stand that room and must have been out of place in the company because Mabel put him down, he wanted to remain and listen to this pack of lies by a prize fighter who was a walking demonstration for the use of a first-aid kit. One of Seetram's eyebrows had completely disappeared under a plaster.

"All right," Ben said, "another ten minutes won't do any harm. Go on, what happened next?"

Seetram went on. Ben was so pained by the interest on Carl's face that he had bad feelings and kept thinking it was a good thing the door was open and the fresh air was gingering him up.

In his excitement Seetram stepped on Carl's tin plate, which he had left as near to the partition as possible. The spoon flew up so high that the boxer had time to catch it as it came down again. Mabel and Claris clapped vigorously, while Ben tried to hide his contempt for his common-law wife's brother.

46

"How many fights you've won?" Ben enquired mischievously.

"Is not how many fights I win," Seetram replied, after he had eyed Ben as if he wanted to murder him on the spot, "is how much I win in the last six. An' that's six out o' six."

"So you're not telling us how many you've won?" Ben insisted.

"I win ten out o' eighteen, an' that's no disgrace."

Mabel snatched Ben's empty plate of of his hand.

"If you say so," Ben said scornfully.

He had known her brother for five or six years, since he began hanging about the Durban barber-shop whose chief barber was also a boxing promoter. In the early days Seetram was meek, even withdrawn. Now he talked as loudly as anybody else, looking you straight in the eye; and if the way he had stared at Ben a while earlier was anything to go by he was prepared to cuff someone down, even outside the ring.

Claris, his lady friend, was confused by the turn the conversation had taken and she sat staring at the screeen which hid the sleeping children. She was wearing a white dress that flared below her knees and gave her the appearance of someone who was accustomed to putting on fine clothes. Ben liked her and felt she was wasted on Seetram; and he was sorry he had made such a fuss about her man's fighting, as if it was important, as if he would not have behaved the same way had he won six bouts in a row. Ben knew that if Carl had not been there he would have acted differently and taken Seetram's boasting in his stride. Mabel knew it too. He could see from her expression that she was saving it all up for when they were alone, to give him an excuse to beat her, so that she could go and show her mother how he was in the habit of manhandling her. And she would do that just after church on Sunday, with the children all dressed up in their Sunday best. She liked provoking him on a Friday or Saturday night, so that the bruises could still be showing on Sunday morning. She would not provoke him on Tuesday or Wednesday or Thursday, for she was too calculating and liked to hear her mother say, "Leave him!" so that the children would end up with four or five fathers, as had happened to her.

"My children are all mine for the whole world to see with their high forehead," Ben said to himself, "and Mabel's mother can't stand that, only on account of the fact that she couldn't keep a man. Imagine being jealous of your own flesh and blood because you had six children with six different men and used to knock about from pillar to post."

He decided to say something pleasant to Claris, but the compliment he was going to pay her about her dress would only have infuriated Mabel.

"You-all been together long?" he asked.

Claris perked up and laughed. "A few months."

"You must make him put aside some money," Ben urged her.

"That's what I tell him, and I make him join a box. He get the last draw, so by the time his turn come he would have time to think what to do with the money."

"Save?" shouted Seetram. "Save what? With the promoter thiefing you money, what you can save?"

His white shoes and worsted suit gave the lie to his remark, but Ben did not want any more trouble with Mabel, so he shook his head in approval. Thereupon Seetram became more expansive and began speaking of his plans for the future.

Carl had lost interest in the proceedings once Seetram broke off his demonstration of the fight, and was now looking vacantly out into the black night.

In less than an hour the two other men were talking like friends, Ben's dislike of the boxer vanishing with repeated offers of Arujo's rum which Seetram kept pouring from the bottle into his broken-handled cup. Ben knew very well why he had been hostile to him on arriving: he had expected Seetram to be hostile to him for the beating he had given Mabel, about which he must have been well informed, since her neighbours kept a tally of Ben's comings and goings and his behaviour on each visit, of the time he arrived and the time he left, and of every groan she uttered, whether from suffering or pleasure, during the minutes of their intimacy. But now Ben was agreeing with him that one day he would be champion of the country and went on to predict his conquest of the West Indies and even of the world, which had conveniently shrunk in the atmosphere created by the boxer's generosity and the women's laughter.

Mabel kept clapping her hands at Ben's expressions of admiration, while Claris, who on this special occasion Seetram permitted to drink the fine old rum, was mooning over her man, her saucer-eyes spinning in their sockets with every prediction of his success beyond the country's borders.

"Yes, man," Seetram told Ben, "I glad we seeing eye to eye, 'cause is your own friends who not able to stand your success. Since I begin winning they find all sorts of excuse to stay away. 'Look how the man batter your face up!' they use to say when I did lose. 'Look what he do to you thick lip! The law shouldn't allow that sort of thing.' But since I don' hardly get cut no more and I does walk out of the ring under my own steam they don' got nothing more to say. Not even 'Congratulations'. This last fight when I get a couple o' bruises, one of them run up to me skinning his teeth. 'You better quit while you winning, boy. I can't bear to see your face like that. Think o' you woman and you mother. Eh, eh!' "

Carl was squatting by the door, and whenever he caught Ben's eye he seemed to be signalling him to get up and go. Ben looked away, for it was he who now wanted to stay. Mabel was sitting cross-legged next to Claris. They were behaving like young sisters, laughing and turning their heads to exchange thoughts in that silent language that never ceased to baffle men. Ben always imagined he saw women like them on his journeys up the Bank, when darkness gnawed at the evening sky, or in the dust of the Public Road, or running along the tram-lines, and even in the faces of haggard old women. They reminded him of the mysterious divisions of the lotus floating among a mass of common plants in unweeded municipal trenches, withering, dying and re-emerging with the April rains. His grandmother never doubted the lotus was female, just as she believed the hibiscus was male, with its long ruby style.

Without warning, the rain came down, clouding the panes, dampening the air and finding them at a loss for words. One of the girl-children whimpered and Mabel half-turned on the expectation that she would cry out for her. Seetram's woman began looking for the pins in her head and then, with a quick gesture, freed her hair, which fell about her shoulders in a dark mass. Mabel, without a word, made her sit on the floor and, as though in a dream, began separating the thick strands with her fingers; and when she fetched a comb from behind the screen, Ben knew the conversation was at an end, that the rain had addled their brains in a manner the rum could not, and that the women were instinctively preparing for bed with their secret gestures — just as inhabitants of a large house, before retiring for the night, go round bolting its innumerable windows, half knowing that what they are doing has a significance beyond the grounds of protection from malefactors who work by night.

Seetram was nodding off. He was not one for communing with himself, as Ben was in the habit of doing, for hours on end, or as Carl

49

did in his strange way, especially if he could fix his gaze on a fire or the night sky or a roadside tree that no one else would notice. Ben watched Seetram and hated himself for making Seetram think he liked him, hated the fact that he had put himself on Seetram's level by professing admiration for him. The boxer's head, his over-developed muscles, his utter confidence in his ability to dominate his boxing division, his self-appointed role as his sister's protector, his belief that his woman was born to idolize him, but above all the careless, approving words Ben had uttered earlier on filled him with rage.

Ben had always admired people like his grandmother and the Chinese shopkeepers, who drew on a limitless pool of patience that without any doubt belonged to a whole culture and must come down and settle on its new-born like an enveloping mist, mopping up all evidence of individual traits. He was not of that kind. One day he would let Seetram know what he thought of him, clear the air so to speak, so that there would be no need for dissembling or false words. And then he, Ben, would be able to visit Mabel with a sense of freedom, show displeasure at Seetram's laughter or even lock the door against him if he arrived and found him there.

They were now at peace, with the children stirring inside and faint noises of the night from outside. Yes, they were at peace, even if it was only for a time. Had Mabel come and sat by him, Ben would have put his arm round her and felt her heart throbbing under her left breast and felt the belly that had carried his three children with their high foreheads. His mind settled on the peaceful recollections of his own childhood in Skeldon: the fish-seller blowing his conch to call the women; the far banks of the Courantyne side of Surinam, a passing corial on the river with an aboriginal Indian paddling at the back and his wife and children sitting in front, strung out like crabs in a line; green caterpillars migrating towards the shade, and those hot, wind-less afternoons when all the women seemed to be asleep at the same time, deep in their hammocks hung up under the house. Those becalmed afternoons were made of boats and cottages and hammocks all drifting gently up and away to that calm the aboriginal Indians had always known, that had never ceased to elude him.

No one spoke and even the insects were silent, and what stirring there was came from the beating of heir hearts.

Ben said goodbye to Mabel and Claris and Seetram, and was soon breathing the night air and trying to keep in step with Carl, who was not walking as if he was on his way to Regent Street. Then Ben remembered they were supposed to visit Tina before returning.

"It's too late to go to Tina," he told Carl.

Without a word of protest, Carl bowed his head and slackened his pace.

8

A COUPLE of weeks later Ben was lying in bed on a Saturday morning. The three boy-children of the Franker family in the room next to Fatpork were screaming because they were about to be given their senna pods. One of them kept protesting that he had asked for castor oil and that his mother was only giving him senna pods so that he should spend half of the day in the latrine at the back of the yard, out of her way. When he grew up he would buy a cannon, tie her, his father, his grandfather and grandmother to its muzzle and blow them to bits. Only his two brothers would be spared, since they also had to endure the weekly purge that kept them from their marbles and other games. All of a sudden he was silenced with a slap from his father, who had not yet gone to work.

The bawling awakened Ben, who was permitted to remain in bed till ten on Saturday, unless the master had somewhere special to go and would not walk.

Ben was in the grip of his reflections again. There was a good deal to reflect upon, a lot that needed thinking out. For instance, he *did* beat Mabel, as he had promised himself. He had not gone round to start a quarrel. Far from it! He had gone in a spirit of reconciliation, to make amends for the way he had conducted himself earlier in the week, when her brother and his lady friend were there. But she wasted no time in picking a row with him and dragging the children off to her mother, Bamford dressed in his best short pants and Sunday shoes and the girls in their red ribbons. Anyway, he had got it out of his system, Ben reflected: *All that resentment masquerading as worry, when in fact it was hatred of her mother who, if I was living with my family, would not be allowed to put her scrawny fingers on my window-still, much less cross my door-mouth.* She claimed all their quarrelling came from the fact that he had not married her daughter. But everyone knew about her character and the six men in her life, who all got what they could out of her before bolting for the safety of another area.

Other things more important were bothering Ben. The master was going back to work on Monday and he intended to use the carriage for hire. He was worried less about the police than the cab-drivers who plied for hire, a collection of characters who would smash your fingers as a warning so that you could not hold the reins. They would stick together, help one another, do anything to get one of their number out of trouble; but all outsiders were enemies, especially if they drove a private cab. When Ben had first conceived the plan he could only think of the master finding out, and more especially about the police. Now the longer he thought of it, the more foolhardy the whole business seemed. However, there was nothing for it but to go ahead. He had already paid out his first fifty cents in extra rent and Carl needed money to prance round Georgetown in search of phantom conquests.

Ben could hear the clang of the pillarbox closing down the road and he thought of the inquisitive constable who had been put on the beat. He knew him pounding the road since he was a very young man. The policeman had never had promotion, yet he strutted about as if it was his first beat in his first uniform. He was expected to be on by nine o'clock.

Yes, yes. The most important thing of all: the mistress was going to New York, she had announced the day before, and they were throwing a party next Friday for their friends. Ben wondered if her best friend, who for some reason had been avoiding the house, would be there. If the mistress's friend was indeed coming, Edna would have to buy aniseed bread, for she only ate aniseed bread. What preoccupied Ben was that he was required that night and had been given a week's warning, lest he take it into his head to slip off when he was needed. Normally he hated dancing attendance on them when they entertained, but once he knew it was, as it were, the introduction to the mistress's going away and the master's recluse-like existence till she came back, Ben minded not a bit.

Carl said he would help by getting things ready in the kitchen for Ben to take into the dining-room. Last night he was seen looking out of the house opposite where, according to Ben, loose women lived. He was glad for Carl, believing that every man needed a lady, even to quarrel with. And sooner or later one of the women would feel sorry for Carl and open up her legs.

Saturday morning, and the few waking hours during the week

52

when he should be in harmony with himself, Ben thought. But how could he be, with these thoughts about plying for hire in someone else's cab without a licence and in competition with indigent mad dogs dressed in black who could not tell a smile from a scowl and who were in the habit of greeting one another by raising a whip?

"You're sleeping?" Carl asked. He was lying on the floor with one leg crossed over the other.

"No. I'm just thinking. About Monday."

"Why you worrying?"

"Because . . . . I'm not really worried."

"What's that noise?" Carl asked.

There was a shuffling of feet up the front stairs, as if someone was scouring the steps with Edna's metal scourer.

"It's the beggars," Ben told him.

Every Saturday morning they did the big houses in a group. And the group that did the master's house was the most repulsive collection of wrecks you ever set eyes on — one-eyed, gaunt-faced, sore-covered fugitives from the sugar estates, who had barely enough energy to get up the stairs and hold out their cigarette-tins for a cent or, on a good day, a cent and a handful of rice. Ben shuddered and began to think how lucky he was and how lucky Carl was and that the secret was sticking together in a narrow dependence that brought the miseries of love but compensations as well, like being able to look at those symbols of destitution with the knowledge that your midday meal was guaranteed. He also thought of Mabel and his children and Tina, like a rock alone on the landscape, like those termite hills rising out of the Mazaruni savannahs that an axe could not destroy. And the Frankers, husband, wife, mother, father and three children all piled up in one small room, stuck together as the Arawak clans used to be in the days before their voices were stilled.

Life was as much thinking as doing, as much the inside as the outside, he reflected. So when he indulged in those inward journey-ings, probing here and ferreting there, he no longer felt ashamed as he once used to. There were corners he had learned to avoid, though, not those dark corners in which people were afraid to look but those twilight ones where doors stood ajar and tempted you to open them wide, and you could almost hear a voice saying, "Come in, ne? Just push and come in and follow the half-light. What's a big experienced fellow like you frightened for? Now your father, he was a man! He would have kicked the door and stood in the doorway with his hands

53

akimbo and laughed at the riddle of the half-open door. But he was born in the last century, when men could turn their hands to anything. I tell you, come in. Follow the . . . . " And as soon as you put your big foot inside, *bodoom*! The door would close and there would follow a deathly silence and you would be alone with your panic.

Ben was terrified of becoming a beggar and that was one of the reasons why he had always taken in people from the street and was forever becoming reconciled with Mabel and hated her mother because she threatened their togetherness. And the coming of Monday and all, with his sortie into a different kind of crime, was almost making him die of fright. He was not a coward, but there were limits to what a man could bear. He was expected to be beholden to the master for saving him from jail, and come to terms with being condemned to drive a carriage for the rest of his life, while frothing at the mouth in secret at his dependence on his employer. With this business of using his cab illegally, Ben was giving him a chance to nail him to the cross; and if the master did not get him, the cabmen would. But how else could he raise money to support Carl?

What for Ben was a torture had given Carl new life. On the day the master went out to work, Carl got up before his friend to clean the stables and look after Ben's plants and the new ones he himself had put in, cassava, sweet potato and tania.

We'll play cards when I get back from the Treasury, Ben thought. *Not as we had to do before I started paying rent for him, but in the open, on the back stairs or out in front.* And in the afternoon Carl might go visiting the loose women opposite. They were in the habit of calling him with a peremptory hiss. "Ss! Ss!" And the time would come when he would hurry over there like a pawn-fly on its diaphanous wings. Carl, who used to lie down for dead from morning till night, had sprung to life on Ben's fifty-cent sacrifice.

The trouble was that even if Ben wanted to get rid of Carl because he could not afford the sacrifice, they had become inseparable, doing everything together except riding in the carriage. They did repairs on the house together, ate together in the kitchen upstairs, drank in Rosemary Lane when Ben got money from a published article, rode the trams together and went to see Tina together.

That night, Ben decided to ride the trams alone. The Sea-Wall, Camp Street, Broad Street, Saffon Street, Ruimveldt, Meadow Bank, Houston, McDoom, Eccles, Bagotstown, then Peter's Hall, where the candleflies lit up the cane fields. The end of the line. Silence.

54

9

BEN WAS ashamed on that Monday morning when he was about to do wrong by plying unlawfully for hire. The sun was out to see him break the law. People were going about their business, the pumper-cart men were nowhere to be seen. Schoolgirls in their blue slip uniforms and ladies with parasols were bound for school and nowhere in particular, while cartmen in rickety donkey-carts were making for the Big Market, all braving the sun on that hot December morning.

He sat waiting on the master in front of his house, while the horse was pawing the ground and licking his muzzle after swallowing the few grains of sugar Ben had given him. The door to the covered staircase of the house opposite was wide open, but the old beggar with the yellowing hair had not yet taken his place on the pavement next to the barber shop. The servant working next door was going through the gate, as punctual as ever, which meant that the master would open the front door at any moment.

"There he is," Ben said to himself as his employer appeared, lifting up his testicles with a swift, practised gesture of the hand. The mistress remained unseen, behind the jalousie that opened upwards.

"Right!" the master ordered.

And off they went. Lately, Ben had been driving right into the Public Buildings yard itself, since the master had been promoted. He savoured the experience of bringing the carriage to a halt and then driving again past the cannon, which was pointing at St Andrew's church across the road, where the young plum tree grew on the opposite side, waiting to blossom wildly in February. He always turned off into High Street to go by the Magistrates' Court and that day he did just that in case the master might be watching from one of the ground-floor windows of the Public Buildings. But as soon as he was out of sight he doubled back into South Road and made for the Vlissingen Road area where the family was not well known and few people were around to witness his misdeed.

Now that it came to it, he was not nervous at all. He looked out boldly for his first customer, while running over in his mind excuses he would give if he were stopped by the police. He would refuse to admit having taken money, so that it would be the fare's word against his. That ruled out well-dressed ladies or men. Since Vlissingen Road was too obvious, he branched off into Irving Street. Thinking he had seen someone waving as he went past Sandibab Street in Kitty, he stopped. But no one came, so he drove on past Pike Street and turned right into the Public Road. Why had he not thought of Kitty before, where the master knew no one and would not want to know anyone? On and on up the coast he drove the horse, which was striking sparks from the stones and sweating from its neck and flanks under the merciless yellow sun. The ocean was always with them on the left, sometimes disappearing from view for a while, but always reappearing in a flash of grey and white. Trotting with its head down in a dogged, monotonous *clop-clop*, the horse looked as if it could go on for ever. Ben drove past Plaisance Police Station where his heart nearly fell out, thinking he had already done wrong and that the police would soon be after him or, worse still, wait for him to come back with a blocked road and battalion of blue-clad constables.

Ben thought he would soon have to make a decision to stop, for however many miles up meant so many miles back and it never entered his head to give the horse more feed that morning or to bring a can of molasses with him. But less than a mile on he was forced to turn back, for the road became impossible with its deep ruts, narrowing where the rains had eaten into its sides.

Back along the road he felt a sense of relief that nothing had happened, mingled with annoyance that he had gone all that way without making as much as six cents. At that rate the enterprise was going to be a failure and either he would have to show Carl the door for lack of money or give Mabel less and face the wrath of her mother. Thinking these thoughts and worrying about the horse at the same time, Ben drove on, looking neither to the left nor to the right for a while, wondering what a man had to do to earn a little dignity to carry with him into the next world. He passed shops of every description, cake-shops no bigger than booths, tailor-shops with their hangers-on sitting on benches, butcher-shops recognized by their signs only, barber-shops hiding behind kaleidoscopic windows, dark enclosed shops, others opened along their whole front, empty shops and shops on the point of exploding from a surfeit of merchandise. He saw them fleetingly, shadows that joined memories of an impressionable childhood, the lean and the fat, the welcoming and forbidding, shops that reminded him of people long dead and swimming in the seas of eternity, a general store recalling his grandmother, who was not a person but a keeper of monumental silences.

The carriage crossed the train lines and re-entered Georgetown,

56

where Ben sank into a state of dejection. He made for Rosemary Lane, and on arriving at the shop of forbidden drinking he tethered the horse to a tree and crossed the two planks that served as a bridge. He was obliged to call out several times before the owner came out from the back.

"I was choppin' wood. You been callin' long?"

"A mauby," Ben said, without bothering to answer him. "Put two schnapps in it."

"You buck frien' been in here."

"He bought anything?"

"No. Two o' the girls been and they call him as he was passing. He like one o' them bad and she does only laugh at him. That's why she call him in, to laugh at him."

"How much those hire cabmen make a week?" Ben asked him.

"Oh. . . . If they work every day maybe eight dollars."

Cheese and rice! Ben thought.

"An' they got to feed the horse and keep up the cab if they own it. If they work for somebody they'd get anything from two-fifty to three dollars a week. . . . Why? You thinkin' o' branchin' out 'pon you own?"

"Me? I've got more sense than that."

"The thing is . . ." the owner went on.

"Thanks for the information," Ben said, cutting him short. He sat on the single bench and looked out on the road where the horse was cropping the grass, more to slake its thirst than to fill its stomach. It had pulled the carriage further into the road than was safe, but Ben could not be bothered to shorten the tether.

The shop was empty, apart from Ben, since the shopkeeper had gone back again to split wood. He watched the horse cropping the grass and shaking its head from time to time to annoy the flies that enjoyed lapping up its sweat. Then suddenly he decided to get up and go back to the house where he was a prisoner. He had three dollars and twenty cents in the bank, which gave him a few weeks to decide which road he was to travel.

Long before, he had noticed something about himself: when he had to face up to a problem he relied entirely on himself. Now he wanted to confide in someone for the first time. And he knew whom he wanted to confide in, which came as a shock to him, thinking he knew a lot about himself: he wanted to confide in Edna. But he could not, for a man should not confide in a woman, he told himself, however burdened he was with troubles.

Ben sat down at the kitchen table and listened to Carl washing his hands at the stand-pipe in the yard.

"You got to hurry through your food to get to the Public Buildings in time, I suppose," Edna said. "It serve you right! I had it ready a hour ago. Is where you been?"

"To the blacksmith," he lied.

Carl took his place as Edna put his plate on the table. She was annoyed at him because he would not eat without Ben.

"All-you married that you kian' eat without one another?" she taunted.

"You know I don' eat alone," Carl responded.

"Th! I know how men stay," she said, "but you not going be there when I got to account for the firewood I use to heat up you bittle again, though."

She joined the two men at table, and Ben thought she was looking at him for an unusual length of time.

"For a educated man, is what you doing workin' here?" she asked him.

"You always asking that," Carl put in.

"Mr Gaston is better educated than I am," Ben remarked, "and look what he's doing."

"It still funny to me, though," she said, after reflecting on Mr Gaston's position. "Why you don' get a job 'pon the newspaper?"

"I didn't go to high school long enough, in the first place," he told her. "And in the second place, because only red people can get a good job on the paper."

"You better be careful," she said, "because I hear the master telling the mistress that you got to behave when she gone abroad or he goin' get rid of you."

Ben mused at the way he had cursed himself that morning for not getting a fare, when in fact it was the best thing that could have happened.

"You never know," he said aloud. "It might force me to get a job."

Edna did not realize that he was not permitted to look for another job because the master would not let him, on account of the hold he had on him; and that one side of him liked working there, since at his age he did not care to look for work; that another side enjoyed the hatred he bore the master, and that a third liked the freedom the

58

imposition of living in gave him from having to account to his women-folk for all his movements.

"If you eat so fast, you goin' get indigestion," Edna said, thinking to console him with those words.

A few weeks earlier Carl would have been devouring her with his eyes; but since he had transferred his attentions to one of the women opposite he ate with his eyes on his plate.

There was a plague of flies, out of season, like a foreboding. They were hugging their plates and shooing the insects away with their spoons between mouthfuls.

"He's too stingy to buy flypaper," Edna observed.

"He's too stingy to buy anything . . . . " And for a moment Ben balanced on the brink of a confession of his dilemma, in order to show how mean the master was.

The conversation turned to the Friday night get-together for friends of the master and mistress, and Carl informed them that in the bush he and his family and friends met at least once a month, when the men drank paiwari and the women had to restrain them from fighting. Sometimes the men saw visions and began describing journeys across the savannah at the dead of night to the edge of the forest beyond where jaguars ventured to attack the cattle. And people from the Arawak tribe were worse, for some of them made these visionary journeys and never came back, falling victim to Bush Dai-Dai, a monster of the forest.

"You buck people does make my skin crawl!" Edna said, hunching her shoulders and shivering. "If you does do all them things, is why town people does go and take them pictures of your women naked?"

"What difference it make," asked Carl, "if they naked or got clothes on?"

Edna looked at him, nonplussed. Several seconds later, she thought of an answer: "There's a time an' place for everything. All-you bucks in' got morals?"

"You go on talking abut the Macusi and Arawaks," Ben urged Carl. But Edna's irreverent remark had interrupted his recollections.

"Go on, ne," she said as well. "I not stopping you."

"What's the time, Edna?" Ben asked, suddenly aware that he might have taken too long over breakfast.

She went inside and came back with the news that it was twenty minutes to twelve.

"I've still got a little time," he said to Carl, in the hope that he

59

would change his mind and tell them more.

"Me mind in' give me to talk," Carl said, with that finality that even Edna, who despaired of ever understanding him, had come to recognize.

She looked at Ben as if to say, "I can't help it if he's touchy."

Ben left them sitting opposite each other, Edna picking her teeth noisily and Carl, expressionless, unmindful of the congress of flies on his empty plate.

With the hot sun raining down on him, Ben set out for the Public Buildings along the pitch road, thinking of visionary journeys, the lairs of jaguars, black-water creeks and whistling anacondas dragging themselves along the beds of dried-up rivers. Carl's world, at once real and legendary, possessed the quality of a projected vision that one saw on the white screens in the new picture-houses of Robb Street and Middle Street, moving images that rivalled life itself. He could be there next week, but now he was here in Georgetown, which paraded its precisely measured avenues, where animals were harnessed and people no longer needed to be harnessed, being so docile, where nakedness was a vision of conquest or immorality. Ben's heart pounded at the thought that Carl's world really existed, that the stuffed alligators in shop windows, with varnished skins and gaping red mouths, were real tokens of a dripping forest.

But his fascination with this world could not hide his disappointment at the discovery of a blemish on Edna's character, a slight insnnsitivity that spoiled her as an ideal. He remembered when his grandmother's eyes had begun to fail she had cut the gall bladder in a pullet she was preparing for the pot, and he could not then understand why the whole fowl was ruined and had to be thrown away. So it was now. A single remark had killed off the Edna he had driven about after dark, pretending she was a fine lady from a mansion in one of the exclusive districts of the town.

He parked the carriage behind a line of three others that had come to pick up their owners, and waited for the master to come out.

10

ONE NIGHT, after Tina and Ben had been talking for a couple of hours, she got up to go. Sensing that she had something to tell him, he asked what was wrong.

"Ma wants to see you."

And so he went at the first opportunity, anxious to show her mother that he was not in the least put out by her knowledge of his thieving. He went at about nine o'clock one evening, when a number of the houses in their street were already in darkness and traffic had been reduced to a trickle. Although the window-panes bore the pale reflection of an electric bulb, the windows and shutters were all closed. She knew that he was coming, yet she had locked up for the night.

Ben rapped on the door and waited.

"It's you, Ben?" his mother-in-law's voice came through the jalousie adjoining the porch.

"It's me."

The sound of the bolt being drawn and the grating of the lock seemed unnecessarily prolonged.

"Did Tina tell you her father and I going away?"

"No."

"Well, we're going away and you'll have the whole house to yourselves," she said, motioning Ben to sit down.

"You know how things are, though. I'm obliged to live in."

"Obliged . . . . Yes, obliged. If you hadn't been arrested I would've said you didn't want to have Tina all to yourself in the house. But facts are facts. Aren't they?"

"You prefer me to go to jail? So that when I come out I could live with Tina?"

"No, not that. Not jail. That would be a disgrace she'd never live down. But what a strange coincidence. Just when you were about to enjoy the freedom of the house, you did do this thing."

"I want to know what you've got against me," Ben asked her. "I've never raised my voice to you. In fact —"

"What?" she interrupted him with unusual haste.

"I was going to say that the difference between you and Mabel's mother is so great."

She looked at Ben as if he had struck him, but said nothing.

"We can't have a conversation with each other," he remarked, affecting an annoyance he did not feel.

"We can't have a conversation because you are not what you make yourself out to be."

"And you?" Ben said angrily. Immediately he regretted his words, which appeared to bring the conversation to an end. "Can . . . " he began.

"Tina said you don' pray. Well, you ought to pray. You ought to kneel down and pray till your knees bruise and much longer, till you feel no more pain and begin to tremble with ecstacy. No, you men don' pray. And yet that's where all the consolation lies, for the bruised knees and the bruised insides. I saw you coming in the distance and should've warned Tina about you. Men like you announce yourselves long before you come and spread yourselves around us like some enormous bat when you arrive . . . . What you know about me? If I'd tried to protect Tina from you you would've cursed me. My husband used to *ride* a horse; he didn't have to groom one like a workman."

"At last . . . at last," Ben said with satisfaction. "We don't have to pretend any more."

"I did tell you I never approve of you, Ben. I did never pretend."

He still could not work up an anger against her, though she had insulted him at their very first meeting. No doubt Tina had something to do with it. But there was something else, an unmistakable dignity that transcended anything she might say, however disparaging.

"I'm not going to quarrel with you," Ben told her.

"You think I've forgotten so many things? Your taking up with Mabel, for instance? Every child she gets does drive you away from Tina."

And he believed she was glad of it, only from the tone of her voice. Then Ben realized all of a sudden that relations between her and Tina were not what they appeared to be. Did she hate her? Thinking back on her past behaviour he saw that this could not be so. If she was jealous of Tina that could explain nothing of the hints, the things unsaid, the unease he felt in her presence, her over-scrupulous behaviour, her fanaticism. He was convinced she disapproved of him as much as she liked him and that those contradictory feelings explained her character, while concealing secret movements of emotion like eddies in the tide of some wide-sprawling estuary.

"We've never spoken to one another, Ben," she said. "Shadows, shadows! That's what we're like in one another's company. But, you know, shadows have shadows too. For instance, I *think* I know what

62

you're like. But dangerous people like you pretend and add pretence to your pretence."

"I understand what you mean," he told her, "but you're wrong. I'm just what I seem to be. I can't stand pretence and don't pretend myself. How can *you*, who's never been straight with me, now accuse me of pretence? One day you approve of me and the next you act as if I was born in a pigsty . . . ."

"You're raising your voice, Ben. That's how I like to see you, in your true colours. You would like to hit me, wouldn't you?"

"I don't hit . . . " he began, but hesitated.

"*We* know, Ben. Tina, her father and me, we know how you beat the mother of your children. And we also know you don't beat her because of her hot mouth, but because you're not sure of her. Now you understand why I see you as a hypocrite. Tina does know you're a hypocrite too."

Ben's expression must have changed because she shrank back. He could longer speak with her, since, as he saw it, she had just furnished proof of her disapproval of Tina's feelings for him. Time and time again he had given her the opportunity to be frank and she had refused to be drawn. He was now sure that had she the courage she would end up being brutally frank and testing his patience. But when it came to it she was afraid of rousing him. The calm woman with the strangely agreeable manner he remembered from the beginning of their acquaintanceship was in fact bitter and unforgiving.

"We're not coming back," she said at length. "At least not for a long time. Can you imagine my husband leaving Georgetown? He does dream of ice and departing ships and crowded wharves . . . . I love my husband, whatever he's done; but he should never've got married so soon. He should've worked on a ship surrounded by the sea, which I detest with all my heart. How can you trust anything that can't keep still? When the earth starts to move we panic and rush around like wild animals, yet there are people who spend their lives crossing the seas. You should've gone to sea, Ben, far away, to Brazil and Africa and America and Europe. My husband, if my husband had gone to sea I would've imagined he'd left me and was never coming back. And I would imagine his scent on the bedroom walls . . . . Sometimes it's the unsaid things that are important, but at other times . . . . Soon after we married, my husband went around telling everybody how he regretted deciding to become hooked for life. Oh, it was common knowledge in Georgetown. People used to meet me and say, "Poor thing," as if I'd just had a limb amputated. He told them that as soon as he caught sight of me coming up the church steps he was struck down. My people said he did it out of vengeance. Vengeance? I hadn't done him anything. How can you avenge yourself on someone who didn't do you anything? Probably that's the way all men feel. After all, he was free the moment before I entered the church; why should he rejoice at the loss of his freedom? Yet *I* was rejoicing at the loss of mine. I remember looking round the church at all the young women, and thinking that I had something they hadn't got and might never get. Truly, it was like winning first prize in a lottery. Do you know, the little girl who was waiting to lift my train when the bride-groom arrived kept hopping about on one leg; and my mother was doing her best to keep her still, while *I* was indifferent to her conduct because nothing could turn me away from the feeling of elation I'd only had once before, when I was a very small child, travelling along a deep-red river."

She was now talking as though under the influence of a piaman's drug.

"That little girl's conduct was as natural as the marriage that was to be, as natural as the beds of heliconia alongside the church. She kept floating up from the ground on one leg, waiting to seize my train and *behave* when the ceremony began, like the good little girl she was expected to be. And soon after that afternoon of people assembled, soon after that bright October afternoon, my husband went about telling people he regretted getting married, just as he did arrive at the church door. I see . . . I see. Is there any reason why a man and a woman should be *confined* in a house for life? I've never understood it. Yet that sort of thing never does seem to bother anyone else. He humiliated me by telling strangers he felt differently at the church door; yet he's a good man and I've never known him to harm anyone or speak ill of anyone, not like so many of the men who think it their right to break rules and enter into . . . 'I've entered into a pact with the devil, and with Hell am I in agreement . . . . ' So, so. But watch out for the quiet ones, the domesticated ones, those who have nothing to say for themselves, those who love to nurse the sick and who never quarrel or raise their voices, those who claim they never does dream or dream only of harmony and light . . . . I used to dream, as a little girl, of barbers thrashing about with razors, of gardens pierced with heliconia. No sooner my head touched the pillow I started dreaming. Hm! As if you don't understand . . . . Would you like to know why my

64

husband suddenly didn't want to get married? There was a reason: he saw the expression on my face as I walked up the church steps, leaning on my father's arm. I was looking at him in triumph. I had *landed* him like a fish and I was triumphant. He never did tell me that, but I know. For years I did tell myself I couldn't forgive him for rejecting me, while deep down it was my own . . . . "

"Was Tina triumphant when I married her?" he asked.

Taken aback by his sudden question she could not conceal her confusion. "Tina's got her work, so she doesn't have to land anybody. She didn't have to bind you to her by marriage."

"Was she triumphant?" he persisted.

"I just answered you, Ben. But why not ask her?"

All the sympathy he felt for her on hearing about her past vanished at the thought that Tina might have married him with the same sense of triumph as *she* had married Tina's father. Looking back on their courting, on her actions, her words, he realized that that was not Tina's style. She was not calculating like her mother, nor given to endless reflecting. If she was not studying, she was tidying the house or getting things ready for the next day. Not once had he seen her passing her time by looking through the window; not once had he known her to be involved in any intrigue or to show interest in any intrigue. In fact, analysing her character for the first time, he could find nothing with which to reproach her, despite the muddy waters stirred up by her mother.

Ben had no wish to continue speaking to Tina's mother. Then, all of a sudden, it occurred to him that they had been talking without any thought of her husband in the room at the back of the house.

"Suppose your husband heard us?" he asked in a muted voice.

She smiled like someone who was overwhelmed by good news and could not take it in all at once.

"If he heard us," she said in the end, "it's because he wanted to hear us. And when all is said and done, I *did* speak the truth. You want to go, don't you? Well, why not get up and go? To the house you're *forced* to live in. You're not afraid of the dark outside, are you? I know what country people are like. A moon's come out to light up the road. But you country people believe in Moon Gazer, I forgot. When it's dark you're afraid of spirits that hold meetings under the trees; and when the moon's out you go in terror of Moon Gazer standing at the crossroads."

"If I had brought property into the marriage," he said, "you would've forgotten where I come from or that I work with horses. Yes, I come from the country, where people don't spend half their lives praying or torturing themselves. An aunt of mine used to boast to her husband that she had set out to catch him, but far from holding it against her the two of them used to laugh about it together . . . . "

Now Ben was constantly aware of her husband sleeping in the bedroom at the back, and of the fact that nothing pleased her more than that she had finally roused him. He wanted to taunt her with his belief that she had been prepared to give herself to him while Tina and he were courting; that she could never forgive him for not having touched her; that what dismayed her about being obliged to go away with her husband was not the distance she would be putting between herself and Georgetown, but rather that she would be unable to keep an eye on Tina, whom she could not bear to lose. He was silent about these things and much more, which gave her away as a hypocrite who laid camouflaged trails whenever she spoke. Ben wanted to say that it was a mystery to him how Tina had escaped her influence, which hung around the house like the rank odour of locust fruit.

"I suppose I should say how you offended me and that I'll tell my husband, so that he'll know the kind of man Tina married," she said. "Well, I won't. Not yet, at least."

"I feel sorry for him," Ben could not help saying. "And I can understand how he came near to abandoning you at the church door."

"Now I can go away, because I've got to know what I always wanted to know, Ben."

"I didn't start it," he told her, getting up abruptly. "And if for once you're prepared to face the truth, it's the best thing for Tina, your going away. Please tell your husband goodbye for me. He's one of the finest men I've ever met."

"I think so too," she said. "That's why I stick by him, in spite of everything."

"Goodbye," Ben said, and put out his hand.

But she declined to shake it.

"You must never do what you don't mean," she said.

"I do mean it," he insisted, suddenly gripped by an impulse to make amends. "You always reject any attempt to be friends."

"For Tina's sake."

"No," he protested. "You were kind . . . in the beginning."

Ben shook her hand and was about to complete the gesture by

placing his left hand below his right. But she drew away and faced the door.

He opened the door and heard it close behind him, and the bolts being drawn, and was aware of the silence of the yard and the silence of the street and of the worlds they all inhabited, like bubbles, briefly illuminated by the reflected light of others. And though he knew he should be glad that the burden of Tina's mother was to be lifted from their lives, he felt a great sadness accompany him down the well-scoured stairs and along the pavements littered with paper from the nut-vendors' stalls. He had always wished her somewhere else, because she troubled him; but he could not take pleasure in her imminent departure.

Then other things occurred to him, like the possibility of her disclosing to her husband things that would reduce him in his estimation. Little as Ben knew him, he shared her view that he was a fine man, whose strangeness was the strangeness of the human heart. Tina had taken after him, preferring quietness to turbulence in her relations with others. Ben did not believe at all the story of how he had gone around telling strangers how he regretted marrying, because it was so uncharacteristic of him and so characteristic of the way *she* saw people.

That night he lay awake thinking of Tina's mother and wondering how she would adapt herself to living in the bush.

11

THOMAS SCHWARTZ was sitting at the casement window of the tower-like structure which crowned his house. The book in his hand was held up in a reading position, although he was no longer reading. His wife, who had set in motion all the preparations for their party that night, was lying down in their bedroom, having put off her mid-afternoon nap until a half-hour ago. The small alabaster clock on the chest had struck six a while before, so that there was only an hour left before the first guest arrived.

His wife was leaving for New York in three days' time; in fact the ship that would take her there was in harbour and could be seen out of one of the tower windows. She went every two years to see her sister who pestered her with letters in the intervening period, complaining that she was lonely and found it impossible to wait out the time until she came. At first Mrs Schwartz disliked his wife going off like one of these women who did as they pleased and flaunted their independence to the chagrin of their husbands. But he had come to understand his wife's needs and thought it wise to indulge them, since the price was a small one to pay for the advantages marriage had brought him. Up to the time when her brother had got himself into trouble, their marriage had been as perfect as it could be in the circumstances. The young man's need for money had dragged him down and now that the embezzlement matter had been cleared up for good, Schwartz was no more than well-off and only just able to maintain the front of middle-class respectability indispensable to his status as a senior civil servant.

While Mrs Schwartz's relations with her servants were unconstrained Schwartz was always uneasy in their presence, so much so that he felt obliged to exaggerate the authority in his voice when speaking to them. But this uneasiness also afflicted his intercourse with minor civil servants, his barber, his tenants and beggars. When prisoners were sent to weed his yard under the supervision of their guards, he had no idea what to say or what tone of voice was suitable for explaining what had to be done. In the end he decided on a harsh, abrupt manner, because in that way his status would not be at risk. He would retire behind the venetian blinds and watch the prisoners wielding their cutlasses in a desultory fashion,while reflecting on the fact that nothing prevented them from overwhelming the guards and penetrating into his house.

Apart from the distress his brother-in-law's conduct had caused him his chief source of worry was the moodiness and impertinence of his cabman Ben. All working people should know their place, because order depended on everything being in its place. Mr Schwartz had conceived a hatred for Ben that was even greater than his hatred of East Indian beggars whose manner and physical deformities warranted, in his opinion, urgent action by the authorities. Two considerations had prevented him from teaching Ben a lesson once and for all. The first was his wife's disapproval of any harshness towards their servants and tenants; the seond was Ben's competence. Few people knew as much about horses or could cope with repairs that required the combined skills of a gutter-smith, carpenter and plumber. But his wife would be away for weeks and he would seize the opportunity to make an issue of the slightest impertinence or disobedience on Ben's part.

Mr Schwartz reckoned that a confrontation with Ben was inevitable, for not only was his status threatened but a hatred similar to his own was consuming the cabman. As a Civil Servant in authority he knew that a matter like this had to be settled once and for all before it got out of hand. Ben was no more than a criminal or a beggar with a job, only different from most other beggars in that he was spared a physical affliction. The prisoners who came to weed his yard were not paid, yet they dared not look him in the eye. Ben, on the other hand, who was paid a wage and given free accommodation, was in the habit of gazing at him in a manner that enraged him to the point of distraction. The fellow had to be put down and the time to do it was while his wife was away.

His obsession with Ben often merged with his dislike of East Indian beggars, who would "take over the country one day", he often told his acquaintances during private conversations in the course of which he elaborated his violent solutions to the colony's problems with a fervour that some of them found repugnant.

It was not that Mr Schwartz had no sympathy for the poor. No, no. His father's house had once supported a number of hangers-on and he himself had allowed Fatpork the freedom of his own home until he discovered that he had become diseased. Rather it was his personal contact with the poverty-stricken that uncovered certain deep-seated prejudices when they did not respond in a certain way. Ben was impertinent and conspicuously lacking in gratitude, while the East Indian beggars represented a threat to the very order that tolerated and indirectly supported them. In fact, Mr Schwartz would have drawn the attention of anyone who pointed a finger at him to his early work as a Civil Servant, when he was head of the Poor Law department and travelled the length and breadth of the colony to conduct a survey of poverty and destitution. It was he who drew up a report on conditions in the New Amsterdam hospital and intimated that action was necessary to alleviate the misery its inmates were obliged to endure. He recalled that two patients shared one bed and in a few cases three. The cats allowed to live under the hospital to prey on the rats had bred so successfully that, to sustain themselves, they had taken to stealing the patients' food, so that those who were not vigilant or the unfortunate ones who were too weak or frightened to defend their plates did without food until the next meal. In the yard, throughout the day, the cats could be heard squabbling with the stray dogs that multiplied as freely as they did. Lacking the cunning and boldness of the cats, they were unable to penetrate into the hospital, and they dragged their skeletal frames from one part of the hospital yard to the other in search of the remnants of anything edible which might have been thrown out of one of the windows. The infernal scenes within the hospital and in the surrounding area confounded him, and for days afterwards he looked down deep into his conscience to find out if he should summon up the courage to write an account of his experience that might well stand in the way of any promotion. In the end he composed a report of everything he had seen, ending it with the vision of more than twenty vultures perched on the mortuary roof with wings outstretched after a torrent of rain. He had seen them in Georgetown but never in such numbers, and they seemed to him a precursor of the end of the world. They flew down into the yard to consume the corpse of an animal, hopping about indolently when worried by the dogs, but returning as soon as the ground was clear.

Ben, however, and those like him were the aggressive aspect of poverty that did not flinch from staring you in the face. Charity could not avert their gaze and indulgence simply made them bolder. Such people could only be dealt with in a certain way, Mr Schwartz told himself; they understood only one tone of voice. When his wife came back from abroad the matter would be settled once and for all. And in the last resort he could always get the police, to reactivate the charge of theft from which he had saved Ben.

His wife appeared in the doorway, a tasselled shawl thrown over her shoulders against the cool evening air.

"You fell asleep?" he asked her, placing his book on the window ledge.

"Yes, thank Heaven. You don't want me to go, do you?"

"Claire, of course I do."

"Four weeks — it's not the end of the world, is it?" She was now standing by the window in front of which he was sitting.

"It's *not* the end of the world, and in any case I'll be well looked after. Between Edna's meals there'll be a lot to do."

"When we got married you used to behave as if I needed protection from the demons of this world. Now all the demons have vanished, eh?"

"Not in New York," he said jokingly.

"Ah, if I knew what you meant . . . . "

70

"Nothing, dear Claire. Nothing. Your beloved New York is waiting for you, your sister's waiting for you, and I'll be waiting for you."

"You used to protect me in the beginning. Don't I need protection any more?"

He answered with a gesture that indicated how powerless he was to maintain the régime to which he had once subjected her. The more she leaned on him the more his grip on her weakened, exposing what lurked beneath the contrivance of marriage. He knew that if he said to her, "Don't go," she would stay. And that, above all, had damaged his pride, the fact that she never resisted. When he had asked for her hand in marriage he had not underestimated the weakness of his position: he was, after all, fourteen years older than she and had presented himself at a time when, as everyone knew, she was still in love with the small-islander. But the day she said, in answer to his complaint that she had not grown to love him, "Don't I do everything you say?" he realized that she was her own mistress, that beneath the compliance, the refusal to fight, was an unflinching determination. He would not take the risk of saying, "Don't go."

She stood by the window holding the shawl around her neck.

"Those women opposite, there're more of them," she said, gesturing with her head towards the house across the road. "I've seen Carl visiting them."

"Oh, well," he put in, "with Ben as his mentor what do you expect?"

They talked of Ben, of the party that was to start in a couple of hours, of the way the neighbourhood was changing and of his favourite topic — how the East Indian beggars would slaughter them in their beds one night and would be seen looking out of the window of the mansions the next morning, leaning on their deformed hands.

"I mean what I say, you know," she said. "If you don't wish me to go I'll stay. Don't you wish me to go?"

"Of course!"

Mrs Schwartz's question was not an idle one. The longer her husband spoke about Ben and the East Indian beggars, the more overwrought he became. From experience, she knew that something else was bothering him, something he was unwilling to talk about; for when all was well he went for weeks without mentioning the beggars. If he was particularly annoyed about the forthcoming trip she would not hesitate to put it off.

"You're sure you don't mind, then."

"My dear," he said, standing up and closing his book, "if I were worried, it would only be about you not being there to supervise Edna. I can manage for four weeks. Why don't you go and get dressed? With all your womanly things to do, your powdering, perfuming, lipsticking, nail-varnishing, and all. . . . "

"All right, all right," she said, smiling as if she had not detected the nervousness in his words. She left him alone in the tower with his book and his reflections.

"O my God!" he said to himself. "This thing'll go on for ever and ever, until I am grey, until I lie down on my death bed, still pretending to be indifferent. And this sister who entices her across the sea with a nod! Yet she hates travelling and detests New York. Edna says Ben has trouble with his in-laws too. The rabble have our troubles as well. Even they are capable of suffering! Fancy that!"

He suddenly became aware of having worked himself up to a pitch and he opened his book with trembling hands. But, unable to concentrate on the text, he kept staring out of the window. The street lamps had come on and the passing carriages and cycles were lit with feeble lamps whose rays barely reached the surface of the road.

"It's a lie," he thought. "I don't have trouble with my in-laws. Her brother didn't ask me to lend him money; it's I who sought him out and suggested I could help, because I was afraid of the repercussions his embezzlement would cause. And as for the sister, all she did was to ask my wife to come and visit her, as anyone in her position would do. This continual lying to myself as though I can't bear to see my actions for what they are! Everything I did was out of love for her, out of this corrosive love, this lump that stops up my mouth when I should say 'No.' And to think that an ugly, vulgar cabman like Ben has two women drooling over him. I hear he keeps them on a string, says, 'Do this, do that,' and flogs them if they disobey. So I *hear*."

And if Mr Schwartz could have looked at himself he would have marvelled at the wild look of elation in his eye, for *he* was incapable of striking a woman.

"*And the spirit and the bride said, 'Come.'* " That a lackey, whom he paid a wage, should be able to achieve what he could not was as incomprehensible as those words she had inscribed in her "Book of Restraints", which she had read and re-read, and the pages of which were blotched with gutter-like passages made by insects over the years. "*And the spirit and the bride said, 'Come.'* "

Mr Schwartz was looking across the road without seeing the con-

72

tinually changing traffic, nor did he hear the hooting of horns or the ringing of cycle bells. His eyes were fixed on the house where Carl visited, yet he was unaware that a light had illuminated the two sash windows of the room where the women were in the habit of eating their evening meal when they came home from work.

"Tom!" his wife called out from the foot of the short staircase that led up to the tower. "It's time you started dressing."

"Right away! I'm just finishing this page." He closed the window and prepared to go down to their bedroom, where she would be sitting in front of her array of jars and boxes with her shoulders exposed.

Ben was to stand by in the drawing-room during the party for the mistress. At first it was to have been in the kitchen. His duty was to help Edna bring in anything heavy; but the master thought of Carl and came down to the room to ask him if he would assist in the kitchen while Ben remained in a dark corner of the gallery. Ben was making signs behind the master's back to get Carl to say no, but Carl, having nothing against the man, agreed to fetch and carry without payment.

"Put your best clothes on," the master told Ben. "And stay in a corner of the gallery in case you're needed out front. The guests will be using the drawing-room . . . . Oh, and one thing more. Keep a handkerchief on you. You sweat so much!"

"I know I *perspire* a lot," Ben said defiantly.

But the master only pursed his lips and continued giving instructions for the evening.

"Can I use the bathroom?" Ben asked.

"Yes. Find out from Edna when it'll be free."

"Can Carl use the bathroom too?"

Mr Schwartz nearly choked at the request, but was obliged to agree. Up till then Carl had never had a shower upstairs.

"By the way," he said, "if any of the guests ask about the *little* pieces you get in the papers, don't go on about it. Some of them are kind people and don't know what you're like."

Ben let him have the last word, but slammed the door as the master was mounting the stairs. Everything about him irritated Ben, the way he tucked up his balls, and his belief that he had the right to say whatever he felt to others.

Yet Ben was looking forward to the gathering that night, to the drawing-room being lit up for once and the possibility of the master's daughter playing the piano for her scarred husband and the company; and especially to seeing the mistress's best friend who, like the mistress herself, was a born lady. They had quarrelled many times before, according to Edna, but she was not a churchgoer for nothing and would not bear resentment. So she always came back to the house, wearing low-cut dresses and smoking menthol cigarettes that gave her a permanent cough.

Ben stood before the mirror, adjusting the bow-tie the master insisted he should wear. He wanted to speak to Carl — who was lying full length on the floor struggling to read the previous day's newspaper — but did not, for fear of waking Edna. She had been working all day, and although her sixteen-year-old sister had helped her until four o'clock she was exhausted and decided to stay on the premises rather than walk all the way to Lodge and come back later.

Now that all was well with his face, his bow-tie and shoes, Ben looked around for something to do in the hour or so that remained before they were required to go upstairs, more especially as he was in the grip of an irritability he could not explain. Then, out of a quiet evening, when only the shuffling of Fatpork in his room reminded him they were inhabitants of a bottom-house tenement that was taking no part in the evening's entertainment upstairs, out of that stillness which would have been offended even by the sound of church bells, came the thud of a rubber ball on his door.

Edna sat up at once. "Is time?" she asked.

"No," Carl answered, turning to look up at her.

Bam! came the second thud.

Ben flung open the door, leapt the few steps to the ground and grabbed hold of the eldest Franker boy, who was about to throw the ball again. With both hands on the child's collar he hauled him into the room and slammed the door with his right foot.

"So you're playing ball against my door, eh? Listen here, you little pervert! You little double-twisted cunt of a yo-yo!"

"Yes, mister," the boy whined.

"You've never had nightmares of a horse baring its teeth and tearing at the banister, have you? And every time it reared on its hind legs it got nearer to the window of your bedroom?"

"No, mister! Pl. . . . "

"And those bared teeth at the end of its V-shaped head haunted you till you were even afraid of going to sleep and wetting your bed?"

"No, mister!" he begged.

74

"Well, when I lock you in with my horse for the night and release the broken bits the next morning so that they can barely crawl to your grunting mother and father, then you will begin to have those nightmares."

"Please, mister. . . ."

"If you ever take your fat ball and bump it against my clean door again, I promise you a life of hell on earth! Do . . . you . . . under . . . stand?"

"Oh, yes, mister!"

Ben thrust him out of the door and closed it behind him.

"Suppose he tell his father?" Edna said.

"Let him bring his father, his grandfather, resurrect all his relations from Le Repentir, I'd give them the same treatment. If it's not him, it's his younger brothers disturbing my afternoon sleep when they're on holiday."

"What get into you at all?" Carl asked. "Since this morning you jump if fly buzz round you."

Ben did not answer. He opened the door without a word and went up to see the master.

Edna lay down again and drew the blanket over her, tucking in the loose ends so that it clung to her hunched-up body like a garment. She wondered at Ben's growing touchiness, thinking that nothing good could come of it.

For two years Ben had had a vague idea of what was at the bottom of his relationship with Mr Schwartz, but it was only while he was standing alone in the room one morning and caught a brief, imagined glimpse of the master standing before him — though he was upstairs and not in Ben's room — that he understood fully. He was possessed by the master. There was no doubt that he was obliged to thrash the matter out with him once and for all.

"Now, pig," he wanted to say now they were alone; but he held back, remembering that there were rules of conduct, even in the most vicious encounters.

"Now, sir," Ben began respectfully, telling himself that possession was an everyday occurrence, that children were possessed by their parents, husbands by their wives, wives by husbands and dogs by their masters; that you could hear every day in the market, "My husband say this," "My husband say that. . . ."

"Now, sir, you've got to understand that you only employ me; you don't own me. I'm not your horse or your land. No, let me finish,

75

please. You do not have the right to say what you like to me in front of my friends. Even when I'm alone, my pride is awake, if you understand my meaning. You just dismissed them with a wave of the hand."

"You're very articulate. . . ."

"To ass with my being articulate! Look, I'm sorry. . . . You can afford to keep your head."

"Can't we discuss this another time?" the master asked. "If I've offended you, I apologize."

"You haven't offended me!" Ben almost shouted. "You don't understand, it's more than that. Have you ever imagined you saw someone standing before you?"

"But," the master stuttered, "If my wife. . . . Are you being impertinent? I mean, at a time like this. . . . " He took out his watch and consulted it anxiously.

"This. . . . just now, earlier, I mean," Ben told him, "I saw you standing in front of me when I was parting my hair. I pretended that nothing was happening because Edna was asleep, and in any case you were upstairs. But you were there, as plain as. . . as. . . as plain as a photograph on a piece of paper. What I'm trying to tell you is that for the couple of years I've been working for you, a closeness has developed — on my side, I mean. The upshot of the matter is that you occupy my thoughts too much."

"I might need you tonight, but I'm not going to be insulted like that," Mr Schwartz spluttered like a lamp without any oil. "You come to the point quickly, and with a display of good manners, or else. . . ."

"All right, all right. I *want* to be brief, but you keep interrupting me. I've got this problem, but can do nothing about it. I can at least insist that *you* display good manners when dealing with me. Not only in front of Edna and Carl, but in front of your guests tonight as well. Oh, yes! Now, that's the only condition on which I'm coming upstairs, is that clear?"

"Of course," Mr Schwartz agreed. "You're certainly entitled to respect. I agree entirely."

"Good, good," Ben said, quaking at the unexpected victory and the pleasant way in which the demand was conceded, even though he knew that the master's manner was a sham and that he was seething inwardly.

"Right!" Mr Schwartz said. "I'll see you upstairs in a while. . ."

76

and here he consulted his watch again.

"Yes," Ben replied, "in a while. . . . Before you go, if you have it in your mind to take it out on me after your little party, remember how much it would cost you to repair the carriage at Grant and Company, Carriage Repairs and Harness Makers, Saffon Street. And all the other things I do around the house for you. Just remember."

Without another word Mr Schwartz turned on his heel, and Ben believed the master was pondering the fact that he could no longer maintain the house in its former splendour with several servants, and that he relied heavily on Ben and Edna to put on a show of respectability.

He went down to his room feeling dissatisfied with himself. What he had said was not what he had intended to say. He was *not* articulate. That was why he got angry when Mr Schwartz said he was, for between what he said and what he thought was a yawning gulf.

Slowly Ben completed his preparations and got ready to go upstairs and pretend that nothing had happened. The night was fresh and the smell of vegetation came from the yard next door, a half-acre of forest in the centre of town. The light was on in Fatpork's room, but the thick window-blind prevented anyone from seeing inside. He liked his privacy and did not suffer from the inquisitiveness of women and people who did not work, Ben reflected. An urge came over him to speak to Fatpork, only to hear his drawling voice. Out of his rotting body came a reassuring sepia sound, like his grandmother's. But there was no time. And often it was so in Ben's job: the inclination, but no time. He could hear the sound of harness out front and instinctively he hurried up the stairs, thinking that the first guests had arrived and he might be needed.

The table in the dining-room was set with crockery and cutlery and napkins in bone rings, with turned-down glasses and turned-up wine-glasses. Despite the two tilley lamps, there were candles placed in among the table things, ready to be lit at the approach of the guests; but the gallery was not as well lit as the drawing-room.

Carl and Edna appeared from the staircase to the upstairs rooms.

"Where've you been?" Ben asked them.

"Instructions for the night," Edna said. "You should've been there, but they treat you special."

"In any case," Ben said, "I know what to do. I'm in the gallery." He walked away, but immediately went back to them.

"You all right?" he asked Carl.

"Sure. We been in her room," he told Ben, evidently pleased at the privilege bestowed on him.

"If you want help," Ben said, "come to my corner." He tapped Carl on his arm to give him the impression that he was in good spirits.

"You worry too much," Carl said in reply.

"I know, I know," Ben answered in turn, with a broad smile, and made for his place at the far end of the gallery, where he sat down in a straight-backed chair that no one ever used.

12

BEN SAT waiting and watching. It was the custom that the master and mistress should remain upstairs, descending in a huff and feigning surprise that anybody should condescend to come. They were probably listening for any arrival and trembling with anticipation, earhole to the floorboards and batty in the air, all dressed up in their evening clothes, he thought. When the mistress came down it would be, "My dear, I'm so glad you could come!" And *he*, "Nice to see you," when all the time he wanted to say: "You're two hours late, you hairy cunt! You and your Guyanese idea of time! You wait till I've got to come to your place — I'll arrive when your food's got cold and you'll have to laugh and pretend you didn't want to stick the bread knife in my back."

Without his noticing it a carriage had stopped outside and now someone was about to get out. Ben leapt up, not certain what was expected of him. He could hear the master's heavy tread on the staircase. How could it all be happening so fast? It was just ten past seven by the clock on the piano.

The master went to the front door and as he opened it made a sign to Ben to stay in his corner.

"Hello!" said the son-in-law. "Lovely evening, isn't it?"

"Good to see you."

"Father!" his daughter exclaimed, taking his arm.

"Hello, my dear."

"Where's Mother?"

"She'll be down in a minute. Leave the door open; it's so warm. Don't sit there — come into the drawing-room."

78

So they passed through, the daughter with her arm round her father, the son-in-law wiping his dripping eye with a handkerchief he kept handy.

Ben was astounded at the daughter's youth. She could not be more than twenty. He recalled the story that the couple had married in the islands. The usual fiction for a wedding ceremony that never took place, he thought: *All fictions are permitted in these circles, if you please. But she is like her mother, a sweet sacrifice to a deformity. . . .*

Another carriage arrived and, disobeying instructions, he went to *do* something. He took up position at the gate and showed an old couple in, saying in his best voice that the mistress would be down in a moment. But less than five minutes later the master came tearing down the stairs.

"Who asked you to use your initiative?" he hissed.

"But I wasn't doing anything in the corner of the gallery."

"The more precarious your situation is, the more insolent you become. You know that?"

"What am I to *do*?" Ben asked. "Tell me what I have to do and I'll do it."

"No, you won't," the master declared. "What you're to do is to remain standing where I told you."

"And do what?"

"O Lord, give me strength. Nothing! Just stand there and wait in case you're called."

"To do what?" he asked again.

"Anything, you. . . . To help in the kitchen, or out front if there's a problem with a carriage. *Anything!* Just do as you're told."

"Very well," and Ben went back upstairs.

But all of a sudden the flowers in the vases gave off a scent which sickened him and the humidity grew oppressive, and there came to his mind a warm night at Skeldon when the whole family was gathered on the stairs and their attention was drawn to a crowd. Attracted by the children's excited shouting, he had run to join them. In the centre of the gathering a man was belabouring a huge snake, which kept slithering slowly towards the trench. Two other men fetched sticks and added their blows to the assault without seeming to do the slightest harm to the reptile. A man in the group persuaded one of the assault group to lend him his stick, and with a single blow on its head he stopped the snake just short of the water, so that its body kept shuddering. Now why, Ben wondered, should he have thought of that incident at that moment? The blow on that diamond-shaped head came back to him with the clarity of a vivid dream. Perhaps he was dead and only his body was shuddering, like the snake at the edge of the trench. Was Carl's indifference to his plight in that house an acknowledgement of his non-existence? And this personality he attributed to himself, was it the freedom of the slave, who was allowed to wriggle without getting anywhere? He inhabited a corner of the gallery with orders to be inconspicuous, to show life only when his name was called. He reflected that his life consisted of tiny, ephemeral freedoms in a long twilight of humiliation. If he had Tina's or Edna's good sense he would not show fight; but being what he was, like Mabel, he was destined to receive blow after blow until someone, judging that he had too dangerous an idea of his worth, came and dispatched him with a thump on the head.

The guests arrived in twos and threes and were welcomed either by Mr Schwartz or his wife, who had meanwhile come downstairs. The mistress's brother was late; and the mistress's friend, the one with whom she was continually being reconciled, arrived wearing a dress with such a low-cut front she would not even dare to laugh; and others arrived too, who visited from time to time and had warm relations with the family.

Ben stood respectfully in the shadows, listening to the laughter and the swish of long dresses; to outbursts and compliments being paid, the mannered observations of the men and the sniggering of the women. On the edge of it all he was invaded by a sense of superiority so profound that if the master had stopped him he would have smiled and contemplated him without uttering a word, without the slightest show of contempt.

By the sound of it, the mistress's friend was becoming the centre of attention. It was a mark of disgrace for a woman to smoke, and precisely because she was smoking the men were drawn to her, for that and the opportunity to gaze down the well of her bosom in the hope of a glimpse of immortality.

They talked of the mistress's impending trip to the United States, of some working people's demand for free washing facilities for the wives of unemployed men, of the drought to which no end was in sight, and of everything except the things that preoccupied them most: sex and the disconcerting way in which Mr Schwartz's son-in-law kept mopping his dripping eye. They talked and drank and ate to the background of humming lamps and the collision of

80

insects against incandescent chimneys.

Everything was going smoothly and no one called on Ben. Perhaps they had forgotten him, he thought, since for the night the gallery was out of bounds, reversing roles with the drawing-room.

Ah, Skeldon! Childhood! he recalled again. A cluttered night sky over the fan-like expanse of decorative palms. The world then was a view from a protective skirt, imported toys, an empty cotton-reel, scissors laid aside, a nodding head, the scent of wood-smoke, an itching foot infested with chigoes from the warm sand. . . . *Thoughts of death never enter my mind,* he reflected. *My mind, like a carriage incapable of travelling forward, is always presenting images of a faraway past. Carl thinks it's the kind of work I do and the fact that I am forever looking down on the back of a horse, which is not a normal animal but is like the silk-cotton tree that bewitches people and only brings misfortune. That's the way he thinks and why no one else understands him. . . . I suppose if I think hard enough I'll arrive back at a time before birth. Our journey through life is like the sun's, from twilight to twilight. Birth, waxing, waning, death. . . .*

Another burst of hilarity. How hard it was to listen to people laugh and not take part!

It occurred to him that some people destroy all opposition with a smile, like Edna — "Come, ne. Come within my circle, I don' mind!" She was there, serving, fetching, carrying, silently, goodness incarnate, with Carl holding the fort in the kitchen with the same calmness he would have shown were a Macusi aiming an arrow at his neck. The Patamona Indians lay down and died because outsiders tampered with their culture and trod the lands where their spirits lived. They lay down as calmly as they did during sickness. *This country's the graveyard of cultures and the plague of priests, who roam the savannahs and forests for souls to convert. And if they catch you, they put the cross on you and watch you collapse because your muscles are already atrophied from wage-earning. I once loved a woman old enough to be my mother. She never laughed at me as that loose woman opposite laughs at Carl — not until later, when she found out that I saw love as something spiritual, a disease brought about by the wind blowing on you while you were asleep. Even in those days I did not laugh and was offended when she said, smiling all the time, "What is it you want?"*

The guests were shrieking with merriment again. Ben looked around the corner and saw the mistress's friend creased up with gaiety and holding her hand to her bosom to prevent the pair of eagles from fluttering out and blinding the onlookers with their beaks.

The mistress's daughter was going to play. The sound of the first chord shone like a lamp at night; and before she had got past the second, silence fell among the visitors and the only noises were the piano notes and the high-pitched humming of one lamp. And Ben thought of the mysterious eleven-year-old girl who used to live upstairs in the tower, long ago, who never came downstairs, then of a sudden left for good; and of the little nephew with the whip, who had gone back to his parents. This instrument that took hold of the guests as only a guitar could, pricking their bowels, was not ordinary, and suggested affinities with horses and with silk-cotton trees in December, displaying their mamillary pods and distended trunks. Ben imagined everyone weeping in the presence of such music and forgiving the mistress's daughter for being hitched to the crippled son-in-law who, his handkerchief dripping with eye-fluid, was standing proudly above his acquisition. He would never leave this malarial hole to return to England, however many quinine tablets he swallowed in his lifetime, for wherever he came from would be the equivalent of death when compared to the delights of this seductive land.

"Moon of my delight,
Who knowest no wane. . . " she sang, bringing everyone's eyes close to tears.

Ben dared not look round the corner again. *These men from outside should not be allowed to interfere with our women,* he thought. Just imagine him rising and falling over her in bed, dripping his eye-excretions on to her face, since it could not be possible to perform the feat of wiping one's eyes and making love at one and the same time!

The temperature had fallen and the insects were no longer assaulting the lamp chimneys, or perhaps they had migrated to the drawing-room where the guests were. Probably they were propping themselves up by the piano, listening to those incredible harmonies, Ben fancied. And the mice, too, for that house was full of "rats", as Edna called them. In the morning you saw their black rice-grain droppings strewn about the kitchen floor as if they had been holding some kind of celebration. The mice and the beetles and the mosquitoes must all be listening and taking it all in, since the mistress's daughter never played when she came alone, only when there was laughter and jollity.

"Moon of my delight,
Who knowest no wane. . . ."

The guests were making her play it again. This time it was the mistress who began singing in her New York voice:

"Mooooon . . . of my delight . . . Who knowest no wane. . . . La-laaaa-la-la . . . lala . . . da . . . . Pam . . . paaaaam . . . ."

Ah, what is this life so sparing with joy? Ben reflected. *You're born, you flutter awhile then die, leaving a smear on the floorboards. Th! Chords and discords, all shaken up in the bag on one's back. And you're brought to your knees with a song, eh?*

The guests began to clap and call for more. The mistress wanted to be urged on and they understood. Then she began again. She was sweetness itself, like her bosom friend; small wonder they kept forgiving one another, even after the bitterest of quarrels. The men did little: they did not sing, neither did they play the piano. But they applauded, and their clapping could be heard over a radius of a hundred yards. The loudest clapping came from the mistress's brother, because his whole life was devoted to a show of gratitude towards his sister and brother-in-law and because he needed to leave his four-year-old son there on occasion.

The next time Ben peeped round the corner to find out what was happening, they were all seated at the dining-table, which was cleared of its glasses. They were about to play bischka, their favourite card game.

Over the houses and shops opposite, a moon had risen among wild shapes in the sky. Ah, yes, Ben thought, there were tides in the blood, storms and calm stretches like September afternoons. Certain mistakes could never be redeemed. You could not go back to school or recall the dead. Yet life was a constant return, twilight to twilight. He missed the laughter and the sound of the piano, now that there was hardly a murmur, what with them being far away in the dining-room playing their genteel game of bischka.

At midnight the infant next door began to cry, an incessant wailing that would go on until foreday morning. What did they expect, those eaters of tripe and skin-fish? Could they have normal offspring with that kind of diet?

Ben had most of the next day off and intended to spend two full hours in bed after he woke up, listening to the drone of the mara-buntas.

13

TO EVERYONE, the house seemed empty with the mistress away. The week after she left for New York, Mr Schwartz went down with his periodic bout of sickness and was unable to go to work. Ben came and went virtually as he pleased, but felt sorry for Edna, who had to take the master his split-peas soup and brown bread three times a day. Carl and Ben did what had to be done about the house and spent much of their afternoon time in the place of forbidden drinking.

One afternoon Carl said, "Tell him the horse need exercise, and we could go for a ride in the cab."

The idea of plying for hire had not died; at the same time Ben had no excuse to get the carriage out. So he went up to the master's bedroom and added his lie to Carl's — Mr Bruce the vet said that the horse was getting sick from lack of exercise; cooped up in the stables night and day it might get colic. The master agreed at once.

"Strange, but he didn't look sick to me," Ben mused. "In my opinion he's laid up with a bout of loneliness. Who would think that a man in charge of destroying the country's currency notes and the printing of the signature on the new ones would confine himself to bed when nothing was physically wrong?"

That morning the mistress's friend and her brother had come visiting. Ben noticed how modestly she was dressed. What he did not realize was that that very visit had saved him from the master's wrath. It was the mistress's friend who had dissuaded Mr Schwartz from getting rid of him at once. He had decided to give Ben a further week, when he would still have enough time to show him the door before his wife came back if Ben's conduct did not improve.

While Ben and Carl were talking there was a knock on the door.

"Come in!" Ben called out. Then, "I thought it was Tina," he said to Fatpork, who put his bandaged leg through the door and slid in. "Your leg's getting worse?"

"Yes. I just came for company. You're a man of leisure these days. I in' see any of you articles in the papers recently."

"One's coming out next week."

"On what?" Fatpork asked.

" 'A holiday at Sixty-Three' it's called," Ben told him.

"I never been there," Fatpork said, "but I hear about the beach. I did read a book the other day. It call — I can't remember now. It say

84

the whole of the country used to be a island sea. You believe that?"

"It's true."

"Hmm. You live and learn. . . . That lil' four-year-old boy that been staying here for a few weeks, where he is?"

"It's the mistress's nephew. He comes and goes," Ben said.

"Say that again."

"The mistress's brother has a son."

"I know that," Fatpork told Ben testily.

"So he's the mistress's nephew."

"Ah," Fatpork said, having at last understood. "You know a lot about loyalty?"

"Why you ask?" Ben said, believing he was referring to the way he had ignored him of late.

"Don' matter, don' matter."

"Go on," Ben persisted. "Why?"

Fatpork paused for a long while, then, turning towards the door he addressed it:

"I got a sister. She younger than me. I could've get married to a woman with property when I was twenty-four and I didn't get married just so I could send my sister to school, pay her school fees and thing, and buy books for her. She go to secondary school for three years. So she meet this young man. And as one thing lead to another they set up house. By this time my lady friend with the property get hitched too. And you know that women with property don' hang from trees like star-apple. To cut a long story short, I write to ask my sister if I could go and live with her and her man. She's a lady who don' like answering letter; but a answer come back quicker than you could blink. No, she say. . . . You believe in loyalty?"

"You can't force her to take you in," Ben said.

"I did actually come to ask you to write a letter for me, obliging her by your journalistic language to do her duty to me as I did do my duty to her when she was a girl."

"I could write it, but it wouldn't do any good."

"You think so?" Fatpork addressed Ben directly for the first time. "So you don't believe in loyalty."

"That's why she wrote so quickly," Ben added, ignoring his talk about loyalty. ("Haul your ass out of my room!" he wanted to say. "Haul your syphilitic carcass from my bed and don't come back.")

"Why not go and speak to her man friend?" Ben suggested. "It could be she's afraid of taking you in on his account."

85

"Naw!" he said emphatically. "Is *she*. Is so she stay. She does drown her dogs when they get tame, and her neighbours call her Shallow Love. She isn't what you'd call a loyal lady. He's going to be in for it too: if he go down with a bad sickness she'd take a look at him and say to herself, 'I give you three months to get off your back.' And if by that time he not up and about, she gone! She'd pack her grip when he was sleeping, and *swuuuuu* . . . like the wind. She does like her men healthy. You know any other women like that?"

"No," Ben answered truthfully, but certain that for every woman he knew who was not like that there would be one like that. "You don't have any other family?"

Fatpork did not answer. At last he said, "Tell Carl, don't trust them women living opposite. They does play hard to get jus' so as when they got you in they grips you don' get a chance; and when you dead you only leave behind a heap of rags." He was one of those men who had no luck with women and believed that all men had a hard time with them.

"Why you don't tell him so yourself?" Ben asked.

"'Cause Carl in' got no conversation. I used to know a woman like Carl. I did teach her to play bridge and I always loss my money playing with her as a partner. Her conversation was like her bridge."

A long silence intervened until Carl got up and left the room.

"The rainy season coming," Fatpork said after a while. "Las' night I see somebody come in the yard to steal water from the vat."

Ben was annoyed at his indifference, because it was his duty to protect the yard.

"Oh," Fatpork continued, "is such a big vat; and this drought last so long poor people got to buy water from the municipal tank. You think that's fair?"

"If I catch anybody with a bucket under that vat pipe I'll break his hand. Just tell your poor people friends that."

"Well, I'll be seeing you," Fatpork said, getting up abruptly and sliding out of the door.

Let him go, Ben thought.

The drought was going to come to an end any day now; any moment now, in fact. Ben began thinking of the roof gutters, which needed clearing of leaves. But then he remembered that Tina was coming. Quickly he ran upstairs to find out if Edna would cook some mincemeat for him. On coming back down to fetch the meat he heard his door slam shut.

It was Tina, who had just arrived, carrying an enamel saucepan with a lid.

"Why you brought food?" Ben asked.

"The last time you had nothing," she said, the saucepan still in her hand.

"I just asked Edna to cook some mincemeat I brought."

"Keep it for tomorrow."

"Wait a minute," he said and went to the door. He shouted up to Edna not to bother about the meat.

No sooner did he sit down on the straight-backed chair to watch Tina spoon out the food than Fatpork came back, slipping and sliding in his new type of walk.

"Oh, you got visit," Fatpork said apologetically.

"What's wrong?"

"You think I ought to write him or see him?"

"Go and see him. I told you!"

Fatpork had only come back because he wanted to know who was visiting. He sat down on the bed. Usually so sensitive, he ignored the irritation in Ben's voice.

"My wife and I want to talk," Ben informed him. "And —"

"Leave him, ne," Tina interrupted. "You're hungry, Mr. . . ?"

"His name is Fatpork," Ben said with brutal satisfaction. Perplexed by Fatpork's refusal to go, he stared him down, unwilling to spoil Tina's visit by throwing him out. Now that he saw her, Ben wanted to make love, not eat. At her own house he needed time, probably because he always found her in her house clothes. Whenever she came here all groomed-up and wearing her going-out frock with a comb in her short hair and smelling of the perfume from the clothes shop and not of hospital disinfectant, and knowing that she did come for *that* first and conversation afterwards, he used to go mad. He had been expecting to throw her down on the bed all dressed up while the mincemeat was frying up in Edna's pan. That was why he was vexed that she brought the enamel saucepan with food.

So she was going to feed Fatpork!

"You got to go now," Ben told Fatpork, not bothering to hide his exasperation. "The wife and I want some privacy."

Fatpork saluted respectfully with one finger, while Tina stared at Ben in disbelief.

"You wouldn't like anybody to do that to you," she said when Fatpork was out of earshot. But seeing that Ben was annoyed

87

she did not insist.

"Where's Carl?" she asked.

"I think he's opposite. He's sweet on one of the shop women."

She passed him the plate with his portion on it, while she held the pepper-bottle with the other hand. But as soon as they began eating, the first downpour came, a sudden, immense fall of rain. Ben went to the window with the plate in his hand to look at the stables, now a shadowless blur in the barely transparent downpour. Through the dull sound of falling water the morning was full of echoes, for the dry season had met the rainy season, and the chill, damp silence that arrived with it would not prevail.

"You're going on as if you're on eggs," Tina said, watching him look out at the rain.

"I should've cleared the gutter, but I didn't expect the rain so soon. I'm wondering if it's blocked up there. . . . And the horse."

And then he heard it. "You hear?" he said, cocking an ear.

"What?"

"It's overflowing. The gutter's overflowing and he'll tear his hair out because I didn't clear it."

"Is it too late?" she enquired. "Do it, then. You can always change when you get down."

He abandoned his meal and hurried to the stables for the ladder. The horse, thinking he had come to take him out, half turned and nudged him as he went by. Lifting the ladder over the horse, he laid it against the stables then closed the door, on the inside of which the rain had left a rivulet that had already reached the animal's hind legs.

The extension ladder felt heavier than usual, and the difficulty of negotiating a passage between the okra bushes of the dung heap and the trees obliged him to put it down more than once. He finally placed it against the guttering, so that its base was resting against a half-barrel planted with a flowering bush which, lacking water, had been throttled by weeds. Ben mounted the ladder slowly; stung by the raindrops whenever he tried to look up, he could only check his progress by the window of the first floor and then by the sash window of the second, which gave light to the room reserved for guests.

Having nearly reached roof height, he was about to put his foot on the next rung when he caught sight of someone in the guest-bed. *It looks like Carl*, he thought, losing sight for a moment of his precarious position. He peered through the glass, now frosted with moisture, but as the person adjusted himself on the bed Ben saw clearly that it was

88

the master, staring at the wall as though in a trance; lying beside him, naked as she was born, was the mistress's best friend.

Ben stood on that dangerous perch, his eyes bulging. The rain was pounding the roof and spilling over the gutter that was blocked by the leaves. He saw the master lift a plaited fan from the bed and begin fanning his wife's friend languidly.

Unable to stand it any longer, Ben clambered down more hastily than he had gone up. Leaving the ladder against the house, he went to his room and grabbed hold of Tina's breasts like a man starved of love who had just been encouraged by a strange woman.

"You!" she protested, smiling and hardly showing resistance.

She put down her half-empty plate on the floor and started to undress while he bruised her flesh. And, before anyone could have backed a horse out of its stable, he was riding her violently, her legs raised in the air and giving off a faint scent of powder. He rode her to the sound of rain and the recollection of the orgy upstairs; and when she came, in a flurry of distress, he went on and on till she began crying for joy and telling him what a sweet cock he had and how she always forgave him everything because his prick was not ordinary and Mabel could never give him what she was giving him, O God!

The morning was full of violent sounds and happenings no sane man dared hope for; and that room, that eight by nine, was his kingdom where he collapsed over her black nakedness with her clothes abandoned on the floor by the bed.

Tina began biting his shoulder. He knew she wanted to mark him, so that Mabel would know she had had her share and that anything else was only extra for her, which did not really count, at least as far as she was concerned.

Tina would stay for the rest of the day now, and he was bursting his head wondering where he could take her, until he remembered the vaudeville show at the Olympic. They would go there with Carl, if he was not mooning around the women opposite. Once more the plans to ply for hire had come to nothing, when in that rain he would have been certain of making a good start.

He went and bolted the door, then returned to lie down.

Tina got up and set about collecting Ben's discarded shirts and bucktahs, which she stuffed into a cloth bag she had brought.

"When you want them by?" she asked.

"Two or three days," he told her. "I still have a couple of clean shirts under the bed. How's the hospital?"

"Same as usual. I'm in the Seamen's Ward now."

That was all she had to say about a job that he would not have done for all the gold in the Mazaruni. Through her he had learnt how patients hated the night staff, who treated them so shabbily they would beg the day staff to do whatever had to be done before the former came on duty, rather than face them.

But he had learned little else of interest about her work, which, he felt, absorbed her as much as their association. She loved her nursing, though her parents had a horror of other people's ailments, and her father carried around in his pockets various condiments as a guard against infection, so that he was always accompanied by the musty odour of a grocer's shop.

Tina was one of those people who never went visiting, received no friends and devoted all her energies to the cultivation of one or two interests.

"Any trouble with the master lately?"

"No," Ben replied. He could not let himself down by airing his problems with his employer. Yet she would have listened and offered advice in her tactful way, while wondering why people tormented themselves unnecessarily.

Her presence reminded him of the evocation of haunting names, saffron or cinnamon, or the proximity of offerings left by devout Hindus on the seashore, bright flowers in the shadow of prayer-flags embedded in the sand. Yet the absence of children in their association was like a trail of ink across an otherwise unblemished manuscript.

"Carl come by me a few days ago," Tina said.

"He didn't tell me."

"He stay at least three hours."

According to her, Carl was a bit touched; but Ben said he knew him better than she did: "He's different, that's all."

She said he had talked obsessively about the bush and Orealla, where some of the Macusi had fled from the missionaries and the diseases they brought.

"I asked him why they didn't send the missionaries away," she said. " 'They bring axes and lend us them,' he said, 'and later they say they goin' take them away if we din' build a church.' "

Then diseases began to come out of the missionaries' clothes and birds began to fall out of the sky. The missionaries told the Macusi that God was angry because they resisted Christianity, because they

90

wore only a small covering around their loins and engaged in collective orgies after drinking their cassava beer. But when they took fright and abandoned their beer, they suffered from vitamin deficiency diseases as a result; and the new clothes they wore gave them pneumonia after drying on them when they got wet from the rain.

"Why did he never tell me all this?" Ben wanted to know. "The man hardly talks here. But he worships the dirt you walk on. What else he said?"

"Is when he start talking about Orealla I believe he's touched," Tina said. For he spoke of the group being protected from the missionaries by spirits that inhabited the ghostly hawk-moths, and of moonlight shining through the window meshes of their houses.

" 'I come to town,' he did say. 'Is stay I come to stay, because of what happen in Orealla.' "

"So he's staying for good?" Ben asked eagerly, and was ashamed at the way he had betrayed his eagerness to his own wife, who now lived alone. But she did no more than look at him with her sad, dark eyes.

"He's staying, yes. I wanted to know what happened in Orealla, but he wouldn't talk about it."

Instead, Carl had continued talking about the good times in Orealla, where nothing was done in haste, where rain-birds sang in the wake of storms and children collected the pink eggs of giant snails.

"Carl sick in the head," Tina said.

"Because he told you these things?"

"He doesn't talk like ordinary people," she said. "When he did speak about town it was about bathers in the rain and things like that. You ever hear anybody talk like that?"

"You're staying the night?" Ben asked her, knowing that the master was preoccupied with his own business upstairs.

"Not tonight. But if I stayed, where would Carl sleep?"

"Carl sleeps on the floor."

"He doesn' mind the hard boards?"

"Naw! Carl can sleep anywhere," he told her.

In spite of Tina's reservations about Carl's sanity, she liked him for his words, which were like an aviary of glittering birds. Ben knew Carl's quietness appealed to her too. And besides, which town dweller was not fascinated by the aboriginal Indians, however much they despised them, however little they understood their strange ways?

She had refrained from asking about Ben's meeting with her mother before she went away, knowing what their relationship was

like. But she spoke of her father; she was certain he would take time off
to visit her once in a while, as much to see her as to go down to the
wharves to watch the departing ships. She could not suppress the
feeling that she had seen the last of her mother, who was capable of
settling anywhere, provided Tina's father went with her.

Their conversation was accompanied by the noise of the deluge on
the panes and on the almond trees next door. When Tina got up to go,
Ben fetched her the large umbrella and watched her depart. He then
stood at the window looking out on the yard, marvelling at the way
affection grew and flourished, at the quietness of love, at its convulsive
violence, and at loyalty, which was conspicuously lacking in him.

14

CARL AND Ben went out plying for hire two nights later. Ben knew
that the rain would be an advantage, but he was not prepared for their
success, which must have been due not only to the weather but to the
confidence inspired by two men on the perch. They made more than
two dollars, and Ben told Carl to ask for what he liked and he would
give it to him.

"Anything," Ben said, intoxicated by the weight of the coins in his
pocket.

"Come over to the women tonight," Carl said.

"O God!" Ben groaned. "You don't want anything else?"

"How you mean 'else'? You tell me to ask. . . . "

"All right, all right. I suppose your sweetheart's going to be there."

"Yes. Is she birthday."

"I didn't know that women like that had birthdays."

"She in' a loose woman. I don' know why you does talk like that.
She does work in the restaurant down the road."

Carl was right. Ben had no idea why he considered her and her
friends loose. But even while he was telling himself how prejudiced he
was, he decided once and for all that they *were* loose, serving in a
restaurant and living all under one roof like that without mother or
father to curtail their freedom. Besides, going after a woman in her
house was bad enough, like putting your head in a noose. And
walking into a place full of women was like walking into a police

92

station and confessing to a crime. Carl needed protection, because Indians did not know about prison or loss of freedom or the peculiar distress that town life bred. So there was a point in accepting his invitation, if only to see what kind of disaster he was courting.

"I'll come," Ben told him, and not with so heavy a heart. He knew men with more than one woman who used to visit loose women just because they were loose.

"We got to carry a present," Carl said. "Is she who say people got to give a present when they go to a birthday party. I don' even know when I was born, and all-you does make so much fuss 'bout the day you born."

"So you don't know what a present is!"

"I know, yes," Carl said, apparently annoyed. "But in the bush we does give present to people who come to visit, not to people we go to visit."

"Well, it's like that. It's just different."

With all those prejudices whirring about in hs head, all Ben was sure of was that in a peculiar sort of way he was looking forward to going over to the loose women's house, not really for Carl's sake but for his own.

He had not told Carl what he had seen in the guest room upstairs. The night before, when Tina and he and Carl came back from the vaudeville show, he had wanted to go up to the master's room and make him tremble at the knowledge in his possession. But he needed time to decide how to make use of the secret. After all, it would take a lot to make a man in the master's position squirm simply because he shared his secret. In his place Ben would say, "Do what the hell you like; but remember I've got powerful friends." And that would be that, with the boot being on the other foot and he the threatener becoming the threatened and feeling a fool.

He did not tell Carl about the master's orgy, just as he had said nothing about the increase in his rent, which had driven him to distraction at the time but now hardly rankled while his bank money lasted. Something was softening him up, he reflected, Carl's presence or Edna's indulgence, perhaps. As things worsened, his reflections lost that depressing garb that kept dragging him down until recently. Well, it had happened before, but it never lasted, so he decided to enjoy the period of lighter thoughts to the full.

Carl reacted to the seasons in a different way from townspeople, who saw rain as a nuisance. He was forever looking up at the clouds as a countryman would look down at his ploughed field, so you would think there was some message in their elongated shapes. And if Ben asked what he was searching for Carl would stare at him like a man in the grip of a mild hysteria. The clouds came and went, and he, with all the time in the world, followed them although they were not going towards Orealla where a part of himself would have liked to go. "Why the hell you don't go back to Orealla if you miss it so much?" Ben felt like saying to him. "Why you don't go back and live among your naked women and talk to the birds? If you miss the wild guava trees so much and hunting labba at night, I don't know why you don't go back." But Carl would have taken it to heart and gone back in truth.

Ben had once read an aboriginal Indian story about a man who carved a woman from the wood of a wild guava tree. The carving had come to life and lived with the man as his wife. One day when they were working in their garden place, harvesting cassava and paripi, the woman, for no reason at all, attacked and blinded him. He started wandering about the bush crying for help and calling her name: "Kanu, Kanu!" But no one heard him. In the end, driven mad by hunger and pain and thirst, he lay down on the ground and waited for death. Watching Carl lying on the floor by the bed, Ben thought of that woman who changed all of a sudden; and he half-expected to wake up one morning to find that Carl had gone because he had offended him unwittingly.

When Carl did go, Ben thought, he would remember him staring up at the clouds, watching for shapes that spoke to him.

The women wore masks. Thick powder, rouge and lipstick hid their features, so that only their eyes were visible; and they peered through these slits in their masks like aboriginal Indian women suddenly come face to face with strangers while their husbands were away. Ben looked out of a window and saw the master's house opposite, for the first time from that height.

"So this is your friend!" a piping voice said.

Ben took the present he had brought out of his pocket — a pair of doilies wrapped in brown paper — and gave it to her.

"Is he," Carl said, more forthcoming than Ben had ever seen him.

She unwrapped the present, sitting, like the six other young women, on chairs around a large dining-table. Without a word she placed the doilies on the table. One of the other women took them up

94

at once and examined them in turn, then passed them to her neighbour.

"You ever see Carl drunk?" the same young woman asked, "Well, he going get drunk tonight."

"I've never seen Carl drunk," Ben delcared, "and I don't see why he should get drunk tonight."

But before she could reply there was the sound of footsteps on the covered stairway.

"Is the boys," she said, jumping up to open the door for the guests, three men with instruments.

"We thought you wasn't coming," one of the girls sitting at the table put in.

"Violet, is you?" the young man carrying the mandolin asked.

"Who you think it is? Me jumbee?"

The man with the accordion sat down on one of the three chairs against the wall and at once began playing. Small in stature with restless eyes and an impatient manner, he was wearing an old hat, a *sour*. The mandolin and guitar players stood by the table talking to the women.

"Well, I not playing until I see the liquor," said the guitarist. "You know me."

Two of the young women went to the back of the house and returned with a wicker basket between them, in which were piled bottles of rum, beer and soft drinks, which they set about unloading on to the table.

"Please for a opener," the guitarist requested. "Me teeth not what they use to be."

Carl's friend Violet fetched an opener from inside and opened bottles of beer, one of which she took over to the accordion player who, from his trance, signalled her to put it down on the floor by his feet. Ben accepted a bottle and watched the other women talking to the two musicians and Carl drinking from a glass by the window and watching his lady friend taking charge of the proceedings while ignoring him completely.

Two masked faces got up from the table and began dancing with each other to a fragile tune, like the jerky flight of butterflies. The man with the accordion played alone, which no doubt explained the brevity of his pieces; and no sooner were the dancers on the floor than they were back at the table.

What the ass is this? Ben thought to himself. *I'm going, because I can see*

I'm not going to be comfortable in the company of these layabouts. But as he was working himself up to inform them that he had better things to do with his time a chill night wind began to blow through the open door.

"Somebody leave the door open downstairs," Carl's darling said, annoyed because they were not making sufficient fuss that she was a year older than this time last year.

She stood at the door-mouth, peering down the unlit staircase.

"Is who?"

But no answer came. No sound. Only the draught came up the stairs like an invisible guest.

"Is who, ne? Oh, is you! What you want?"

Then, as the visitor neared the top of the staircase they could hear the wheezy sound of his breathing and the shuffle of his footsteps.

"What you want?" Violet asked the old beggar with yellow hair as he stepped out of the darkness.

"I bring a present," he whined, displaying the gloomy interior of his toothless mouth in a forbidding grin. "Is you birthday, in' it? I bring this."

He handed her the small packet wrapped in tissue paper, which was easily unwrapped.

"Is a packet of playing cards!" she said, turning to the gathering round the table.

"It new! It not second-hand," the old man informed them. "And the man in the shop say it got two jokers, not one."

"You want some rum?" Violet asked.

"No rum. I don' drink."

"You want food, then?"

"No, I eat a'ready."

She raised her shoulders in a gesture which indicated she had nothing more to offer.

Then he drew her head closer to his and whispered into her ears.

For a moment she looked at him then burst out laughing.

"Is what?" Violet's friend Nora asked, and immediately her question was echoed by the other masks, who started clapping.

Meanwhile the musician in the hat continued playing as if nothing were happening, apparently put out neither by the noise nor the draught from the street.

"He wan' dance with me!" she declared.

Her friends and the two musicians near the table fell silent, as though the old man had mad a more daring request. But he started

96

whispering in Violet's ear once more.

"He want you to play the new tango," she shouted out to the entranced musician, who stopped playing, disturbed by the peremptory interruption. "He want you to play 'Los Muertos Bailan'."

The old man advanced solemnly, put his right arm round Violet's waist and waited for the music to start, while the others looked on. And then, like a man who has lived in the dance halls, like those demented souls who haunt the music brothels, he led his partner away into an exhibition of dancing that took their breath away. *Tam-tam, tam tam tam tam tam tam-tam.* The accordion wept and gasped, gasped and wept in the hands of the be-hatted musician, whose eyes were now closed. Carl, for the first time since Ben had known him, looked displeased, and the way he was holding the glass of liquor it looked as if it would crack in his grip. Then it was over and Violet stood in the middle of the floor, bewildered and radiant, still holding the pack of cards in her hand.

The old man turned to face the table, bowed low and said, "I've always been happy." Then he left by the front door, and in a trice the draught ceased.

"Play, man, play!" the guitarist said to the accordion player while he dragged a mask wearing high-heeled shoes on to the floor. And his friend took one of Violet's friends in his arms and danced off with her.

"What happen?" Violet asked Carl as she sauntered up to him. "You don' love me no more?"

"You know I kian' dance like that," Carl told her in a suffering voice. "In Orealla we did all dance together."

"You not in Orealla now," she said petulantly. "You dancing or not?"

"No!" he declared, with uncharacteristic finality.

"May I have the pleasure of this dance?" Ben asked. If he was no master of the art at least he knew how to invite a lady to dance.

She started rubbing herself up against him as Mabel used to do before he blew up her belly. And he did not care that it was an unorthodox way to dance the bolero and that his prick was letting him down.

"Is wha' happen to him tonight?" she asked Ben as they went past one couple. "This morning he was different. He so funny with his ways."

"Probably it's the way you treat him," Ben answered.

She said nothing more. He could feel that her right hand was raised

97

off his shoulder and guessed she was looking at the pack of cards in her hand, while collecting reflections about Carl and the old man and the way the evening turned out, with people dancing pell-mell, musicians with the women and the women with other women to the music of a man who took pleasure in giving pleasure only because he was too shy to look you in the eyes.

Outside, the birds were sleeping in the little forest next to the master's house, the baby next door was bawling on the hour, the master was laid up in bed thinking of the next time he would be fanning his wife's friend's flower-bed, and the whole world was oblivious of the drama in which Ben was taking part as a celebration for a birthday. Up and down Regent Street there were theatres enclosed in four walls with actors playing in earnest, a man on his last legs, spitting in a phenol jar to relieve his tubercular lungs, a woman contemplating the mortality of ambition, a youth attacked by sudden dread of a dead ancestor, moist eyes for love-objects unaware of their good fortune. Her hair was down in plaits because she despised Carl, who had withdrawn into himself and saw nothing around him. Like everyone else he was drinking, but unlike the rest he would get drunk as befitted the occasion, and not by accident. The beer was now in Ben's bloodstream and he took to the young woman in his arms, who probably danced in that way with all men, and even more so with men to whom she was indifferent, in that wrong-headed way that men would never understand.

She gave a little start and stopped dancing because she had dropped two cards, one face down and the other staring up at them, gleaming in its newness, reflecting the pale lamplight of the kerosene lamps divided from the wall by a metal shield. Carl's friend stood without moving as she looked down at the exposed card. It was the king of hearts. The Red Man.

"Is wha' wrong?" one of the masks asked, and stopped dancing.

"Is the Red Man," Violet whispered.

"A lot of damn superstition," the guitarist said.

He picked up the two cards and put them on top of the pack, which he took from Carl's friend and placed on the table among the bottles.

When he joined the accordion player the other musician followed suit and the music, amplified by the sympathy of strings, left the young women more sad than before. One lit a cheap cigarette while the other consoled herself with another mask that had been keeping her company at the table.

98

Ben went and sat by Carl.

"You know," Carl said, coming to life without warning, "he tell me he want me to be his cabbie, because he din' trust you no more."

"What?" Ben was galvanized by the disclosure. "The master said that?"

"He say I could do anything you can do, and that the horse know me good now."

"And what you said?" Ben demanded.

"I say 'no'. What I goin' say yes for?"

He only told Ben because he was hurt by his woman friend, who was now cavorting about the room with another powdered mannequin, to music that had quickened since there were three playing. The other night he had told Ben, "In Orealla when you eat with somebody he does become you brother. Here in town all you does eat with friend and enemy as if it's the same." That set Ben wondering whether the woman had given him food; or if he was complaining that since he had eaten Ben's food the two were brothers and he had not yet done anything for Ben as a brother should. Ah, yes, he must have said no to the master's offer of a job because they were brothers.

The disclosure about the master's offer decided Ben once and for all: he would tell him what he saw while risking his life on his ladder with the rain pelting down on his head. This resolution not to be ruled by his instincts came back to him but he rejected it, preferring the intoxication of an irresistible desire to do the master harm.

Carl was now drunk and could not even take advantage of the looks Violet was aiming at him. He was no dancer; the three musicians were all playing, but the women continued to dance with one another, a wild look in their submerged eyes, as if it were Carl's woman's last birthday.

All of a sudden Carl got up from his seat and started dancing by himself with steps that could not have been made up in town. Ben was sure they were from the Macusi and tried to suppress the shame he felt, especially as no one took the slightest notice of him, not even Violet, who had been eyeing him a minute earlier. She came over to Ben and started talking.

"It get so hot! You don' like me," she said. "I can see that. You don' like my style. You don' like my friends neither, or the house or our drink. They all clean, you know. . . . "

"I didn't say I don't like you," he answered. "I don't know you, that's all."

99

"You jus' like that Edna who does work for your people. She's a servant, like us, but she does turn up her nose when she go past the house, as if it got a bad smell. You jus' like her. Carl's the only one in that house —"

"You and Carl!" Ben said angrily. "Carl's lonely, that's why he comes over here regularly."

"Regularly? If he come over twice a week he come a lot."

"It's your birthday," Ben said, half-forcing a smile.

And the hostility vanished from her face.

"Yes, is my birthday. An' every year less and less men does come to my party. Is not that I kian' find them; is just that I get more choosy every year. I kian' stand rowdy men, especially Regent Street rowdy men. . . . I get my first child when I was fifteen and did bear three children in my mother house. They use to call her 'Ma' and call me Violet, even though that's not my name. My last child father invite me to town, but when I arrive he wasn' there to meet me. I been here ever since, knocking from pillar to post. What I goin' get hitched to a buck-man for, who kian' do nothing for me? Me and the girls join together to rent this place and all we get from you men is bad talk. But let one of us crook we finger and all-you come running."

One of the lamps went out, and in the near darkness the women's faces floated about the room like unhappy spirits with holes in their heads.

"Put some oil in the lamp, ne?" Violet shouted.

"Nora!" one of the other women shouted in turn.

"Put it in yourself," answered a strange voice from inside.

"Last year," continued Ben's companion, "one of the girls did bring her man to live here, and he didn' loss no time tryin' to boss us round. But we turn on him and show him the door."

"All of this talk," Ben declared, annoyed by her confidence, "all of this talk, when the simple fact is you don't like men. Look how you treat Carl, yet you know he does spend half the day looking over here. Even when you're at the restaurant he looks over here at your broken windows."

The lamp was lit once again and it revealed the musicians, who were playing a piece in the rhythm of the Santapee bands of Christmas time, to which only two of the women were now dancing.

"I don' got to account to you for the way I does treat Carl," she told Ben. "Take him home, ne. He only making a fool of himself, dancing alone."

100

And, indeed, two of the women sitting at the table were laughing at him. The young woman with high heels went to join him and began dancing in the rhythm of the piece the band was playing, while he was crossing from one side of the room to the other in a demonstration of his Macusi joke dance. Ben got up and grabbed hold of his right arm.

"You don't see how they're laughing at you?" Ben told him. "Come home, man. You don't have any shame in front of women? They don't ever let you forget that kind of behaviour, I'm telling you."

But Carl wrenched himself free and carried on.

The newly lit lamp was smoking and giving off a faint, sickly smell; and when the music stopped there was an oppressive silence in the room, the women being sprawled on their chairs and Carl on the floor like a dead dog.

Ben stood by the door surveying the room in its twilight, its objects perceived rather than seen, the disembodied powdered faces of the women, the musicians preparing to play another piece, his Macusi companion crumpled on the floor not far from Violet's feet, the lamp chimneys glowing like trumpet-flowers and the expanse of bare floor trampled only by women day after day. He opened the door and closed it behind him.

15

IT WAS half-past one by the drawing-room clock when he scratched the match and placed it near the clock face. He was in two minds as to whether to go upstairs, and cursed the softness that had taken hold of him these last couple of weeks. It came and went like his anger in an ebbing and flowing that controlled his character even. But climbing the staircase brought back his resolution. He heard the accordion from across the road and could see Carl sprawled on the floor at Violet's feet through the open window, and Violet herself teasing him with the sight of her drawers. Somehow Ben's resolution was stiffened by thinking of these things and he went and knocked on the master's door. He knocked again, harder.

"Who's it at this time of night?"

"It's me, Ben."

"What the devil's wrong?"

"I've got something important to tell you."

"Tell me tomorrow morning," he said, with that tone Ben could not even bear thinking about.

"No, it's got to be now!"

Silence fell in the house and only the wailing accordion penetrated through the skylight.

Eventually the master came out, tying the cord of his dressing-gown.

"D'you realize you've woken me up?"

"You would've woken me up in the circumstances," Ben countered.

"Don't let me have any of your damn impertinence. You're getting above yourself when you've nothing to be above yourself about!"

"When I tell you what I know, you won't be so cocky."

"What?"

But Ben could hear from his voice that the master was not so sure of himself.

"You? Know of me?" he said.

"I saw you through the window, you and the mistress's best friend. She was lying down on the bed naked."

Ben stopped deliberately, but the master did not react so he went on.

"I came to tell you I knew and that. . . . "

"Who would believe I saved you from the clutches of the police? You always complain you don't have any freedom; here's your chance! I won't stand in your way if you want to go. Of course I'll give you something — thirty dollars and a reference."

Ben laughed in his face, a mirthless laugh, when he recalled his stingy ways and the fifty cents rent he had to pay for Carl, and the string of humiliations he had endured in front of the women of the house, the mistress and Edna, and the way he was ignored at the party.

"Listen to me, *Master*. You *are* going to give me a reference. I'll write it myself. . . . "

"All right, all right. You being a *journalist*, you'll know what to write. I'm always telling my wife how well you write."

"No, Grunt-Hoo."

"Grunt what?" he asked.

"I call you Grunt-Hoo because you look like a pig."

"Damn you! It's the police for you. You go around sulking all day, spread lies about me stealing the Treasury's money and now you've got another lie under your hat you think you can frighten me with. Go on. Get out!"

Ben decided to test him and turned to go.

"Look. . . . Have you told anybody about what you thought you saw?"

"Not yet."

"Come. Let's go down to the drawing-room and talk about this unfortunate thing. You're a man who knows about women."

Mr Schwartz slapped Ben's back; then, holding his arm as they went down the staircase, he continued talking.

"You people expect your employers to be perfect," he said, "while you yourselves indulge from time to time."

"Oh, I don't mind if you indulge. Indulge as much as you like. Oh, no. I'm concerned about the extra rent you make me pay for Carl, and about the low wages you pay me. And about how you offered Carl my job."

"He told you that? My God! You've got to admit you're a difficult man to deal with. The night of the party my guests refused — *refused*, I can tell you — to ask you to do anything. One of them, my son-in-law in fact, got Carl to fetch a cab because you're so rude whenever you speak to him. Now you've got to admit you're not an easy man to get on with. Do I treat Edna badly? And Carl?"

"No. But they're docile," Ben snapped.

He began descending the staircase once more; and when they were in the drawing-room he had the satisfaction of seeing the master go into the kitchen and light a kerosene lamp himself, which he brought into the cheerless drawing-room and set on the table at the foot of the stairs.

"Let's talk this business over like two educated men who don't despise . . . a bit of . . . you know what."

Ben sat down and saw his face lit up by the spotless brass lamp with its elegant smoked-glass chimney.

"What do you want?" Mr Schwartz asked in a wheedling voice.

"I want to have Carl by me without paying any rent," Ben told him.

"You're asking a lot; but I'm a reasonable man."

"I'm not finished. I want seven dollars a week."

"That's impossible! You tell my wife whatever you like, I can't afford that sort of money."

103

They sat bargaining for a long time, while the music from across the road arrived on the breeze, bringing hallucinations of powdered women. Ben offered to keep the house in perfect condition. He reminded his employer of the vegetables Carl grew in the yard, which ended up on his table for free. But in the end it was Ben's threat to tell his wife when she got back that made him settle for six dollars and fifty cents a week and the concession to allow Carl to eat at the kitchen table. And when it was all over the master could not resist reminding Ben that he was able to revive the police charge he had saved him from. But Ben was quivering at the thought of being able to give Mabel two dollars a week on top of the dollar he gave her and still have two dollars and fifty cents in his pocket!

"You understand you've got to keep your part of the bargain?" the master said. "You know that. . . . "

"Don't threaten me. Those days are over."

"We mustn't threaten each other, you mean. Just as a matter of interest, do you ever . . . . Oh, it doesn't matter."

He spoke bitterly; and Ben was sure he was thinking of the days when slaves used to be strung up and beaten for minor offences.

"Yes, one more thing," he began again.

"Haul your ass!" Ben said, putting out his hand to prevent him from coming nearer.

Mr Schwartz stood looking at his lackey with murder in his eyes. Then in a high-pitched voice he spoke:

"The worst thing we could do in this country is to educate people of your class! You're my servant and, whatever hold you've got over me, you'll remain my servant. If you cut my throat, while I'm dying I'll have the satisfaction of knowing you're my servant. You'll always address me as a servant should. Never you use insulting language to me — never again!"

He kept slapping the fist of his right hand against his thigh as he talked.

"You've finished?" Ben said, pretending that Mr Schwartz's words had had no effect on him.

"Yes. Now get out!"

Ben felt he had never been closer to knocking out the master's teeth, but he smiled before leaving. Then once at the foot of the staircase he felt tempted to do violence to something or other, all the more so because of that damned accordion which kept intruding on the night silence. To escape its sound he went down to the stables to see if the horse was all right. On the way back to the house he saw light in one of the upstairs rooms. The master had not yet gone back to bed! He could not find peace of mind! And Ben's dejection was immediately transformed into an indescribable joy. He saw nothing except the wan lamplight through the panes of the sash window and the open skylight below the eaves; he stood watching that part of the house, thinking that the worst thing that could happen to him would be to witness the blowing out of that lamp that could signify the return of a peace of mind sufficient to allow the master to settle down and fall asleep.

Ben had always dreamed of flattening him, either in the flesh or in the spirit; and here before his eyes was the evidence of his extinguished spirit, a window smudged with yellow light.

He went and lay down to savour his feelings. Oh, the satisfaction of hatred that did not have to masquerade as what it was not!

After a period of confusion in which his thoughts alternated between anger and dismay at his helplessness, Mr Schwartz stood rooted to the spot, hardly crediting his ill luck. If it had not rained Ben would not have climbed the ladder and witnessed what had happened. Furthermore, his wife's friend's first visit with her brother was uncharacteristic. She never came to the house when his wife was away. And the second visit, when she came *alone* — he would have considered it unthinkable if someone had suggested that she might — was another link in a chain of unlikely events. If the idea were not absurd he would have said the whole thing was a conspiracy between her and Ben, designed to trap him into committing his indiscretion. Everything about the incidents was strange, even bizarre. Never had he seen her in a dress or bodice that did not have a deep neckline; yet on the occasion of the two visits she was buttoned up to the neck. In fact the dress she wore the second time had a turned-up collar secured just under the chin. It would never have entered his mind that, dressed like that, she had come to provoke him. All his acquaintances desired her, but in the way one desired an object that could not be dislodged. His wife had told him once that since the friend became a widow no one had proposed to her because she was considered unattainable. How could he, married, portly and plain of face, conceive of attaining a prize like that?

She had come, she said, to see how he was faring alone; and immediately he thought of Edna who was capable of misconstruing the visit and gossiping. And while she was standing in the gallery, the

105

sky darkened and the wind began to shake the panes. And when the season broke he knew from the hollow sound of rain on the roofs and the gurgling of water through the pipes that the downpour would last a long time. She sat on the couch while he closed the numerous windows at the front of the house and watched water accumulating on the warped stairs; and as he bolted the windows, one by one, he could not suppress the feeling he was shutting in something that belonged outside. He could not offer her green tea since, at all costs, Edna was not to know he had a lady visitor.

"I'll have a shot of rum. Would you . . . ?" he asked, knowing that women in his circle did not touch alcohol.

"A tiny tot. I can't drink."

"Ah . . . tiny." He took out the decanter, a bottle of ginger-beer and two schnapps glasses, then poured a suitable shot into each glass, adding some ginger-beer to hers.

"Here's to your loneliness," she said, lifting her glass. And for the first time since she arrived she seemed herself.

Soon she was talking volubly and he, thinking only that Edna might hear them, thanked God for the rain, which had the pervasive sound of waves on a nearby shore.

"I should never have drunk this," she said, laughing softly. "Never, never, never. It only leads to indiscretion. . . . How close it is! Can you open a window? Oh, I must lie down; I'm not accustomed to alcohol. Tom. . . . "

Mr Schwartz, obsessed with the idea of Edna coming out, suggested that she took smelling-salts rather than lie full-length on the couch.

"I must lie down, Tom. I've got eye-turn."

"All right, but not down here."

She leaned on his arm and allowed herself to be led up to the bedroom where guests slept. . . .

Mr Schwartz suddenly realized that the pleasurable recollection of his experience had displaced the grim thoughts of a while earlier. He turned his mind to Ben. The reasons for crushing him were now twice as strong. Just as, up to a few years previously, all his energies had been devoted to securing promotion — mainly to impress his wife — now he would never be at peace until he destroyed Ben. What a fool he had been not to have followed his instinct and shown him the door soon after his wife went away. He had waited, so as to sound out Carl, and after that because of the advice his wife's friend gave him. Reason had always been inferior to his instincts as a guide, he reflected bitterly.

But the longer he thought of the matter, the clearer it became that Ben's position was unassailable. He need only disclose what he had seen with his own eyes for the clouds of scandal to gather, the very scandal that he had spent most of his savings to avert when news of his brother-in-law's embezzlement of government funds reached him. Besides, how would he be able to face his wife's scorn if she found out?

Mr Schwartz finally put out the light, and immediately heard the music from across the road and the laughter of the women through the rain. For a while he was filled with indescribable envy of these poor people, who possessed no carriages and had no husbands to stand by them; who worked for a precarious wage that would be insufficient to maintain his horse. And for the first time in his life he was prepared to subscribe to the view that the individual had no control of his own destiny, which was mapped out from birth to death, as the East Indian palmists would have their clients believe. He listened to the accordion and the singing violin, and wondered why, with his education and upbringing, he had not been able to avoid the mistakes that bring anguish in their wake. His life was, in his eyes, a failure. At the same time there was no turning back. Nothing could be undone.

Ben woke up from a dream of beggars under the front windows, lining up to receive their weekly stipend. It was Carl who had just come in, bringing with him a gust of night air and the reek of rum.

"Shut the door!"

Carl kicked it shut with his foot, looked about him, then tottered to the foot of the bed where he hunched down on the floor, without his backside touching the ground, in the way aboriginal Indians squat.

"Is what now?" Ben asked.

"You people," he said, "who does eat after dark and allow strangers to bury you dead, I don' care for you, you know." He had more than once spoken of undertakers, who were permitted to bury people they did not know; but it was the first time he mentioned the habit of eating after the sun had gone down, which Ben knew he despised.

"Even if you wanted to eat, there's no food," Ben told him.

He remained in the shitting position when, with the long, distressing night behind him, he would have been expected to lie down and look for sleep with the utmost speed. But he sat as if he were over a

107

latrine hole and did not want to contaminate his backside with the surrounding wood.

"Go to sleep, ne," Ben said, not wishing to rouse him.

"When I go anywhere it'll be back to Orealla."

"What happened, then?"

"That's the las' time I crossing the road," he said, wishing in his roundabout way to convey his intention never more to visit Violet, Nora and their friends.

"So you say," Ben commented, concealing his delight. He had not dared to admit, while at the party, that he enjoyed Carl's humiliation at the hands of the women, that although he started the evening defending him, disquiet at the way they were treating Carl was built on a solid foundation of satisfaction at the knowledge that the house was not a place where he could be happy.

"I say so, yes," Carl said, then lay down as though he had put down a burden.

"Don't worry," Ben told him, disclosing what he had not intended him to know before morning. "Tomorrow we're going to drink in Rosemary Lane and I'll give you a present to take to Mabel."

"Why?"

"Because I came into some money. And if you like you can go to the whores that live on the edge of town. They're clean. . . . You're listening?"

"I listening."

"That's all. Tomorrow we're going to do whatever comes into our mind. You can even ride the horse if you want. Or we can take a trip in the tram."

Ben was sorry for him all of a sudden; for his isolation in town, his dependence, the way he paraded his barefootedness, and, when all was said and done, for the distance between him and Orealla, and the wild savannahs spaced with termite hills and stunted trees.

He fell asleep with thoughts of the sad accordion music and of the master pacing up and down in a cage adorned with windows.

16

CARL WENT out the next morning and came back with news about Mabel and a report of what had happened. Her hair was dishevelled and she was feeding the youngest. According to him, when he put down on the table the ten dollars Ben had sent him with, her expression did not change. She went on feeding the child.

" 'Why he send you?' That's what she say. Why you send me? As if she din' know. I tell she was better she get the money from me than not at all. Then she ask is where you get the money, if I been working. I tell she you giving she a lot more every week from now on; that you get a raise 'cause the master does handle so much money at the Treasury."

She had cooked for Carl and asked him to take some cooked food to her mother's house. *But it was not her mother I married,* Ben thought. The old lady would quarrel from morning to night if you gave her the chance and thought Mabel was a monument to patience when in fact her character was not very different, except that it had a tender side that must have come from her father, who preferred to lie down rather than spend a lifetime with the mother.

"And when you left the house how was she?" he asked.

"When I lef' she was joking with me, although I know she don' like me."

"You don't miss a thing, do you?" Ben said.

"Hm! If I did tell you all!"

"What?" Ben asked anxiously.

"You better go round quick," he said. "She want a man bad."

"Why you're saying so?

"'Cause I know."

"How d'you know?" he demanded.

"I don' know. I jus' know. But I sure she thinking it."

Ben had neglected her because he was afraid of her eternal complaints about money and of the frequency with which he met her mother there of late. But he decided it would be best to go at once, just after his gift of money.

He took a bath upstairs and set off as the sun was setting, while Carl was picking his teeth on the stairs, his calloused feet jutting out of his new sandals.

"Wait up for me, however late I am," Ben told him. "We're going to Rosemary Lane when I get back."

"Right," Carl said, making a hissing noise as he drew a swift breath to test his teeth. "You goin' find me right here, if the rain don' start falling."

Just as Ben feared, Mabel's mother was there.

"Howdye," he said, intending the coolness for his mother-in-law, and putting Mabel into a temper straight away, because she believed he was vexed with her.

She started knocking the furniture about and bombarding him with cut-eyes.

"Is why you come if you in' in a good mood?" she blurted out at last.

"I'm in a very good mood," Ben answered, but directing his gaze towards her mother. She was sitting on a chair with one hand in the other and her flat chest half-exposed. *Why do I put up with it?* Ben thought. *I put up with it because of the mistrust in Mabel's eyes whenever I speak to her mother or about her.*

"Once and for all," he found himself saying to the old woman, "I don't dislike you. But you come between me and Mabel. You used to come once a week, then twice, and now it looks as if you come every day. If you really did care about how the two of us got on you would give us a breathing space."

"There in' no law that say how many times you can go visiting," she said drily.

"But you don't care about how we get on?" Ben persisted.

"Is what I doin'? I sittin' here thinking m'own thoughts. Talk, ne! I not stoppin' you from talkin'."

"Let me ask you something?" he said angrily.

"Stop it!" Mabel intervened. "Is true she in' doin' nothing. When I alone all week . . . ."

"I'm going to ask you something," Ben addressed the old lady truculently. "You're living here or not? Because if you're living here this is the last time I'm visiting, and you can support her yourself."

She raised her knobbly, bloodless hand to brush away his words. Ben got up.

"It's only because of Mabel I won't tell you what I think of you," he said.

Mabel had meanwhile put herself between Ben and the door.

"You come," she said acidly, "and you go with the slightest excuse.

110

You leave a little freck 'pon the table, then goodbye. Well, if you leave like that today, don' bother to come back. An' you know me: I not going come runnin' after you like you wife who worship the dirt you walk 'pon."

"I come to talk to you, not your family," he said. "Six times out of seven I meet your mother, and the seventh it's your brother. Well, he's tolerable; but this. . . . Look, where're the children?"

"In bed."

"Bring them out."

She bit her lip, looked at her mother and then went inside.

Bamford came out first and then Laly, the second. Ben picked Laly up and asked her how she was. In reply she gave him the empty matchbox she was hiding, but when he showed some interest in it she demanded it back. Ben questioned Bamford about school, only for appearance's sake, because he had grown sullen of late. When Iris was presented to him he took her on his other arm and chatted to her with baby talk, while Bamford went and sat down against the partition to wonder, no doubt, why his sisters were receiving all the attention.

"You are six years old, young man," Ben told him. "When you were two I used to pick you up just like this."

Ben walked round the cluttered room with the two girls, grazing the cane-seated chairs and forgetting his malicious feelings towards their grandmother, whom they saw more often than him. He recalled how his own father used to give his mother's mother the leavings of food, because, in his quiet way, he did not care for her. It was not in his nature to be strident in his objections. Yet for him she was the spring from which the world had oozed, and who, in her decline, was being devoured by some invisible fungoid growth that brought decay to her head and body. These old women were deified in Africa, where he would not even venture to eat in Mabel's mother's presence. Calmed by this reflection, he stole a glance at the strong, veined hands that lay on her lap, and wondered if he was being unjust to her and to the mother of his children and to the children themselves, who had witnessed more rows between their parents than tender exchanges.

"Take Iris for me," Ben told the old lady, to show her some respect.

She got up hurriedly and took his third child from him, avoiding his eyes as she did so. He watched her out of the corner of his eye, knowing all the while that he would rather see her dwelling in the Alms House in Upper Brickdam, in the company of old people who

111

had lost their ties and were rotting slowly between the pitch road of Brickdam and the rutted avenues of Hadfield Street.

Iris fell asleep soon after she was taken by her grandmother, who had spread her lap wide to accommodate her. Now that all was quiet in the room they could hear the noise made by the coffee-grinder's machine next door, accompanied by a woman's singing. No lamp had been lit and no light came from the unlit street, so that he could barely make out Mabel's figure. From her posture he guessed that she had pursed her lips tight and was making an effort to bend back her thumb to reach her arm. Like him she was violent and spent much of her time holding down the lid over her strange ideas. When she was a girl, she once told him, she used to gape at the world, until suddenly she became a woman and chased away her fifty-year-old uncle, who was in the habit of visiting the house when she was alone and putting his finger up her vagina.

"Why you does send me away whenever he comes?" a girl cousin once asked her those many years ago, and she answered without forethought in her gaping way: "Because he goin' lift up my dress."

So it was, before she grew into a woman and became violent. She was now folding her arms, watching Bamford and feeling sorry for him because she thought Ben did not like him on account of his ugliness.

Carl once told me that his father, like all Macusi men, dared not look at his mother-in-law, reflected Ben. *Dared not! They were frightened of their wives' mothers. Now look at that, eh? Now look at that! The Macusi were trapped in that time when men knew fear of their mothers-in-law.*

Laly was dropping off as well, so Ben went inside and laid her on the bed. Mabel's one going-out dress was draped from a hanger against the wall. He saw behind it the pair of trousers he had left in her care, pressed smooth by her weight and the children's through the straw mattress.

"Go to bed, Bamford," he heard Mabel say.

In his docile, bovine way, the boy came behind the screen and lay down next to his little sister.

"They're putting pitch down in Regent Street," Ben told Mabel when he came outside again.

"Why not write about that?" she suggested.

He shrugged his shoulders, not having given it any thought.

"I don't know why they bother," he continued. "The pitch in Brickdam does melt in the sun and that's not good for the horse."

112

"Why?"

"It slows him down," Ben answered.

"You does go on as if the horse is a human being," she said.

"Mm. . . . But it slows him down, though. It slows him and the carriage down."

It was clear that the old woman did not intend to budge.

"Come let me show you something in the yard," Ben said to Mabel.

"What?"

He ignored her and went outside, leaving the door open, and when she eventually joined him he closed the door and kissed her. He pushed her behind the tenement because he knew if he had asked she would have said no. And just by the window under which the children's bed was he touched her vagina and found that she was ready, and must have been ready while they were quarrelling in front of her mother. And in that standing position he eased his cock up her where it belonged, like a sword in its sheath. She held on to him and begged forgiveness for the behaviour of her empty-headed mother and confessed she was in heat, being near her time of month. Ben forgave her with all the violence he could muster in a standing position, but said nothing in reply.

She went and sat down on the stairs when it was over and would not answer when he talked to her. All the noises coming from the yard had ceased and only occasionally a bicycle went by, zigzagging between the ruts of the badly made-up street.

"Some day you're going to realize I'm not a bad man," Ben ventured. "You stood by me when I had little to give. I'm going to stand by you now the money's coming in."

Then, several minutes afterwards, she sucked her teeth in contempt and went inside. How in the name of God he was expected to fathom this woman, he thought. The only time she ever calmed down was after he beat her.

It would have been the worst thing he could do to announce that he was going, so he went inside and sat on the chair. She had lit the kerosene lamp and was folding the children's clothes.

Iris was sleeping with her mouth twisted out of shape by the pressure of her head against her grandmother's chest. She was the best-looking of his children, just as Bamford was the ugliest, with his protruding eyes, as if he had been born too soon.

The night was deathly still. Ben watched the sweat trickling down the face of his youngest child, who cleaved to her grandmother as he once did to his, in that perfect consummation of a relationship that rarely existed between adults. He was as foolish as those he was in the habit of condemning because they crossed him and denied him that strange nectar of love and hatred to which he himself was addicted. He thought of that red dress behind the screen and of his pressed trousers as if they were keys to unlocked doors; and of the nature of love, like a kind of madness, for which they should not be expected to accept any responsibility; of the attraction of locust-fruit to children, while its foul pith was reviled by adults; of the ups and downs of ambition, hatred and pain, which tortured the soul to little purpose. And these thoughts flashed through his mind like a howling wind as the lamp burned and twisted their shadows.

"Well, I gone," he said, still sitting on the same chair.

"What, already?" Mabel asked suspiciously.

"I'll come tomorrow again."

"Oh!"

But he remained in his seat, plagued by a feeling that he had left something undone, for which Mabel might never forgive him.

"I gone, then."

"Go, ne."

"See you, right? Tomorrow."

"Eh-heh," came her laconic reply.

He went out into the black night past the sign advertising windows and into the deserted street.

Carl was sitting on the steps as he had promised, and on catching sight of Ben got up without a word.

They hurried towards Rosemary Lane, knowing how erratic the owner of the shop of forbidden drinking was. One night he might put up his shutters at eight, while the next he would remain open until past midnight, defying the law.

As soon as they stepped into the shop Ben knew that something was wrong. The owner was wiping a glass with exaggerated gestures; and then, exasperated at Ben's obtuseness, he went into the back room. He looked round at the customers who were occupying every available table in the shop as well as the two metal ones in the yard by the window.

Carl whispered to Ben without turning his head, but he did not understand.

"I goin' order the drink," he said more audibly.

114

Instinctively, Ben turned around and saw the sergeant from next door sitting at a table alone, his gaze fixed on the counter. He got up and came over to them.

"What're you frightened of, cab-driver?" he asked. "I'm drinking liquor too." He lifted his glass to show the rum he was drinking.

"We don' drink rum," Carl said. "We're mauby drinkers."

"I know," the sergeant declared. "You prefer paiwari. But you're not in the bush now."

The owner returned, still wiping the glass.

"Two maubies," Ben said.

"You're a pair," the sergeant went on, measuring Carl from head to foot. "A cabman and a buck-man. People say none of you's got any friends. Is that true? They say you're protected by your boss, the man who prints the signature on bank notes and destroys them later. It's true he protects you?"

"I work for him," Ben said, looking him in the eye. "But nobody protects me."

"This place," said the sergeant, "reeks of vomit and rum, yet everybody's drinking mauby. How you explain that?"

"Ask him," Ben said, and nodded towards the owner, who was cutting off the white froth from the top of a glass with a knife.

"Ask him?" the sergeant said with scorn. "He does deny everything. If you said to him, 'You've got a son,' he'd say, 'Me? I don' got no son!' Yet he's got six sons. He's like that. When you live next door to somebody you get to know everything about them, down to the smallest detail. You see how he's trembling? It's not only because he does sell liquor without a licence; it's not only because he does give public dances upstairs without getting a licence for that too. It's because I know so much about his private life. It's not surprising, though. Neither he nor his sons go to church. It's his wife who goes and prays for them on Sundays. She hopes that the vice waters that threaten to drown them will recede one day. A woman from a good family sinking with them deeper and deeper. . . . Go on, drink your mauby. But let me warn you! If I catch you buying rum here or leaving here with rum on your breath, it's better you were never born, or your buck friend with the new shoes, who doesn't have any visible earnings, but's got skin as smooth as a plum.'

He emptied his glass and left angrily, more because Ben had said nothing to him than on account of his futile visit. And promptly the counter was besieged by customers wanting their liquor, although there was a rum shop less than ten minutes away where one could get drunk in peace. Carl and Ben brought a cuttie and settled in a corner of the shop from where they could see the road and so have time to dispose of the rum if they saw the sergeant coming back.

"I don't know why people bother to drink here," Ben told Carl, not having yet recovered from the excitement.

"Why you does drink here?" he asked in his flat voice.

"Ah, that's another story."

Soon things returned to normal again, the owner reading one of those American cowboy books he devoured and exchanged with his customers for others he had not yet read.

When he left Mabel Ben had been dying to talk to Carl about his mother-in-law, but the encounter with the police sergeant had supplanted her in his preoccupations. Yet, by the third or fourth shot of rum he started to unbutton his mouth.

"What you think?" Ben asked Carl. "You think I'm a family man or a free man? Because it stands to reason that I can't be free if I'm a family man."

"A family man, I suppose," he answered.

"So I'm a family man, with a mother-in-law sleeping in my family place whenever she likes; coming and going whenever she likes?" Ben said.

"You're a free man, then."

"But how can I be free with three children and Mabel?"

"Then you're a family man."

"I'm nothing, that's it," Ben declared. "I'm not a free man or a family man. One day I decided that the only way to free myself was to kill the old woman. . . . "

It was the first time Ben had ever seen an expression on Carl's face. But it was gone in a trice, and left his features blank as before.

". . . and after thinking and thinking," Ben went on, "for a whole week, forgetting my troubles with Grunt-Hoo, I decided I'd frighten her to death. I set out for her room late one night and when I reached the deserted streets around her house I circled and circled like a chicken hawk with my heart thumping and my hands sweating as if I'd dipped them in water. The black cloth with the slits for my eyes was tied round my waist under my shirt, and as I was preparing to undo it a dog began to bark. It must have been chained because it was working itself up in a frenzy; but the sound wasn't getting any nearer. I walked off again, thinking that the barking must have awakened

116

someone in the area. I should have gone earlier, you see, when people's lights were on, so that if anybody looked through the window-pane of a house I would have seen him. All those dark windows could have concealed prying eyes, for all I knew. When I got to the next street I peed behind a kind of shed, out of nervousness, because hardly a dribble came. And I told myself that if on my way back to the room the first fifteen houses had no light it would be a favourable sign and I would walk straight up to the old lady's room. There was no light in the first fifteen houses, so I hurried my step, still shaking. This time the dog didn't bark, even when I turned into the yard which was covered with high bushes on each side of the path. I undid the cloth and adjusted it so that I could see through the holes. Then I knocked on the door and waited. I'd have gone away if she hadn't answered; but after a short while I heard her voice behind the door.

" 'Is you, neighbour? . . . Is you, Vibert? . . . Is you, Mabel? . . . Is who then?' "

"And by the time she came to 'Is who then?' there was terror in her voice. If I tell you I could *see* that woman through the thick wooden door, see her bony hand on the bolt and the eyes popping out of her head you wouldn't believe me. But it's true. I could see her; and I'm sure I saw her put her hand over her mouth at 'Is who then?' And all I had to do was pretend I was Vibert or Mr Cobb her neighbour, who had a wheeze in his voice.

" 'Is who then?'

"But I turned away and tiptoed down the path between the high weeds forming a hedge all the way to the gate. And you know I had to go and pee again! I went behind the same shed and peed into the wet grass. When I got back to the house I asked myself why I hadn't done what I set out to do. I knew then I was no murderer, that it was hard to take a life."

"You din' kill she 'cause you frighten of she," Carl said calmly.

"I've got nothing but contempt for her. If you knew the contempt I had for her — I have for her!"

"You frighten of she, just like my father did frighten of his mother-in-law and din' dare look at her like all the Macusi and Arawak men. They had a town man living at Crabwood Creek who was always abusing his mother-in-law; and one day he admit he was frighten of she. Is the same thing, except that Macusi men don' lie like town people."

"You full of shit, buck-man," Ben cursed. He wanted to thump Carl on his back for talking so calmly, as if he were God.

Ben was suddenly aware of the muttering and humming around him, as if he had his good ear to a beehive, and smelled the rum-reek through his own drunkenness and saw the shifting and twitching of this cut-off of the human race, like the corner of an ant-heap in Rosemary Lane. *At least I am alive and conscious*, he thought. *At least I am part of the consciousness that is the plague of the world. Our problem is not one of coming to terms with what wells up from below, but rather with this damn conscious self, longing to fly away on its own to the detriment of our mental health. . . .*

There was a commotion outside in the yard, but he was so befuddled he had not realized what was happening until he saw the sergeant from next door appear in the doorway. Confusion broke out as if a signal had been given; and before Ben knew what was happening Carl was jumping out of the window and he was following.

Losing sight of Carl in the dark, Ben pressed on until he reached the alleyway and was able to scale the paling-fence behind the stable. The horse snorted and raised its head, but he walked the length of the yard to his door, trampling the cassava bushes in the dark.

Carl's hammock was empty and Ben immediately jumped to the conclusion that he was caught. He went out again, not knowing whether to go up or down Regent Street to look for him or to take the side street in case Carl decided to come in by the alleyway. He stood in the dark, ears cocked to pick up every sound — the shuffling of alfagats in Fatpork's room, the after-call of a late car horn in the distance and the incessant breathing of the wind in the almond trees next door. Carl was caught, he was now certain, and would worry himself sick, for to lose his freedom would be a sort of death to his kind. Ben went and stood on the bridge, looked up the road where the street lamps mounted guard above the parapets. It was the hour when pumper carts spilled their stench on the air and filled the night with the chugging of vacuum pumps.

In the end he went back to his room, where he found Carl lying full-length in his hammock.

"Where you've been?" Carl asked him.

"I've been waiting outside. I got home a good fifteen minutes ago."

"So you hear Edna sleeping with a trumpet," he said, and laughed softly.

In truth, Edna was sleeping on the premises that night, and the

118

noise of her snoring came down through the floorboards. But Ben could not understand how Carl could ignore their adventure, as if he, Ben, had imagined it. There was so much he had looked forward to talking about, the way they had shot away like two arrows from a single bow. At least they could have laughed at themselves.

Ben changed into his old pyjamas, while wondering at his friendship with a man who was so different from himself.

17

THE MISTRESS was due home from New York and Ben was to fetch her from the wharf. The master would come immediately after an important meeting at work, provided it was over before the boat came in. It was to prepare for her arrival that Edna agreed to work late the night before and get up early this morning, rather than travel all the way from where she lived even before the five o'clock gun was let off.

Edna knocked on the bathroom door and shouted to Ben that the master wanted to see him at seven in the gallery before he sat down to breakfast. Ben heard her footsteps going down the stairs with the bucket from the commode to the latrine in the yard, carrying the master's night-pail while tucking her see-through nightdress between her legs.

What did his employer want to see him for, Ben wondered, when he already had all the instructions about picking the mistress up at the wharf and had anyway done it once before, in greater style and with more courtesy and aplomb than the last cabman, she said?

At table Ben was as nervous as on the morning of his wedding.

"He's sprucing up himself upstairs," Edna said, smiling like a little girl.

"It's not every day your wife comes home from New York," Ben said. "All this long time without dootal. . . . "

"That's all you men does think about," Edna retorted, pretending to be annoyed. "He love his wife and wan' see her again."

"He loves her, yes," Ben said.

"What you mean? You know something?"

"Me? He lives upstairs and I live downstairs. How am I going to know something?"

119

Carl looked at him with his blank expression.

"All I know is," Edna went on, "I glad she coming back. You should've see him haunting the gallery and looking out of the window as if the mistress did jus' go to see her brother and she was a lil' late coming home."

"Yes," said Ben. "You know them better than I do, Edna. After all, you're closer to them."

"You girl friend opposite been here las' night," Edna said, talking to Carl. "She sit 'pon the stairs and although she did know I been here with the light on and all she din' come up and ask."

Carl did not take her up.

"She stay 'pon the stairs and wait for you and then go home."

"How long she stay?" Carl asked.

"'Bout a hour. You don' care?"

"We done with one another," Carl said.

"It in' look so to me," Edna took him up at once. She got up and cut another slice of bread from the loaf then, sitting down again opposite Carl, dipped the unbuttered slice into her bowl of coffee and edged it into her mouth slowly.

"I thought she didn't like you," Ben said to Carl.

"I don' know what she come for," he answered. "I don' know what she want." He got up and washed up his bowl and saucer as he always did.

"Where're you going?" Ben asked.

"I goin' clean the carriage lamps."

"Give the horse a brush-down too."

Carl placed the still dripping crockery on the empty dresser and went through the open door.

"What's wrong with him?" Edna said.

"The other night," Ben told her, disclosing what he would not normally have disclosed, "he was lying drunk at the woman's feet and she was behaving as if that was where he belonged."

"What wrong with being at a woman foot? A lot of women does spend all their life at men foot." She said this in her colourless voice, pretending she had no passion like other people and did not suffer like other people, so that had Ben not known her longer than Carl he would have said she was copying him.

It was the longest conversation Ben had had with Edna for some time and he imagined there would be many more, since he now ate all his meals upstairs. He watched her fish out a dead fly from her coffee,

120

which she threw away before coming to sit down at table.

Her hair was in plaits, and he got to thinking how little one knew people one worked with, who arranged their hair before they went out, ironed their clothes and put on their masks.

As the sun gradually brightened the room, the flies began to descend on them in a plague that had begun a week or so before and threatened to smother the table. Edna fetched a new fly-paper from the cupboard in the dining-room and hung it up on the nail on which she kept the aluminium frying-pan, now turned down on the table.

"Why you're fidgeting so?" she asked, and the way she said it she must have had her eyes on him all the time. "With Carl to look after the horse and carriage you don' got nothing to worry 'bout."

He could not humiliate himself by admitting that he was nervous about seeing the master who, since their agreement, could not even look him in the eye. *Why did he want to see me when he was incapable of looking me in the eye?* Ben wondered.

"You want some more coffee?" she asked, as much as to say: "I did peep behind your show-mask and you're not as strong as you make out to be."

"I can't understand," he told her, "I can't understand how you remain so placid all the time. You never get vexed?"

"Your wife placid, jus' like me."

"Tina isn't placid," he corrected her. "She's neat."

"You want some more coffee?"

"No. I've got to see your master."

By the time Mr Schwartz came downstairs Ben was in a foul mood, having been kept waiting fifteen minutes.

"Ah, Ben. Ah. . . . Oh, yes."

The master dropped his eyes as soon as he caught Ben's. Then in a high-pitched voice he spoke like a teacher addressing a class.

"Ben. On no account must you breathe a word of what you *thought* you saw to anyone. Not to anyone. Not to Edna, or your wife, or Carl or your . . . lady friend. A careless word when — you know — when you've been drinking. I'm not suggesting you can't hold your drink. But the best of us do that, confide in others, in at least one person. . . ."

"Who you take me for?" Ben demanded.

"My goodness, it's just what I was afraid of. I trust you implicitly. But, as I said, we *all* confide in someone."

"I don't!" Ben said firmly.

121

"Very well. If you realized how implicitly I trust you, you wouldn't lose your temper. Anyway, that's settled. On other thing: when you fetch the mistress. . . . "

And he began giving careful instructions in his Civil Service tone, while the marabuntas from the nests under the roof gutters threw themselves against the window-panes, intoxicated with the sun and the heat. From the drawing-room came the scent of ripening sapodillas which Edna had piled in a drawer, a gift from the servant next door. They filled the house with their sweet smell while the master spoke. He spoke, though he was aware that Ben was not listening, and that he knew exactly what to do since he had lectured him twice before on the same points and was only repeating himself because he had become afraid of him and because that was the manner of Civil Servants who had to account for everything they did, and believed that the world was a whole series of Civil Services joined together, whose very existence depended on following rules. But for Grunt-Hoo, he might have gone to fetch the mistress with his heart roaring, Ben thought.

Now he knew that, despite his triumph over his master, he wanted to take his life and was certain that the violence he aroused in him had nothing to do with the derisory wages he paid, nor his contempt for Carl. If he made over to Ben all his money it would not put out this feeling of hatred and dread he harboured towards him.

"Very well," Ben said, when his employer was no longer speaking.

Mr Schwartz went and sat down on the dining-table, tucked his napkin into the top of his shirt and rang the table bell for Edna, who came promptly with a meal on his tray.

Ben left by the kitchen door and went aback to the stables to see how Carl was getting on.

18

THAT NIGHT the house was full of people, women with their children, husbands and wives, the mistress's best friend, her brother, her daughter and wet-eyed husband, who had given up his white handkerchief for a pale blue one, and many of Mr Schwartz's Civil Service cronies. They had started dropping in from about two in the afternoon, soon after Ben brought the mistress back from the wharf. From time to time she would put on one of the records she had brought from the States, so that the old phonograph, which had not been played since she went away, wheezed and puffed out tinny music through its funnel, to the wonder of the guests hurrying to gather around it. The mistress looked ten years younger and kept bursting into laughter. She threw her head back and displayed her fine teeth, one of which protruded a little, giving her a slight pout when her mouth was closed. The men were all looking at her, some openly, others out of the corner of their eyes. If some of the women were jealous, none showed it, all hugging and kissing her as if she were a plaything that had to be fondled. Mr Schwartz put his hand on her arm now and then, to assert his proprietary rights.

She did not go to bed until well after ten. Asked by Mr Schwartz to put out the lamps as Edna was not sleeping there and he had had a hard day's work, Ben went about the house, raising the chimneys and extinguishing the lamps one by one, gently, so that they would not smoke and ruin the scent of bodies the ladies had left behind, in the corners especially, where it clung to the wood of the partitions in the tepid night air.

Just as he had put out the last lamp in the drawing-room he heard the creaking from upstairs and came to the conclusion that the master was asserting his marital rights in no uncertain fashion.

The next morning when he came back from his daily trip to the Treasury Ben went upstairs, as the master had asked, to enquire of her whether she needed him to get anything special for her. He was standing at the entrance to the drawing-room, where he saw her winding up the phonograph slowly, as in a dream. When he spoke she turned around, startled by his voice. And before he knew what was happening she hurried off up the stairs to the top storey, but not before he saw that she was crying.

"What's wrong with her?" Ben asked Edna, who was scouring the floor. "She's crying."

"I don' know. Where is she?"

"She's gone upstairs."

"I don' know," Edna repeated. "He did look happy before he go out this morning. He look as if he did jus' get married. That's why he ask you to get whatever she want. . . . I don' think is the mistress who come back. It must be her sister."

123

Ben stared at her, not knowing what to say. He could see no difference in the mistress, except that she had seemed happier the night before.

Downstairs Carl was tending the plants in the yard, but seeing Ben, he said he was going to take the horse to the race course for a couple of hours. And, as fate would have it, hardly had he turned the corner than his fancy woman from opposite came asking after him.

"He's gone out," Ben told her.

She looked out to the back of the yard, evidently believing that he was lying. Then she sat down on the bed and crossed her legs.

"I thought you-all had broken up," Ben remarked.

She stared at him, then looked away without answering. Suddenly, as if on an impulse, she got up.

"You're his father or somet'ing?" she asked. "Then why you don' let him run his own life?"

"I tell you something," Ben retorted. "The next time you come and he's home I'll go out. You can't get it through your head he doesn't care for you any more?"

"Who say so? He say so?"

"No," he replied. "I mean, yes. He told me so."

Ben's contradiction now convinced her he was lying.

"What you've come for?" he demanded. "You used to spit on him one time."

She gave him a vindictive look. "I love him, that's why. You don' understand that. Everybody round here know you, how you does live away from Mabel and you children like if you was a stranger. Yes! And how Mabel going to do for you!"

Seeing that he did not react to her remark she became bolder.

"The girls want Carl to come an' live opposite, 'cause he not the sort to bully them and let them down."

"So they want him to live opposite?" Ben said as sarcastically as he could. "And who he'd be screwing? All of you?"

"You think you talkin' to Edna?" she asked. "I in' Edna. He'd be screwing me."

"And why you want him back so badly? When he was ready to kiss your ass you didn't want him. Now he doesn't give a damn whether you're alive or dead. . . ."

"Carl love me!" she insisted.

"Love? You push him too far and he'll go back to Orealla before you could stretch out your hand. I know Carl! He doesn't want

124

anyone in town to tie him down."

Ben had only said so to put her off, but when all was said and done he felt he had spoken the truth.

"Carl doesn't think like us," he said. "You can't tell when he's unhappy or when he's content, because he's got the same face day in day out. A couple days after your birthnight party he was holding the reins of the horse while I was sitting next to him, and you know what happened? With the same expression on his face he let the reins drop out of his hands. He'd just gone off into a trance. You don't believe me? Ask him!"

"That in' got nothing to do with us," she replied.

"You're right. It's a fact, though, that he doesn't give a damn for you and your dolled-up women."

"I in' surprised you don' got no friends," she taunted.

Ben laughed, knowing that the reaction would be more powerful for her than anger. He laughed in her face as if she had been the butt of some joke; and as he expected, she lost her temper.

"You sicken me, cabman," she said, gesticulating with her right arm. "Why you clinging to Carl so? As if he was a woman? Why you come over to our party when nobody did invite you? Is why you buy shoes for Carl and clothes, as if he was your woman and had a cunt between his legs, eh? You bitch! Is which way you facing? That's what the girls want to know. You're a tom-cat or a queen, eh? Everybody know how you does go riding the trams in search of what you don' got; and how the mother of you children does live on the edge of madness and that people waitin' to point they finger at you. You don' got to laugh at me, 'cause I got friends, you bitch! An' Carl is one of my friends and I don' got to account to you for my friendship with him. I love Carl and you can stick your bastard hate up your ass, 'cause I don' depend on you for shoes and clothes or for nothing! Hch! One day is me who goin' laugh at you. . . ."

"The way you were laughing at Carl at your party?" Ben asked, remaining outwardly unperturbed. "And inviting your powdered whore-friends to giggle with you because they don' have a mind of their own?"

Her lips were pursed and she answered Ben's gaze with a murderous look.

"If I was a man, you couldn' talk to me like that," she fumed. "None of us is a whore. We does all work. Is no disgrace to work in a shop. One day your master goin' find out he harbourin' a snake. But you jus' watch you'self when it come to our business, 'cause I would hire somebody to smash your balls good and proper, and knock all that talk out o' you."

"While you're hiring somebody to do that you haul yourself off and don't come back here again."

She screwed up her mouth in a pout, but did not move from the spot.

"Go on, get out!" Ben ordered.

"Touch me, ne," she challenged. "Go on, touch me! Touch me an' you goin' find out I'm a pistol ball!"

"You're going or not?" he asked.

"I goin' when the spirit give me, not before."

"Please yourself."

He took out the key to the room from his pocket and made as if to go out; but she did not move. Then he pulled the door towards him, inserting the key into the lock from the outside.

"What you doin'?" she asked.

"I'm locking you in," Ben told her calmly.

"I going. But I'll take Carl from you if I dead doin' it."

She went, leaving behind the scent of her sweat in the room.

Ben had never seen her in any other dress but the one she was wearing. She was made up excessively, just like her friends at night when, provided they were off duty, they would sit at their windows or in chairs in front of the covered stairway, their powdered faces standing out above their black dresses.

Her rank sweat lingered like the stench of locust fruit when exposed to the air.

"They're a pair," he told himself.

But his thoughts were centred on Violet's remarks about Mabel. He intended asking Carl that very night. As far as Ben knew, all was well with Mabel since he had increased her allowance. Yet, so strong was the premonition of disaster, he made up his mind to go at once, even though he had repairs to do around the house.

Laly and Iris were at home, but on catching sight of him Iris ran inside, nearly falling over the threshold. Mabel appeared in the doorway and smiled at him.

"She so shy," said Mabel, referring to Iris, "she make shame-bush look like jump-up-and-kiss-me." While saying this she picked up Iris, who buried her head in her mother's armpit.

126

Ben put his arm round her as he had not done for weeks and he felt her flesh yield to the bone as in their courting time, seven years ago.

"I've come to take you and the girls on a picnic."

"Where?" she asked, not taking him seriously.

"To the Big Gardens."

"What about Bamford comin' home to eat?"

Ben had forgotten Bamford.

"I could get neighbour to look out fo' him an' give him something to eat," she suggested.

He nodded, thinking that she had found the solution only because she wanted to.

The girls' hair had already been done, but Mabel herself had not loosened her night plaits. She sat down on a chair and began undoing them, from time to time looking up at him and winking as if they were children.

Mabel had always been strange. He was warned about taking up with her by none other than her brother, who claimed that from childhood she had disturbed the family by her powers of healing, which she practised on children and animals. Her father, who regarded her talent as an illness, sent her to stay with his sister's family in Malgré Tout on the West Bank; and to his great relief he found that she was well again when he went back to fetch her. But according to her brother all that had happened was that she had learned to pretend in order to be accepted back into the home. And indeed, for Ben, being hitched to her was like an association with two separate women. Some days she even looked different, as if she had borrowed somebody else's appearance. But today there was no brooding. Everything was straightforward, as on bright days when one knew that birdsong would be followed by the sound of drays and street-sellers shouting their wares, and then the silence of afternoon when the women were all asleep. She smiled whenever he caught her eye, answered promptly when he spoke to her and was patience itself with the children. Perhaps it was because they were alone, except for the children, or because he had given her a substantial increase, or even because she had at last discovered in him an abiding fondness for her. Ben looked at her hands coursing through her hair, and they seemed to be extraordinary manifestations, like the place where her teeth and gums met. Although she had given him three children he still lusted after her as he did when she was hardly a woman and he used to drag her to those shaded places where the smell of urine was

127

washed away by the fat rains. And this talent for healing and arousing passion in others, where did it get her? Ben's brother, who wore women's clothes as a child, was afflicted with a similar call, and in the same way caused those around him to grieve.

"Laly, get Iris ready fo' me," Mabel said. "Put on she good frock."

"Ma say you got to, so you got to," came Laly's voice from behind the screen. "If you don' put up you hands I goin' hit you."

There was a hardly audible whimpering, but no more talk.

Mabel was looking at Ben brazenly and her whole manner and the way she was sitting said, "I belong to you." For today at least.

To avoid her eyes he kept pretending to brush away the flies from his face.

"We goin' in this hot sun?" Mabel asked.

"I could make paper hats for the children."

When Mabel was ready she went next door to her neighbour and asked her to look out for Bamford and feed him.

"You glad we going?" Ben asked the girls.

"We walkin' or we takin' you cab?" Laly enquired.

"We're walking," he answered. "One night I'll take you on the tram."

And on saying this Ben felt a shadow settle on his thoughts, for Carl's woman friend's remark came back to him, suddenly.

"Or for a drive in the carriage," he added.

"After bedtime?" Iris asked, while she drew circles on the ground with her feet.

"Yes."

Laly wrenched her sister's thumb from her mouth and she began to cry.

"I goin' tell Ma!" Iris complained.

But Laly just sat there, unmoved, waiting dutifully for her mother's return.

"Laly's right," he told Iris. "Your finger'll get all wrinkled if you suck it."

"She does suck she finger too," accused Iris, "when Ma not there."

"You want me to tell you a story?" Ben asked Iris.

"No!"

"Tell me, Pa," Laly said, out of spite, it seemed.

But at that moment Mabel came through the door. "You wash Iris?"

"I bathe she this mornin', Ma," Laly replied.

128

"Look how she face full of sweat. Wash her again."

Laly obeyed, taking Iris by the hand.

"I comin'," Mabel told him.

He could hear her going out of the back door to the bath in the yard. All this to-ing and fro-ing, when he imagined they would have been away as soon as Mabel agreed.

It was to be a good half-hour before they left with the two children, who were wearing the newspaper sun-caps he had fashioned for them. They walked up broad pitch roads and past streets that went widening to the sea, before settling in a long line on the wall. Proud of his family, he scrutinized the faces of passers-by to catch their admiration. He thought of his uncle, who married a young woman with three daughters, only to discover too late that he had married four women. He thought of Mabel next to him in her broad-brimmed hat, swinging her arm gently, walking ahead of him with a bearing that wore down the heel of her right shoe on one side. Her skin, covered with tiny beads of sweat, smelt of carbolic soap. On the way past a school they heard children chanting their multiplication tables.

"You're glad?" Ben asked her.

"I glad," she answered.

As they approached the eastern edge of the town birds descended from the trees in flocks and settled on the parapets, only to take flight at an exclamation from the children. A man was repairing his punctured cycle at the roadside and the spokes of the upturned wheels glistened like lines of silver when they caught the sun. Sounds of closing doors and barking dogs chained to their pillars mingled and alternated with the stillness of mid-morning away from the main thoroughfares. Yes, Laly, they were dahlias, flowers few people would put in a vase because they were reserved for wreaths, and were in any case too lovely, even lovelier than roses. Unwholesome gardens. He was not made for contentment and the blessing of children, for already he was thinking ahead to Mabel's moods.

"Why you so quiet?" she asked.

"I was just going to say something," Ben lied, his resentment thwarted by her voice.

"What would you've done if I hadn't come?" he said.

"Me? The same as every morning. Why?"

"I just wondered," he declared, looking ahead without seeing.

Mabel smiled at him again.

They made small talk, about Bamford's schooling, how she would

129

miss Laly's attentions when she went to school, and about everything except what they meant to say to each other. Was it true that a man could only find happiness through a woman? Through her fingers and mouth and thighs? Or did that kind of happiness rob you of your freedom? For most of the last two years he had been striving for freedom from his employer, while at the same time gloating over his good fortune in being associated with the unpredictable mother of his children, who came to him in his dreams as a speck on the horizon and whose feet never touched the ground. Perhaps his lot was to breed and leave a furrow of memory in his children, just a little more than every horse and dog that roamed free.

They camped by the water-lilies.

"I only bring a flask with chocolate and some guava cheese," she said.

Ben bent over and kissed her, and she eased her arms round him gently.

"Pa going?" Iris asked.

"No, he staying,' Mabel answered. "I love Pa, but Pa don' love me."

Ben could not believe his ears. "You know what you're saying?" he asked.

She smiled as if she had said nothing of significance. She whispered into his ear, so that the children would not hear what she was saying:

"If Tina was to dead, you would marry me?"

"What're you saying?"

Then she whispered again, gently blowing the words into his ear:

"If Tina was dead you would be free to love me. Would you? Don' look like that; I mean it. . . . I feel like dancing 'cause I can hear strumming in my ears. . . . Tonight I goin' visit you when you sleeping. I goin' lie in my bed and visit you."

And he felt like weeping in the shadow of the palms. Suddenly he knew how he lied to himself, even in his sincerest reflections. In bargaining with the master he failed to make the most important demand of all: that he should be allowed to live away from his house. Ben hated being at his beck and call, yet neglected the one demand that would have given him a measure of freedom and, above all, reunited him with one of his women. His children were more accustomed to their uncle than to him. And how could he reconcile this longing to be near Mabel with his silence on the matter? All of this was unknown to her, yet she managed to strip him with a glance.

130

"Everything I have I give you," Ben told her. "I don't give Tina anything. Not a cent."

"Eh-heh."

"You don't believe me?"

"I believe you," she said. "I din' say I din' believe you."

She rummaged in the cloth bag she had brought and pulled out a photograph of Bamford. Ben guessed her brother had arranged for it to be taken, but he did not ask. He scrutinized the picture, which showed more clearly than in real life how ugly the boy was becoming, with his bulging eyes and idiot-like hairline.

"He good-looking, eh?" Mabel remarked.

"Yes," Ben answered, for fear of offending her. Then, after a while, he said: "I come visiting whenever I can."

"I know." She took back the photograph.

"Let's go over to the manatee pond," Ben suggested.

They all got up and he heaved Iris on to his shoulders.

There was a young couple at the edge of the pool. The man was pushing handfuls of grass into a water cow's mouth, but the woman, too frightened to try, stood aside each time the animal thrust its head upwards.

"Look the holes at the top in it head," Iris said, pointing to the manatee as it slid under the water.

"You want to feed one?" Ben asked her.

"No. Let Laly feed it."

Laly took the tuft of grass he had pulled out and went right up to the water's edge, only losing heart at the very last moment.

"He take half of it, though," she said.

At her next attempt she was able to feed the animal all the grass in her hand.

They sought out the shadow of a flowering bush and dined on hot chocolate and guava cheese. Then Mabel made the children lie down, and soon they were both asleep, Iris with her thumb in her mouth.

"How's your mother?" Ben asked.

She looked at him suspiciously. "You sound as if you getting human," she remarked. "She all right."

"One day you'll see," he told her, "I did everything for the best."

"One night she nearly dead when somebody come knocking 'pon her door. I din' tell you 'cause I thought you wouldn' care."

"Old people are always imagining things," Ben said.

"But she see the man walking out of the yard."

131

"Oh . . . why she didn't call out for help?"

"That's what she say afterwards. If she'd called out they might've catch him."

Ben was afraid of changing the subject, lest she was testing him.

She lay down on the grass, so that her breasts flattened and her thighs stood out under her cotton dress.

"Let's go in the bushes," he suggested.

She got up and followed him through the undergrowth. They sat down under the shade of a fig tree whose roots grew into the water; and there, surrounded by the hum of insects and the green cover that shut out the sunlight, they merged into one another. Afterwards she did not sulk as she had taken to doing after they made love, but drew him to her as if she was going away on a journey. A ripe fig fell into the water and floated like a buoy in the midst of eddies. A pair of black marabuntas settled on the grass a few feet away and flew away lazily when Ben waved his hand.

"You love the children?" she asked.

"Yes."

"You did want a houseful of girls. And God give you Bamford to judge you."

"I like Bamford," he protested.

"You like Bamford just as I like Laly. We are what we are, but we shouldn' pretend. . . . You so full of secrets."

He smiled to ask forgiveness for his character, which he was born with and which was going to be his undoing, he felt sure. Words never mollified her, and she was far more impressed by a gesture. He reflected that it was easier to utter lying words than to make a false gesture.

"I'm all wet and unfomfortable," she said, standing up to brush the bits of dead grass from her frock. "I got anything in my hair?"

He cleared the debris from her hair and then they rejoined the children, who were fast asleep. *Whatever this woman does me,* he reflected, *I'm sure I've just spent the happiest day of my life with her.*

They sat by the children in silence, in the grip of that torpor that follows a mid-afternoon act of love.

On the way back home they passed by the same school, where groups of children were now standing at the gate and in the yard.

"Must be just after three," he said.

"You in time?" Mabel asked.

"Yes. As long as I get to the house by half-past three."

Ben left her and the children at the corner of Hadfield and Camp Streets, promising to look them up the following day.

19

EARLY THE same evening somebody knocked on Ben's door. It was one of the women living in the house opposite.

"Come quick, something happen to Carl."

He rushed out with her, not bothering to put on his shoes. She opened the door to the covered stairway and he ran up the stairs two at a time. But just as he was about to open the door into the drawing-room he heard the crash of the street door through which he had come. Trying the door before which he wa standing, he found it either locked or bolted. He began banging on it with his fists, but no one came to open. Then, recalling Violet's threat to crush his balls, he made his way down the stairs on tiptoe and listened for a while, before heaving with all his strength against the street door to no avail. He was expecting the door at the top of the staircase to open any minute and to find himself faced with two ruffians, but everything remained quiet. Near the top of the stairs were a few bars of lattice-work that gave a view down into the rubbish bins on the concrete surface of the yard. But just as he was about to clamber up on them he heard a distinct hissing noise.

"My God! It can't be!"

Standing stock still he tried to scan every foot of the staircase in the near darkness, relieved by a faint glimmer of light coming through the base of the upstairs door.

If it was a snake the only thing for it was to remain as still as possible. He stood in the dark for about a half-minute, listening to the intermittent hissing that could have been coming from any part of the staircase, until, unable to bear the suspense any more, Ben dashed up the stairs and, using his fists and shoulders, smashed a hole in the rotting lattice-work. The hissing appeared to fill the whole staircase as he jumped down into the yard.

Ben recognized the master's voice.

"The doctor said you're lucky," he told Ben, when he caught him

133

opening his eyes. "It was not a long drop, but you fell on concrete."

For a moment he wondered at his concern, then recalled the hold he had over him.

"Where's Carl?" Ben asked. No sooner had he begun to talk than he was stricken with a violent pain in his head.

"He's gone to fill the prescription. . . . Don't bother. Carl knows enough about the horse to stand in for you. And Edna'll bring your meals down tomorrow if Carl isn't there. . . . The women opposite seem anxious to shut up the matter. What happened?"

"Nothing. Carl'll be back just now?"

"Any minute now. Ah, I'll go now, unless you want anything. Your friend in the room next to the Frankers' wanted to come in, but I kept him away."

"Send him in, please," Ben asked.

He left, and a couple of minutes later Fatpork came in.

"I can't talk, Fatpork, but you can stay."

When Ben dismissed his injuries as trivial Fatpork began talking about himself.

"Man! And to think I been waiting to tell you the good news. I going to live with my sister."

"You go on," Ben told him. "I'm listening."

Ben hardly heard what he was being told, so obsessed he was with his recent experience. All he remembered afterwards was that, to his surprise, it was not Fatpork's sister who wanted to take him in, but her husband.

"You can't hear anything?" Ben asked, forcing him to speak.

"Like what?"

"Hissing. . . ."

"No hissing," Fatpork said. "I can hear the infant bawling next door, but no hissing. They servant say they getting a East Indian woman to beat the spirit out of the child."

"What spirit?"

"The spirit that making the child bawl. If it go on bawlin' like that, something going' happen to the mother. . . . How this accident happen? You look all shook-up."

"Another time," Ben said, gritting his teeth to get the words out.

He gestured to Fatpork to turn the lamp down, and he did so. He wanted him to go on talking, just so that he would not get bored and leave him alone, because Violet was the sort of woman, he felt, who was accustomed to fighting to the death. To tell the truth, he thought

134

Carl might as well go over and live with her and have done with it.

Ben's hands and head were bandaged. He could not understand how the doctor had diagnosed that he was all right. He was certain that his hip was fractured and his skull split open.

The sight of Carl's hammock — one he had bought in town — made Ben change his mind about his going. In his imagination it was like the window, his bed, the flaking partitions and the furnishings in his room, which he had detested for more than a year after arriving in the house. And in any case if Carl was to go he must go far away, to Skeldon or Orealla, and not pester him with thinking that he was accessible and near enough to accompany him to the place of forbidden drinking.

Seeing him on his back like that, Ben reflected, and with Carl available to do everything he was capable of doing, it must surely have crossed the master's mind that it would be to his advantage if Ben died. All his problems would be solved, what with Carl having no ties and considering money as a means to buy two shots of rum a day, and the bare necessities in clothing.

Ben knew that in future he had to be on the *qui vive,* as in his school days. Especially at night; not only on account of the dark, but because Violet was a night animal, like labbas and accouris. Light bothered her. Looking back on the times when he met her she always seemed uncomfortable when the sun was out.

He turned to face Fatpork and listened to his monologue, his loyalty to him as a reporter who knew how to talk and write, who would, in a different country, have been at the top of his profession, instead of writing about things that did not count. He knew now that he liked Fatpork and began to worry about the new neighbour who would take his place, who would probably be some fanatical churchgoer like the Frankers.

Ben recollected later that he must have fallen asleep soon afterwards, because he remembered nothing more of his visit. And so it was over the next few days. He slept more than he remained awake, tossing about in a delirium in which the only regular visitor was Tina, dressed in her nurse's uniform. And in that delirium he learnt many things from the whispering voices around him. For instance, that there had been no snake in the covered staircase; that Violet had fallen in love with Carl only because he lost interest in her. Much of what his grandmother had never spoken about came to him with such clarity he was able to describe in detail the places where she lived, the

135

veranda overlooking the Courantyne river on the other bank from Nickerie on the Surinam side. He saw her as a girl in a long bouffant frock, walking next to her father in the main street of Skeldon. There was only one mirror in the house, and that was kept locked up in her parents' room. At the age of eighteen, when she was to meet a suitor who had been given permission to visit, her mother allowed her to look into the mirror for the first time and discover her face, what the lacquered boxes and water in the rain-water barrel were unable to show. It was in that way she learned to be vain. This handsome woman bore a striking resemblance to Tina and Mabel, who, like her, shunned make-up which did nothing to enhance their looks. She grew old and died, leaving him a pair of silver earrings he gave to Tina, and a gold churia, now in Mabel's possession.

And more than once he glimpsed the master edging into the room under cover of darkness, thinking he could enter without being seen. Each time he offered Ben two hundred dollars before leaving, as an inducement to go away, to Truly Island or Rose Hall. Once he brought the mistress's friend, who was not so indulgent and said bluntly that she did not care whether or not he refused because, in the master's place, she would show him the door and he could do what the devil he liked. Ben recalled her cigarette holder and saw how false her face was. He was told that Carl was a wonderful man, not self-centred and cantankerous as himself; and, besides, the carriage had never looked so well kept. Ben's seized-up mouth prevented him from answering the master and his friend, and in any case he was certain he was dying and believed that any violent display would only hasten his end.

The times Violet came she was invariably accompanied by a hissing sound. The first time, Carl got out of his hammock and went outside, in disgust, as Ben thought, because he could not stay in the same room with her after what she had done. But in a trice he was back with the horse-whip in his hand, and before Violet or Ben knew what was happening he slashed her and she doubled up, holding her side.

"The nex' time I goin' mark your face," he told her.

Yet she kept coming back, and he did not mark her. Neither of the men spoke to her. She would sit on the chair by the door with her legs crossed like a lady. One day Carl told Ben she had gone upstairs and was talking to Edna. A half-hour or so later she came down to the room and said that Edna had allowed her to use the bathroom, something they found hard to believe, knowing Edna. Then she sat opposite the bed showing off the clean, smooth flesh of her arms and legs, exposed up to the knees, where she had pulled her dress up and tucked it under her. Ben could see she would not give up until Carl changed his mind and started visiting again.

However, the most disturbing visit was Mabel's. She came when Tina had just changed the bedclothes. Carl had put the horse away and was talking to Tina, while resting the harness on his shoulder. Mabel sat down, barely able to control herself. Ben could see how Tina was trying to avoid a quarrel, while at the same time she was unwilling to leave on account of Mabel. He wanted to know who was looking after the children, but no words would come.

Carl went upstairs with the harness and stayed to chat with Edna. When Tina sat down on the edge of the bed Ben closed his eyes for a moment, feeling that Mabel must be getting ready to rip her apart. From the sound of tin plates banging in the Frankers' room he guessed that the father had just come home, that they had just said grace and were about to eat. If only Carl were there he could speak to Tina and avoid strife.

"I hear you does come every day," Mabel said.

"Yes," Tina answered.

"You don' have to come every day. I don' come every day."

"Nothing does stop *you* comin' every day."

"I got children," Mabel said haughtily.

Ben knew that Tina was hurt, because she never spoke of her affliction.

"If —" Tina began.

"You got the ring," Mabel interrupted, "but I got his children."

Tina did not respond at once, but when she addressed Mabel she turned towards her.

"So you've got the children. What else?"

These words, coming from someone who had appeared frightened of her a moment before, silenced Mabel.

Something fell to the floor in the kitchen above. Mabel and Tina were afraid of one another; but who could fathom a woman? When Ben looked out front at dusk he knew it was raining only because of the umbrellas. No, he could fathom women no more than he could a horse. Tina never carried an umbrella, even when the rain was pelting down. And as for Mabel. . . . Under the fig-tree she put her arms round him as if she were going on a long journey; and the children

137

were sleeping some distance away — twigs from a massive tree that died in Skeldon. From Orealla, where the clay cooking-pots simmered, to Skeldon, then to Georgetown where mirrors abounded and lamps burned well into night-time. The two women sized up one another like fighting cocks. Tina, whose head was turned to the partition, looked around slowly to face her rival. Her face was hidden under a thick cake of white powder, thicker than on the faces of Violet's friends at the time of the party.

" 'I' this and 'I' that," she said, "and with your children and his frequent visiting you still have to come and pick a quarrel with me. I don't even want to see you or know what you're doing. Ask Ben if I ever enquired about you. Ask him! I'm satisfied to know he saw me before he saw you and that you had to sneak up behind my back and steal what you could from him. That's what's bothering you: that you had to steal him when I wasn't looking. You think I didn't know you used to go visiting him when we got married? He does tell me everything 'cause he trust me. How much he does tell you? How much he does tell you, with your three children and all and his regular visiting? Answer, ne. You can't answer. And me? I know when you first get pregnant, when he been having trouble with your mother and a lot of other things you wouldn't want me to know. I does go from my house to the hospital and from the hospital to my house, yet I know a lot about you. And it'll always be like that, 'cause he's mine. You know how much money he does earn? He ever told you? Or if he's got money in the bank? I know you don't know because he told me so. And the day I want you to know those things I'll tell him to tell you. But not before. I going to choose the time when it suits me. I'll say: 'Go and tell her how much you earn.' And is only then he'll come and tell you."

Tina sniggered and Mabel drew back as if she had been hit.

"You don't know me," Tina continued. " 'Oh, Tina's quiet!' people does say, as if they knew me. 'Tina don' talk.' But they know what I want them to know. I used to watch you at school and I know how you're sly and how you never could keep what you got. If you want Ben to live with you, you have to come to me on your hands and knees and if I did feel like it that day I'd say, 'Yes. Go and live with her and the children. It's good for them.' Yes, Mabel. It's me that's standing between him and you, even though *he* visits you and it's *me* that visit him. And the day I want him to leave you I only got to lift my little finger and say, 'Ben, don't ever go back to Mabel. Don't ever see her children again.' So don't come with your airs, flaunting your children at me."

Mabel, who was getting more and more worked up as Tina spoke, suddenly put two fingers in her ears and shouted, "No! All them's words that come out your midwifery books. I got proof!"

Then, turning towards the door, she screamed: "Bamford!"

He came through the door and stood by his mother, his eyes bulging more than ever.

"That's Ben son! Look at him. He in' got a scar, not a blemish. And he got Ben stamp 'pon him for everybody to see. What you got? You got words that come from books. An' let me tell you something else: I never had to go out and work. When I leave my mother house is Ben who start supporting me. Even if I want to go to work he wouldn' let me. But he does glory in the fact that you work and support yourself. Tell him you goin' stop work and you'll see how much he care for you."

Tina shook her head in contempt. "I pity you," she said quietly. "He made you his slave and you're boasting about it. The next thing you're going to do is boast how he does beat you and drive you home to your mother. Ben never touched me one time 'cause he respect me, madame. When people talk about Ben being a violent man I don' understand. He's like my father, who wouldn't hurt a fly. 'I got this, I got that. . . . ' You've got him, the children and your mother, yet you've got nothing. Every time you talk you say 'I'. . . . "

When Ben looked at Mabel, tears were streaming down her face. He opened his mouth to speak, but the terrible pain locked his words in.

"Even the stammerer can sing," Tina went on. "You were never a child, so he won't live with you, but only does crave the silence of your armpits. Ben don't know you and you know yourself even less. You cling to your mother, cling to her, 'cause Ben can never love you.'

Mabel rose to go, but Tina would not let up. A stream of inaudible words came from the distorted sphere of powdered flesh, and as her rival went through the door she bared her teeth and laughed soundlessly, so that even the droning of the mosquitoes could be heard distinctly.

The child next door died one afternoon. That night its mother wailed for hours on end but, as was the custom, did not go to the funeral the following day, lest she lived to bury her other children.

And the same afternoon the beggars came, more numerous than ever, all in a line. To a man they were East Indian, displaying an enviable solidarity, even in begging.

One night Ben saw somebody standing next to the crabwood wardrobe, half-turned away from him and continually drawing his arm across his face. Braving the pain, he shouted at the man, who stepped out of the shadows at once and came up. It was the master's son-in-law. Ben was about to ask him what he wanted, when he bent down and allowed the fluid from his bad eye to drip on him. Ben twisted and turned in pain but could not avoid being covered with the substance. In his despair he summoned up all his strength and struck him on the face. Immediately the fluid began gushing out of the eye in a continuous torrent, while the young man stood, impassive, by the bed, his arms hanging by his side as if all the energy had been drained from him. Then, on Tina's appearance, he vanished.

Tina was standing by his bed in her nurse's uniform.

"You met Mabel here?" he asked at once. And there was no pain whatsoever.

"No," she replied. "I saw her at the market about two weeks ago, but she turned away."

"You didn't meet her here?"

"No."

"Listen to me," Ben said urgently. "The child next door. . . . "

"It died last week. The police arrested the woman who tried to chase the spirit out. . . . We thought you were suffering from dropsy. How d'you feel now?"

"The pain's gone. You and Mabel nearly came to blows the way she was carrying on."

"You must've been dreaming," Tina declared, furrowing her brow.

She made congo-pump tea on the kerosene stove she had brought him, and sat on the edge of the bed while he drank the infusion. And when she went she left him with a longing to see Carl. He must have taken the master out after work, to visit one of his cronies who, like him, would no doubt talk of nothing else but the new sewerage rates that would be charged when the sewage system, now put down as far as Robb Street, reached this part of town.

Ben could not help wondering how Carl would take it when he was completely better and ready to assume his duties again.

140

Feeling soiled, he decided to go upstairs to have a shower. But his first attempt at standing up was proof that he was far from well; and he lay back, bemoaning his inactivity. Another day had passed with its interminable succession of small images that was his view of life, like umbrellas that tell people it *might* be drizzling.

20

FATPORK MUST have left while Ben was still very ill, for this morning he had seen a strange man come out of his room and hurry off like a criminal. "You'd think he would leave his address, after the long conversations we had," Ben reflected; "but he probably intends writing."

Edna said that, nearly two weeks previously, the Chinese fireworks factory in Charlestown had burned down and people had believed the whole town would go up in the conflagration. Yet only three buildings to the south of it were destroyed. Ben remembered very well the two explosions that preceded the fire, but, in his delirium, had thought that his head had split open at the front and back.

That afternoon he went to sit on the front steps after his first proper bath for weeks. It was just as well that he was able to move around, because Tina was now on night duty and could only drop in on her way to work. The beggar opposite — the old man who had danced at the party — was sitting on the pavement, leaning against the painted glass of the barber-shop frontage, while the servant next door, who plied Edna with sapodillas in the hope of making a friend of her, passed by and bowed elaborately. *Oh, what nights in the land of the living!* Ben thought. Was life so glorious after all, when he told himself a hundred times it was not worth living? The sky was thick with stars, like a vast tree in flower. Carl's constellation had risen to the middle of the sky, and Ben gazed at it and its companions, believing that nothing else on earth could express his longing for life and the infinite pleasure of mortal attachments. A young couple who were passing by on the pavement stopped to look in at the shop window of the cloth shop, but they soon continued on their way. The house of the Dorcas Society further down the road was full of light and occasionally a passer-by would look up to see what was going on; but all was quiet.

141

It was about eight o'clock when Carl drove up with the master, who enquired after Ben's health.

"I'm starting work tomorrow."

"We'll see," Mr Schwartz said, with the same smile he always used since their new arrangement.

Ben could see Carl in the background, waiting to talk to him.

"No," Ben said, "I'm starting tomorrow. I feel better now."

"As you wish," the master said, not abandoning his smile.

And as soon as the front door closed Carl hurried up to Ben.

"Mabel abuse her neighbour and lock herself in her room."

"How do you know?"

"Her brother stop the carriage an' tell me."

"Wait," he told Carl. "Don't put the horse away."

At the risk of offending the master Ben went through the front door and found him and the mistress talking at the foot of the inner staircase. They both looked at him as if he had committed a crime.

"I'm sorry, Mistress," Ben said, bowing slightly. "It's my lady, the mother of my children. She's in trouble."

Then, turning to Mr Schwartz, he asked, with the utmost show of respect, "Can I borrow the carriage?"

"What? You may not!"

"How serious is it?" the mistress enquired.

"She may be in danger, according to Carl," he answered.

"Call Carl up here," the master ordered.

"There's no need, Thomas," she intervened. "Let him go, as long as Carl goes with him to take care of the horse."

The master turned away abruptly and went upstairs. She in turn followed him, turning back half-way up to speak.

"Take the carriage, Ben. But you try and show a little more respect to the master in future."

"I. . . ."

"You *are* in a hurry, aren't you?"

"Yes, Mistress."

"Very well."

Mabel's brother was just locking the room when Ben arrived.

"What happened?"

"What happen happen since yesterday," he said truculently.

"And why you're locking the door?"

"'Cause she and the children at Moma place."

142

"You're going there now?" Ben asked.

"Yes, they makin' her dance tonight."

"And nobody told me?"

"You does live here?" he asked insolently.

"No, but she's the mother of my children."

Ben went off and jumped up on the seat beside Carl. Mabel's brother came running up to the carriage and just had time to get one foot on the footrest and hoist himself into the vehicle, which had already gathered enough speed to throw him badly if he had fallen off.

The houses beside the Princess Street trench were reflected in the water and dragged along like pictures on a slide as they went by. Ben had the curious idea that Carl would have driven twice as fast if Tina were involved.

"Give me the reins," he told him.

They exchanged places and Ben began slashing the horse with the whip. The carriage lurched dangerously as the animal, responding to the blows, flew eastwards at a breakneck speed. At a crossroad a horse pulling a dilapidated cab reared to a stop in order to avoid a collision, and they were followed by curses from the driver.

There were people standing about in the long yard leading up to Mabel's mother's house. Ben told Carl to go home and lay up the carriage and horse, then to return if he wanted to. But he knew Carl considered himself an intruder and would have felt out of place. He was sure he would not come back. The carriage turned around in the street, its lanterns lighting up the surroundings feebly, while Carl waved and the horse set off at a trot.

Mabel's brother left Ben, who shuddered on recalling his last visit to the yard. Not bothering to see whom he could recognize among the knots of people, he walked up to the house and went through the open door into the small drawing-room which was packed with visitors. He pushed his way through the crowd into the bedroom, where Mabel was sitting on the bed with her mother beside her.

Kneeling before her, Ben took her hands.

"May, is what wrong? May, it's Ben!"

She smiled at him. "You come from the Big Gardens?" she asked.

"No, May. I've been sick. That's why you didn't see me."

"I come from the Big Gardens," she told him. "The lilies. . . . Laly did try to lay down on a lily leaf, but it couldn' support her weight and I had to take her off. Moma say you was dead. . . . "

"Why you told her that?" Ben demanded of the mother.

"You been here one night when I was alone?" she asked in turn.

"Me? No," Ben lied, with the same murderous intentions as on the night he came.

Ashamed and frightened that he was under suspicion, he did not probe further about what she had told Mabel, who seemed unusually interested in their exchange.

"Mabel, I'm coming back," he told her. "I just want to talk to your mother for a minute."

He took the old lady into a corner and enquired as to what was wrong.

"She grow up, that's all. She had three children, but was still a girl."

"Where are the children?"

"My son got them," she said with evident satisfaction. "The drummers coming soon. You ever dance comfa? If you dance with she it would be easier. If she din' love you so much it'd be easier. In my family we does love deep."

"All right, all right," Ben said testily. He went back to sit beside Mabel. "May! You know I nearly died."

"So Moma was right, eh? She say when you firs' come visiting she left the milk on by mistake, but it din' boil over. She say that about you. Sometimes she so malicious. She tell me that Bamford ugly. . . . The children was sleeping on the grass when we come back, and I was wet with your milk."

"Why you quarrelled with your neighbour?" he asked. "You know how she likes you."

"'Twasn't with that neighbour," she said reflectively. "When you take a pen in your hand an' dip it in the ink and start writing, then I know what I did want Bamford to be when he grow up. . . . Why you does always suck a new pen nib before you use it?"

"It's hard to write with otherwise," he answered. "You know, you sick, May."

"The day when we been to the Big Gardens I put the children to bed early. That night I dreamed, but I din' tell anybody, not even the neighbour."

"You're going to tell me?"

"Yes," she answered. "If I don' tell you, who I goin' tell? I dream I hack Tina to bits with a axe; then I cook the pieces and give you to eat. . . ."

He put his hand over her mouth and looked around to see all eyes

144

on them, whether because they had heard what she had said or because they were interested in how they would get on, he had no idea.

"Listen, Ben," said Mabel. "Listen to me! If you see me comin' from church you'd say hello to me?"

"Of course, May."

"But if you see me goin' to church would you come up and say hello?"

"May, I'd greet you wherever you were. You don't understand? For me you're the most important person. . . . "

She gazed at him with a look of infinite sadness. Then, hardly opening her mouth, she said, "I used to clap Miranda an' his dog. That was before you stop visiting."

"May, I was sick," he told her in desperation.

"My father send me away when I was small, to live with my uncle and aunt. I could tell you a lot 'bout my uncle and aunt. . . . "

"Hush, May," he said. "They say you're dancing tonight."

"I was fucked when I was ten," she said.

"May. . . . "

"When I got troubles," she continued, "that's the only consolation I want. Never send Laly or Iris to their uncle; sin does bear blossom, but not fruit."

Ben kissed both her hands to show that he understood, that nothing could tarnish his love for her. And each time he touched her she drew closer to him, and he desired to be alone with her.

A drum began to beat softly and the room emptied in a few minutes. Mabel's mother went out, but came back soon afterwards to announce that the drums had come and the *brethren* were out in the yard. Ben led May to the back stairs; and at her appearance the other drum started up. The trees around the wide expanse of the back yard, the low, shuttered houses across the paling-fences, the profusion of stars, the white-robed drummers, the grave faces of the company of friends and acquaintances surrounded and covered them, giving little comfort. Everyone believed, Ben was certain, that Mabel's distress was to be laid at his door, that he had abandoned her. Knowing them, they were probably putting it about that Tina and he had conspired to interfere with her in order to get her out of the way. For was there not something peculiar in their relationship? He had heard once that he was supposed to be under Tina's thumb, that the price he paid for not supporting her was a promise to do whatever he was told. He had

145

heard that it was the good health of the children that made her envious. They did not know Tina and hated her because she kept to herself, and they were envious because she had a decent profession and was in no danger of starving during hard times. Then, all of a sudden, he was comforted by the recollection that more than one girl had crossed the bridge to womanhood in Mabel's way and that the ritual of drumming was reserved for those who did not want to grow up.

The drumming began to quicken and three young women were already dancing, while Tina's mother was sharing out schnapps glasses filled with rum and her son stood chatting with an acquaintance at the foot of the stairs.

Ben asked Mabel where Claris — Seetram's lady friend — was.

She did not answer and he was unable to see the expression on her face in the dark. Only two kerosene lamps lit the yard, one hanging behind them from a nail on the house and the other attached to the paling fence near the drummers.

Everyone left them alone, as if Mabel were a guest. He knew that at some time her mother and brother would come for her and force her to join the others, and Ben made up his mind there and then that he would not dance.

Feeling a hand on his shoulder, he looked up and Seetram handed him a schnapps glass filled to the brim, which he drank all at once.

"Hello, Ben." It was Claris.

"You just arrived?" he asked, glad that someone had spoken to him. He got up.

"How she is now?"

"Still the same," he told her.

"I hear she been talkin' to you. She wouldn' even talk to she mother. You goin' dance?"

"Yes," Ben said, softened up by the effect of the rum and the gratitude he felt for Claris's warmth.

"I feel like a stranger here," he said, aware that his control was slipping away.

"You mus' talk to people. When you talk you don' sound as severe as you look."

"Go and dance, ne," he urged her.

"You vex?"

"No, Claris. I promise I'll dance."

She put her arm round Mabel.

146

"Is you, Claris? It so dark! You see them playin' hide-and-seek in the yard? Why they drumming as if a child born or is nine nights or something? I got three children, two lil' girls and a son who face twist up as if the moon shine 'pon him when he was young. Tch! All this drumming! When the silk-cotton leaves start swirling on the road like spirits the drums goin' stay silent. How many uncles you got?"

Claris hesitated, then said, "Seven."

"I got one uncle," Mabel told her.

"Only one?"

"Jus' one, Claris, You got seven. Seven is a good number. You know the head got seven outlets. Is my uncle who tell me that. He uses to teach me 'bout numbers. Two, seven, nine and forty. . . . Look how all the houses round here in' got no lights. But the people watching, though. When they want to watch, they put out the lights. . . . I use to be a healer; tonight is *me* they goin' to heal. But is not time yet, you know. When is time is not drums goin' heal me."

"I goin' dance," Claris told her, standing up. "You coming?"

"Not now," Mabel answered.

Claris joined the dozen or so people who were now dancing, shoulders hunched and head turned up to the sky or bent towards the ground, as if they were searching for something.

They came for Mabel, her mother and a white-robed man. And she, as though she had been expecting them, rose and walked into the centre of the part of the yard occupied by dancers and drummers. She stared at her feet, then, at a signal from her mother, started to sway like a shadow in the dusk. Ben felt numb, incapacitated by the pain of regret at what he might have done for her. But she had always spoken in riddles and hidden what affected her most deeply.

Men had now joined the dancers, one with a bandaged head and a young boy in short trousers, who danced like a member of the santapee bands, his long legs twisting and bending among the women. The drumming was louder than ever in the long yard, an unbroken throbbing that drew a new dancer to the stamping company every minute. Mabel's mother had joined them, and her brother too, his tall, slender body stripped to the belt. Ben searched for Mabel and guessed that she had been drawn to the edge, where the drums were, to assuage the longing of her body for peace from the ghosts of her childhood which tormented her because she never spoke of them. He stepped down into the yard in search of her, pushed the dancers aside until he came to her mother, who was deaf to his questioning. Then he spotted her dancing alone behind the drummers, themselves stamping violently. And watching her body gyrate in the shadows he recalled stories Carl had told him, of the aboriginal Indian killer who kept his victims' hair, of the clans breaking up into families to avoid decimation by influenza, of the horrors that afflicted a once proud world. Through the music of May's body this world sang to him, to the accompaniment of drums beating like the wings of some thwarted heart, to evoke the presence of long-departed ancestors among the thronging shadows.

He himself began to dance, until the effect of the rum and the shifting mass around rendered him incapable of seeing himself as separate from Mabel, her family and friends, and allowed him to merge into that identity that was for Carl a natural state. How could he have been jealous of her mother's and brother's attentions or resent Bamford's ugliness?

Suddenly he saw Mabel surrounded by several dancers, who caught her as she was about to collapse.

"Get the candles!" someone shouted.

The drums continued pounding, and a number of people who were still dancing were by now possessed by the remorseless rhythm. By the time the candles were brought, Mabel, trembling uncontrollably, was made to sit on a straight-backed chair, while they were lit in turn by her mother, who mumbled incomprehensible words as each new flame flickered uncertainly.

A freshly-lit candle was handed to each of those standing around until it was Ben's turn. He took his and held it so as to complete the circle of light round Mabel's chair, while her mother undid her shoes. But, sick at heart to see the picture of loneliness she made among her own, he gave her his candle, which she grasped without looking up. They stood around in an effort to lift her spirit and send it flying into the sky where the stars shine by night and crows wheel by day in endless circles beyond their panting woes. And Mabel sat all alone among them at the end of her long journey from childhood.

148

21

BEN ROSE after an hour's sleep and got ready to take the carriage out. When Carl stirred he told him not to bother to leave his hammock.

"Why?"

"Because I'm better now."

Carl sat up. "I goin' get the harness down for you, though," he said.

"I tell you it's not necessary."

"You talkin' stupidness," he answered gruffly.

Ben left him without more.

The stables were cleaner than they had ever been. The empty tins in which surplus molasses was kept had been scoured and the feeding trough was spotlessly clean. The horse gave him no sign of recognition, and when he placed the molasses before him he snorted into it before drinking. In ordinary times he might have felt jealous, even though, but for Carl, nothing would have been done without help from outside. But that morning he had other things on his mind that made all else seem unimportant.

Having nothing else to do in the stable, Ben stood around while the horse drank, and after it had finished he placed the can in the corner next to the others, before wiping the animal's dripping muzzle with one of the clean cloths Carl had ranged along the metal rod along the wall. Then he busied himself with the carriage in the adjoining stable. Where the axle joined the wheel it was smeared with new grease, so that when he picked up the shafts the carriage moved effortlessly across the yard through the corridor between the fence and the wall of his room. Leaving the cab at the roadside he went back to saddle and harness the reluctant horse.

With fifteen minutes to go before the master came out Ben went back to his room, where Carl was still lying in his hammock.

"Wha' happen las' night?" he asked.

"She's bad."

"So what you goin' do?"

"All I can do is wait and see if she gets better," Ben said.

"Who lookin' after she?"

"The mother."

"Why you don' go and live with she?" Carl said.

Ben laughed, scorning himself. Then he told Carl that if he was to go and live with anyone it would be with Tina.

"Why?"

"She's my wife," he declared.

"And what Mabel is?"

"The mother of my children," Ben answered curtly.

"I don' understand," Carl said.

"You never understand anything, with your bush ways. . . . I'll come back for you and we'll go round and see my mother."

"All right," he said. "But I got to bathe and eat firs'."

"Put on your good shoes," Ben advised him.

"I'm told your lady friend isn't well," the master said, smiling, as if addressing someone called upon to account for his actions. "Is it true? Isn't she well?"

"I'm told a lot of things about you," Ben answered, "but I don't see it as any of my business."

"Listen, Ben," the master declared, looking around and finally bringing his eyes to rest where a wheel of the carriage had rutted the dew-laden grass. "I'm sorry about yesterday. Look, the fact is that . . . .I'll forget the difference in our stations and make a confession: times are difficult. These sacrifices I have to make — these big sacrifices. . . . My wife's brother is a squanderer. You probably know. Everyone knows. He's a thorn in my flesh. I'd do anything for my wife; and to save her from disgrace. I wouldn't normally tell anyone this, you know; but my wife has. . . had. . .has the highest regard for you. I'm lucky having you and Edna and Carl. Yes. I'm not ungrateful, you see. But this drain on my resources. . . . We once had two horses, you know, and did not let any rooms. It's not that I don't earn well, but just that you and my brother-in-law make demands, exorbitant demands. Anyway, I didn't keep my bargain, neither did you. You were insolent, just a bit violent; and I was rash in turning my back on you. I suspect that we both set great store by our dignity. Oh, you can call me whatever you like, curse me, but I implore you, never in front of my wife. You're the same, after all. You begged me to show respect in front of my wife and her friends. You see . . . dignity takes on such proportions in front of other people. Anyway, I've got it off my chest."

He took out his watch from his breast pocket and after a swift glance at it said, "Good grief! It's the first time I'll be late in twenty years."

Ben drove off when he had barely taken his seat and began turning

150

over his employer's words, slowly, slowly, like a portion of garlic pork served up at Christmas. *Yes, Grunt-Hoo, you're born to suffer. The Creator served you up to predators like your wife and brother-in-law and me. I've got my troubles too. And as far as yours are concerned I'm as interested in them as you are in mine. One of us will destroy the other, and if yesterday that would've meant something to me, today the outcome is of as little importance as the phases of the moon. "I'm lucky in having you and Edna!" You've got us because our kind would lick your kind's ass to get a job. If I hated you yesterday, today I've got an unquenchable thirst for your blood. Edna serves you in the day and her man at night and yet she would never speak ill of you. Not me. . . .*

"Look whey you goin', you big goat!" a man shouted as he sailed over the handlebar of his bicycle.

Ben looked back and saw the riderless cycle travelling over the grass verge in the same direction as the man had flown.

When they arrived in front of the western stairs of the Public Buildings Mr Schwartz jumped out and fled up the stone steps.

Ben went back and collected Carl. They drove about the town, drinking from a big bottle of rum he had bought for the occasion, but did not speak. Every now and then Ben passed him the reins, which glistened in the sun where it was soaked in the horse's sweat.

The denuded silk-cotton trees stood out against the background of wooden buildings. In spite of the sunshine there was gloom in the air, a gloom of people with bent bodies and bloodshot eyes, of buildings in need of repair, of beggars dragging their woes along the dusty side streets, of tailors pushing steam-irons to the rhythm of conversations with their hangers-on; a gloom of sodden fruit, of old people dying imperceptibly. An infant was crawling along the pavement in front of the Chinese stall-holder who measured out nuts in an old sardine tin and sang an interminable song he had brought from Hong Kong. At the corner of Regent Street and Vlissingen Road a group of convicts were weeding the verge under the supervision of a prison officer, distinguished from the prisoners only by his unpatterned uniform. Further on, where the road divided into two, the grass was covered with yellow patches of daisies.

As the carriage rode over the train lines in the outskirts of the town Ben recalled the drive up the coast, when he tried his hand at plying for hire for the first time and fatigued the horse under a blazing sun. The sun was gentler now.

"Miranda!" he called out, when he had brought the carriage to a stop in front of his mother's house.

151

A woman put her head out of the window of the house next door.

"She not there! Eh eh! Is you, Ben? She gone to Schoonord. Come down an' bring your friend."

"When she's coming back?"

"I in' think is today. Come down, man."

Ben got down and tethered the horse to a tree, and called to mind how his mother was always dragging him somewhere as a child, all over the place, from Mabaruma to Kwakwani.

"You been drinking?" she asked, surprised. "In broad daylight? . . . You friend got nice skin. I can see he don' work for a living. You want some milk? I jus' milk the goat."

"I'm not going to say no," Ben said. "Miranda did tell me you moved away."

"That was years ago. I come back. I come back long time. Is a good thing I din' sell the house."

As a youth he had hated her, but grew fond of her when he became a man. She was unofficial midwife to the young women in the district and used to relate the news of new-born babies to his mother, especially the disasters, like the birth of hermaphrodite twins to the charcoal-burner's wife.

He gave the first bowl of milk to Carl and waited for the second, which was rank and warm.

"I kian' believe it!" she said. "She goin' be sorry she was away. She say you only does come when something happen. With you cab an' all, you in' got any excuse. You friend got nice skin." She began stroking Carl's face.

Ben was glad he had come. She had always told him that if his mother died, hers was his second home, an offer he had spurned at the time.

"Your place is still the same," he told her.

"Yes, m'dear; but I gettin' older. . . . You friend visiting?"

"No," Carl said.

And he knew at once that Carl liked her.

"What about my friend?" Ben asked jokingly. "Suppose anything happen to me? He can come and visit?"

"I always got work round the place. With the goats them and the ducks, I don' want for nothing. Who does feed goat and duck? He can always come. He does drink bad?"

"No," Ben vouched for Carl.

Carl smiled, less concerned about his welfare than Ben was.

152

"You come round to see the old lady for a special reason?" she asked, tucking her dress between her legs and sitting on the kitchen stool, which she had dragged to the drawing-room where she was entertaining them.

"Miss Boxhill, I'll tell you: I don't know why I came. It's like a wind that blew me here."

"You goin' stay to eat," she ordered. "You better stay to eat, else I not talking to you no more."

"We'll stay," Ben said.

"What about the master?" Carl asked.

"That'll be all right," Ben replied, relaxed in his first open act of defiance. "He knows I'm not picking him up."

Sitting in a house so conspicuously free of possessions, so many self-evident observations pressed on him; he wondered why he ever neglected to come to this district where his mother lived among simple people.

"I goin' kill a chicken," Miss Boxhill said, smiling at Carl with her eyes.

And within the minute they heard a hysterical squawking, which ceased as suddenly as it had begun. It was followed by the rustling of the sea breeze in the vegetation around, for the place was only a few hundred yards from the sea. Ben looked out and saw the horse cropping the grass, wondering whether he ought to turn it loose for the afternoon.

"Why not turn him loose?" Carl said.

"Do it, ne."

Carl went down the stairs to unhitch the animal; when he had brought in the harness he came back upstairs and, like someone coming home from work, sat on the chair he had vacated.

"You didn't know I had a mother?" Ben asked him.

"You never say so."

"She collects jewellery. If she was home I would've shown you what she had."

In the house opposite a woman was sweeping with a pointer broom, and soon she came out on the porch, directing the dirt over the rim of the floor. A child of about three, perched on the top of the staircase, was protected from falling only by the slender balustrade running its length. A hammock under the house swung gently as if it had just been occupied.

"Howdye," she said, on catching sight of Ben.

153

"Howdye, neighbour," he answered, trying without success to recall who she might be.

"You want to live long?" he asked Carl.

"Yes. You?"

"No. What for?"

"I dunno why," he answered.

"No, I don't want to live long. I don't want to die either. Half of the men in this street are fishermen and they don't get. . . . " His words died without reason.

The clucking of chickens from the yard, the sound of wet garments being beaten at the trench-side, the rapid flight of a bird past the wide-open window, gave to the morning a timeless, eerie perspective. Carl was drumming on the window-still as he looked out on to the street.

"If we didn't like our own excrement we wouldn't live in town."

"What?" Carl asked.

"Oh, nothing. Come down into the yard."

"Miss Boxhill, I'm taking Carl to see the yard," he called out.

"A'right. See if the fowl lay fo' me. If I don' lock her up she does only lay her eggs in your mother yard."

Carl and Ben went downstairs and sat on the long bench in front of which husked coconuts were strewn about.

"She not like town-people at all," Carl was moved to say.

"No."

And Ben told him how as a girl she had come from the Pomeroon to marry a sick pork-knocker who had found diamonds in the bush. She had come with eyes like wine-vessels to live in the house of a man she had never set eyes on before. When he died soon afterwards, his relations stripped Miss Boxhill of everything except the house. She was not even entitled to that, she was informed. Since then she had lived on her own, working as a midwife and raising her poultry and goats. Although she was unattached, people left her alone on account of the calabash trees growing in her yard, home for spirits that protected her, they felt.

Between the house and fence lay the yellowing innards of a recently fallen breadfruit. Ben looked at the palings separating his mother's yard from Miss Boxhill's, with their bases eaten away by the earth piled up over the years, and thought of Mabel's room, now in the possession of strangers, her mother, brother and friends. His children would soon become strangers to him. And these events had occurred

154

so swiftly he was obliged to make an effort to recall them in sequence. All this was the master's doing. Everything that happened stemmed from the condition of employment that he should live in his house. And having lived in his house he had discovered what a certain kind of freedom was and that it was a beast with head and feet and arms and eyes.

"You hungry?" Carl asked.

"Yes. You?"

Occasionally, when a gust of sea breeze blew up, scattering leaves along the road, the clumps of bamboo across the fence in his mother's yard would groan and whimper above the roof tops. The birds that alighted on top of Miss Boxhill's pointed palings flew away almost at once, disturbed by the men's presence. Their coming and going reminded Ben of his grandmother's house in Skeldon when the soft rain fell on the window-panes while she was cooking at the back or the heat drove her to interrupt her work and take to the hammock strung between the whitewashed trunks of two mango trees in the back yard.

"She calling," Carl said.

"It done!" came Miss Boxhill's call.

She said grace after Carl and Ben had sat down.

"You never quarrelled," Ben reminded her as she placed four lengths of fried ripe plantains on his plate.

"What for, I ask you?" she answered. "But you, you was always quarrelling. You change yet, or you still so ruction?"

He smiled, but did not answer.

"You like the bittle?" she said, addressing Carl.

"He eats everything," Ben answered for him.

Two calabashes three-quarters filled with water were placed near to the table's edge, and next to them a cake of soap and a small pile of black-sage sticks. Miss Boxhill then sat down opposite Ben.

"You come from the North-West?" she asked Carl.

"No. From Orealla."

"I from the North-West. You're a stranger to town like me."

Miss Boxhill broke out into laughter when Ben told her of their escape from the place of forbidden drinking.

"I know the shop," she told them. "The sergeant don' bother him no more, though."

"Who says so?" Ben asked.

"You din' hear? He had money troubles."

"Who?"

"The sergeant," Miss Boxhill declared. "And the shop-man lend him forty dollars. Since then the two o'them like batty an' po.'"

Both men laughed with relief, because they had only dared visit the shop once or twice since the raid.

The sound of children's voices came from across the road.

"Is children comin' home from school," Miss Boxhill said.

"When I was ten," Ben told them, "I got a prize for handwriting. I used to use my own nib for handwriting lessons. They gave me a fountain pen as the prize, and from then on my writing went from bad to worse. Ha ha!"

"Them beggars does still come to your master house?" Miss Boxhill asked.

He told her that they did, and she related why the master helped support so many of them. Years earlier two beggars, a middle-aged couple, knocked on his door and asked for alms. Mr Schwartz refused to give them anything; but the husband, instead of going away, started clapping. He remained on the porch, clapping louder and louder. In the end Mr Schwartz gave them a cent to get rid of them, but they came back every Friday after that for several years before their visits stopped abruptly. One Friday afternoon, at a time when the master was at work, the mistress heard a clapping in front of the house, but there was no one there. Once more she came out front on hearing the clapping, louder and more urgent than ever, and went downstairs to search the yard but found no one. Trembling with fear she went upstairs to call the servant who used to live in at the time; but when the mistress got to the front door she saw a sari lying in the doorway. She bent down to pick it up and found that it was covered in blood. After that, the master never turned away a beggar, and that was why he was pestered by so many of them.

Carl and Ben washed their fingers in the calabash bowls and cleaned their teeth with the black sage stick while Miss Boxhill retired to the bedroom for a nap.

The street was quiet again. Now that the effect of the liquor had worn off, Ben began to worry about the master's reaction to his failure to pick him up at the Treasury. He imagined him fuming because he was late and then, with ten minutes gone, preparing to burst a blood vessel. The tranquillity of Miss Boxhill's home, the other-worldly atmosphere of the district, had in no way softened his intentions. The master would suffer as he had suffered on Mabel's account. He could not afford to send her off on a holiday, nor was he permitted to stand by her as a real man ought to. No, he would go back when Carl and he had had their fill of Miss Boxhill's hospitality.

After she woke up at about half-past two they said they would repair her fowl-coop, with wood stacked behind the bench under the house. And so the afternoon passed while the mild sun sank beyond the horizon and finally left a moonless evening in its wake.

In the end they left, promising to come over whenever Ben dropped in to see Miranda.

"She goin' be sorry she wasn' home," Miss Boxhill shouted as Ben was climbing up on to the driver's seat. "You got to come again soon."

"A'right," Carl called out, waving vigorously.

The two pale shafts of light from the carriage lamps travelled before them in the dark street, picking out an abandoned cardboard box or a dray-cart laid up for the night. Along Lamaha Street, plots of cultivated land stretched away towards the railway station, separated from the road by a wide trench. Next to the railway yard piles of imported cubes of coal, like outbuildings with black walls, rose from the ground and blocked the view beyond.

On arriving in front of the master's house Ben could see there were visitors. Two cabmen were chatting between their carriages, parked partly on the verge. Ben ignored them, while Carl and he set about the business of getting the horse and carriage to the back. Mercifully, Edna had gone home, so that Ben was not obliged to explain to her why he had been away all day.

Carl went upstairs at once to have a shower, and on coming down again lit a fire in the yard, as he did at least once a week. He took out a chair and sat staring into the burning heap, his back turned to the house, framed in the yellow light. Ben thought he could never get accustomed to Carl's ways, to his impossible silences, to his reverence for fire and his contempt for shoes. He sat in the yard alone, gazing at the flames and the plants he had put in the ground, as if they were his children.

22

THE NEXT day Mr Schwartz was as circumspect as a pupil in the teacher's presence. Ben played his part well, not wanting to drive him into a corner. The master said not a word about the day before, nor did he leave Ben at the Public Buildings as if he did not exist but gave a quick, dignified wave before climbing the short staircase. Ben had set out to squeeze every advantage he could from his hold on him and, as Ben saw it, yesterday was only the beginning. He needed only to be careful, to calculate how much he was capable of taking.

Back at the house Ben found the eldest Franker boy standing outside his door.

"He gone! Carl gone. He tek he things an' gone."

"Gone where?" Ben asked, hardly able to speak for the thumping on his chest.

"I don' know. I ask him where he goin' and he say 'Away'. And he throw his hammock over his shoulder and piss off."

"In which direction?"

"I don' know,' the boy replied, alarm in his eyes at Ben's expression. 'Don' hit me, Ben," he pleaded.

"Wait, wait!" Ben said, grabbing his shirt collar.

"I din' do nothing, Mr Ben. I din' tell him to go."

"If you do me a favour I'll give you four cents."

"Four cents!"

"Yes. I'll give you two cents now and the rest when you get back. I want you to go to a lady named Miss Boxhill." He directed the boy to the village in the suburb and told him that anybody in the street would know her house. "Ask for the midwife. And ask if Carl there."

"Where the gil?"

Ben took out a penny and gave it to him.

"Thanks, Mr Ben. I goin' run all the way."

Ben went inside and saw that Carl's hammock and sandals, his only possessions besides the clothes on his back and an extra shirt, were all indeed gone.

It was not possible, he reflected. Only the day before they were drinking from the same bottle and sitting on the driver's seat together. Then he recalled Carl's downcast posture in front of the fire in the yard. But why? He had not quarrelled with him. Miss Boxhill had hinted strongly that he could go and live there, provided he was

158

prepared to work. It was not possible that two such blows could fall in a matter of days, Mabel's sickness and Carl's going away. But that sort of thing had happened before. One disaster attracted others, there was no doubt.

Then it occurred to him to ask Edna. He rushed up the back stairs and found her in her maid's headgear, sitting at the kitchen table over a plate of soup.

"You know where Carl gone?" Ben asked her.

"No. He gone somewhere?"

"The Franker boy said he left with his hammock on his shoulder."

"You sure he in' gone to mend it?"

"His shoes are missing too."

"Carl can't go without tellin' you," she reassured him. "He not like that."

Ben was not disposed to argue with her.

"You go on eating," he told her. "You didn't care for him."

"I did like Carl," she protested. "In any case is not moping goin' bring him back."

She got up and ladled out a plate of soup for him.

"No."

"Eat it, Ben. It goin' clear you head."

He pushed the plate of soup away and saw before him the fried plantains and chicken on Miss Boxhill's table, and the calabashes with the pile of black sage sticks next to them.

"You believe in fate?" he asked her.

And her expression was the same as that of the Franker boy when he drew away from him before he grabbed his collar.

"In some things," she answered. "Why?"

"Yesterday," he said, "when we were sitting under Miss Boxhill's house, the bamboo in Miranda's yard was groaning in the wind like somebody in distress."

"Who's Miranda?"

"My mother. It's my mother's name. We drove over to see her yesterday, but she was out; so we went over to see Miss Boxhill. All afternoon the bamboos kept groaning and Carl was so quiet."

"He always like that," she said. "If he was goin' to Orealla he would've say so."

Ben could feel her eyes on him and detested her for her pity.

"I not married, you know," she said. "I don' even got a man. That's why I can always sleep overnight when they want me to."

159

"I thought . . . " he began.

"Everybody got a man, so I like to pretend. I kian' leave my mother and she use to go wild when I go out with somebody. I get accustom to it now and I don' think no more."

"A young woman like you," he sympathized, forgetting his own problems for a moment.

She did not answer. Then, hearing footsteps in the drawing-room she added hurriedly, "I jus' tell you so as you know you not the only one with a cross to bear."

The footsteps went upstairs and ceased altogether.

"That time you take me out for a drive," she said, "when I dress up in my finery, was a big thing. My mother did want to come, but I put my foot down."

The footsteps came downstairs once more and when it was too late for him to leave the mistress's skirt was rustling in the doorway.

"Ah, Ben," she said, "where were you all yesterday?"

"I had an accident, Mistress."

"Were you hurt?"

"No, Mistress. But I was incapacitated."

"Do speak simple English, Ben. How were you incapacitated?"

"My foot, Mistress. It was all twisted."

"Very well, Ben. Is it straightened out now?"

"More or less, Mistress."

"All right. Talking to you is like entering a maze. Edna, we're expecting my daughter and son-in-law for breakfast. Lay the table for two more — or rather three. Sometimes they turn up with someone. If there's time buy a duck or something."

She left the kitchen. All the verve she had brought back from abroad had gone. Yes, Ben thought, we all have our cross to bear, but she was able to lay hers down from time to time, while on her overseas jaunts.

"One day," Ben told Edna, "I was once happy, you know. I wasn't always sour like this. I was happy when I was a boy living in Skeldon. For years I was happy."

"I'm happy now," she told him in a level voice. "I got my cross, but I happy. You must come round to the Brethren Church one night and let the Elder cast out the spirit that eating your inside out. . . . "

"Hm!" he sneered. "You're a strange one. All this time I thought I had you sized up. You'd get along well with the Frankers."

Ben left, slamming the kitchen door, although it was only closed during the day when rain was falling hard.

At thirty-eight he was embittered, aware of the impossibility of tackling his aspirations from the beginning or planning a different course for his life. But inaction was not in his nature. He realized now that by taking Carl in he was attempting to break out of the impasse into which he had driven himself. If Carl had really gone he would have to steer his craft in another direction, this time into much deeper waters. No, he would not lie down and allow life to trample him. Once, as a boy, he was taken to the sugar factory at Rose Hall, and as he walked along the cat-walks, high above the thundering machinery, his grandmother said, "You have to know where to negotiate the cat-walks. One slip and you'd be mangled. But it's so sweet, the smell of sugar all around." She lived into her eighties to bury nearly all her children. And with each premature death she was heard to say, "She slipped," or "He slipped."

Where did Edna stand? wondered Ben. He felt cheated by her deception. There was no cause to practise it on him. Yet, when all was said and done, her behaviour was thrust upon her by the intolerance of people like himself. Carl was from a culture where men and women did not marry, yet entered into life-long associations stronger than the bonds created by ceremonies. The town world, mined with expectations Edna took too seriously, trapped her into lying to those around her, her inferiors in almost every respect. Not him! He was going to break every convention and hack his way towards a condition that existed, he was sure, a condition of the certainty of happiness. There he would welcome Mabel and Tina, his children and even his hideous mother-in-law. Did not Fatpork, even in his condition, find a refuge with his sister and her husband? The last time Ben had seen him he looked healthier than ever. His syphilitic body did not rot in Grunt-Hoo's room, after all, as Ben was certain it would do, even while giving him the advice to go and see his sister. "*I* am healthy, in mind and body," Ben told himself.

He was hoping that the Franker boy would come back before he had to go and fetch the master.

Whenever, as a youth or a young man, anyone asked him, "What are you thinking about?", Ben recollected, he could never give a truthful answer. All manner of thoughts now tumbled over one another in his mind, leaving no trace; and now it was difficult to believe that he was so preoccupied with Carl's going away. He got up to go to the stables. The day he went to the lighthouse, about seven

161

years ago, he was able to look *down* on the flights of birds for the first time in his life, on carrion crows and gulls straying from the sea. He was then taken by an almost irresistible impulse to leap. It was not the height that called him downwards, for since boyhood he had been running up and down ladders. Rather, it was the birds below manoeuvring on the currents like threads in the sunlight, with a freedom that made him envious. And of all the people jostling one another in his reflections it was Fatpork who kept coming back to him. Ben felt he had taken him for granted and had avoided him in so obvious a manner it was surprising he ever spoke to him. Was he happy in his new house, where he would probably not be able to come and go as he pleased? One nod from his brother-in-law and his sister would put him out on the road, so that he would have to drag his healthy-looking rotting body from one room to another, until he ended up in the Alms House. The shadow who had taken his place in the room was as elusive as a yellow-headed snake, a clown without a voice.

Young Franker came back soon after Ben had driven the master back to the Treasury.

"Well?" Ben asked, with the appearance of great calm.

"He not there. Miss Boxhill say he din' come there."

"You looked around the house?"

"I jus' been there and she tell me what I tell you. What about the two cents?"

Ben gave him a coin; but he hung around, no doubt in the hope of earning more money.

"You believe in fate, young Franker?"

"Believe? That's me aunt name. Aunt Fate."

"It *would* be, you little freak. An aunt called Fate. You've ever watched your father fooping your mother?"

"Me mother don' foop me father. Don' say nothin' 'bout me mother!" he protested.

"Look here, you pervert," Ben said, grabbing his hair and easing him off the ground by tugging upwards. "Give me back my four cents."

The boy's eyeballs were staring, fixed in an upward gaze while he emptied his right-hand pocket, allowing the coins to fall to the ground.

"Now listen to me!" Ben shouted at him. "I don't like you or your brothers and sisters or your maniac parents. I believe you know more

162

about Carl than you're telling me and that you didn't go to Miss
Boxhill's house at all. You're not even sweating, yet it's a good three
miles there. If you don't find out something about Carl by tonight I'll
hammer on the wall when your parents're fooping their inside out, or
when they're screaming their heads off singing hymns without words,
you understand? You misconceived little runt! Now get away! But
remember what I said about Carl. By tonight."

When Ben let go of his hair the boy retreated from his reach until he
stumbled against his doorstep when, with a swift movement, he
pushed open his door and disappeared inside.

It was in the afternoon, when Ben was preparing to fetch the master,
that he heard the laughing. "Hoo-hoo! Ha haaaah!" It came from the
women's house opposite and was so loud that one of the barbers came
out on the pavement, his scissors in his hand and his apron strewn
with the hair of his numerous customers. He looked up at the
windows, but went back inside when he could see nothing unusual.
Ben climbed up on the seat and, just as he was about to give the horse
the signal to move off, a window above the barber-shop was flung
open and Violet herself appeared, dressed in the single dress she
owned.

"Ha haaaah!" her voice came across the road. "So *he* gone! What
happen, cabman?"

The three barbers came out as a man and craned their necks
upwards, and at the same time two of the women living in the house
appeared at different windows.

Something held Ben back from driving off and avoiding making
himself a public spectacle. He pretended to be looking for something
under the seat.

"He gone, cabman! But where he gone? I goin' tell you one thing:
he in' gone to Orealla. He in' hiding in the stables neither. Probably
he dig a hole and get inside to hid from you, eh? The trouble is you
don' know who you dealin' with!"

Ben gave the horse the signal, almost blind with the humiliation he
had suffered in front of the women, the barbers, their customers who
had come out on to the pavement as well, and the beggar, grinning up
at Violet with his toothless gums. The carriage set out, more slowly
than was usual, with her words flying after it like vindictive birds.

"Queen! Queen! Is where you man-friend? Boyyyyyy!"

A crowd of people were gathered in the street outside the Law

Courts, where a murder trial was being held. The jury was expected to give a verdict late that afternoon, by which time the crowd would have grown to twice its size. He drove past the flamboyant trees and the Magistrates' Court. The master was waiting at the foot of the stairs. He got into the carriage after giving him a more pronounced nod than Ben used to receive before he discovered his adultery. Ben turned the carriage around and drove back to the house. He could see the women from a distance, waiting for his arrival, and imagined the malicious expression on their faces. The barbers and their clients had gone back into the shops, but the beggar was there, sitting on his box, to the left of the painted glass of the barber-shop. The pitch road, melting at its edges, threw up shimmering patterns which kept receding before the carriage, between the rows of shops with their living accommodation above them. He stopped the carriage on the side where the master's house was.

"Ben!" came Violet's voice. "Is wha' happenin', man? Is where Carl gone?"

The master, getting out of the carriage, looked up at Ben in surprise, but almost at once made for his stairs.

"You're going out this afternoon or tonight?" Ben asked.

"No. You can put the horse away."

When the door closed behind him Violet shouted out: "I know where Carl is. He not far, Ben. That's one consolation. April will be the worst, when the long rains come and you kian' work outside an' you got to stand at the window lookin' out. I tell you one thing. You still got the horse. Haa haaaaaaaah!"

And the girls began laughing with her, and the beggar too, and the barbers, who had come out once more to savour his humiliation.

His pride was swallowed up in that laughter and he knew his life would never be the same again. He knew as well that the slightest show of weakness would be disastrous for him. Aware that people were impressed by his arrogance and apparent indifference, he unhitched the horse and left the harness on the passengers' seat. Then he led the animal in, even hesitating a while on the bridge before leading him round a non-existent obstacle. But he was trembling like a leaf, as he used to do immediately after a burglary, when the tension was over and the long empty street stretched ahead of him.

Ben came back for the carriage and, unable to resist the temptation of stealing a glance across the road, looked up and saw Carl standing beside Violet.

164

"Don' pretend you in' see him, cabman!" she shouted. "Is he! An' he wearing you shoes and the shirt you buy fo' him. Eh-eh! You ever hear such a thing in your life? I tell you one thing. If you come over here to get him we goin' lay you up in bed again, you bitch! Koo-ka-ree-a-koooh! I tell you I'm a pistol ball!"

The barbers laughed aloud at her imitation of a cock-crow and description of herself, and Ben held it against them, seeing it as evidence of some kind of vengeance against him.

Once the carriage was put up he went inside and sat down on his bed, thinking that that afternoon, and the day he discovered Mabel was sick, were the two most disastrous periods of his life. Besides, both incidents were the result of his living away from Mabel. That very night he had to let Mabel know that, whatever the cost, he would come and live with her and the children. In fact, the master would probably be glad to see the back of him, provided he came to work early enough to get him off to work and was able to keep the stable clean and maintain the house in good repair.

A whirring sound came from the Frankers' room, stopping and starting up intermittently. Ben recalled his threat to young Franker who, after all, had told the truth. He had taken away his money, assaulted him and called him a liar. So Carl was there, within earshot! His hammock was slung up in the women's house, where the beggar was a regular visitor. Ben understood too well. He was a creature of company and must have languished in his room, where he, Ben, revelled in isolation. But there was no back yard in the house opposite, and he would miss his plants and the fires he lit in the yard.

Getting up abruptly, Ben prepared to wash down the horse. And it was only while he was drying him that he realized how much work Carl had been doing, that the garden of greens would be taken over by weeds because he was no longer prepared to break his back in another man's service.

After the horse had been groomed and its mane clipped, and its body examined for sores, Ben reminded himself that he must take it the next day to the municipal vet for its periodic treatement against worms.

23

EVEN BEFORE he reached Mabel's doorstep Ben heard her brother. He knew that he had narrowly won a points decision a few days ago and hoped to see him badly bruised and his face swollen. But when he pushed the door and searched him out among the roomful of people he was unscathed and might have been a stevedore, rather than a brute who fought for money. His lady friend Claris was there as well with a piece of silver jewellery round her neck and her white teeth sparkling. Mabel's mother was squatting on the floor, flanked by Laly and Iris, who lay full-length beside her grandmother, fast asleep. Bamford was sitting in Mabel's lap as if he were an infant, while about three feet away stood a stranger, a well-dressed young man, smoking a thin, black cigarette. Ben seemed to remember having seen him the night of the ceremony for Mabel.

"Mabel?" Ben said.

"Hi, Uncle," she answered.

"Put the child down. I want to talk to you."

She looked at those around her for approval. Seetram got up.

"You come near me and I'll lay you flat," Ben said calmly. "And it's not my fists I'll use."

"Stay there, Mabel," Seetram told her.

But, apparently stung by the prohibition, Mabel got up and came over to Ben, who kept an eye on her brother. He was still standing on the same spot, uncertain what to do next.

Ben slammed the door with such violence that he could feel the step shudder underfoot. Mabel followed him into the yard and down to the gate, where he stopped under the signboard.

"I brought the weekly money early," he told her. "And I came to tell you I'm moving in with you."

"Uncle . . . " she started.

"Don't call me uncle!" Ben protested.

"Uncle," she said, "I sick. And they not goin' let you."

"You want me to?" he asked her.

"Yes, Uncle. You shouldn' be living away from home. And I know Tina does come and spread sheself 'pon your bed. . . . "

"You want me to come back?" he repeated. "That's all I want to know."

"Yes. You not lyin' to me?"

"No, Mabel. But I've got to give the master notice. This is February. By the middle of next month."

"As long as you come back."

"But you must stand up to your family," he enjoined.

"If I know you comin' back," she gave back, "I goin' stand up to them. . . . You think I sick?"

"You're not sick, Mabel," Ben told her, genuinely believing what he said. "Come in with me and face them."

"What about Seetram?" she asked.

"I'll deal with him."

Ben put his arm round her waist and walked towards the room, marked out by a line of light round the ill-fitting door. When he reached the stairs he stopped and looked at Mabel, more certain of her loyalty than ever. Opening the door he stood in the door-mouth, his hand in hers.

"I'm coming to live here next month," Ben said. "And anyone who doesn't like it had better get out now. And I mean you more than anybody else, Seetram. I'm master in this room."

"You might got education," Seetram said, "but you in' goin' talk to me like that."

"I'm going to talk to you how I like because I pay the rent for this room."

"You . . . " Seetram said, raising his hand. But his mother and Claris jumped up and grabbed hold of him, while Mabel placed herself in front of her man.

"Let him come," Ben said, picking up a chair. "Claris wouldn't want to look at him when his face looks like his batty, split down the middle. Let him come!"

Seetram made as if to tear himself away and the women held him even more firmly.

The young stranger, embarrassed by the set-to and bewildered by the speed with which the situation had arisen, could only step forward with an ambiguous gesture, and then step back again.

"Go home now," Mabel told her brother. Then, addressing Claris, she said, "Take him home. I don' want no ruction in front of the children."

"I goin'," Seetram said, shaking himself free of the women. "But you touch my sister and you in' goin' set foot in this room again. Don't think I don' know you does beat her. I see the marks 'pon her body."

He swaggered towards the door and when, looking back, he saw

167

that Claris wasn't following, he said, "Is what you waiting for? The six o'clock gun? Come on!"

Claris did as she was told and the young man followed her. And with their going Ben's anger collapsed, inexplicably. He felt no ill will towards his mother-in-law. She had taken her place on the floor, where Laly was propping up Iris, who had not woken up during the altercation. Laly was as calm as at the moment he arrived, and looked as Mabel must have looked when she was a little girl. Mabel's mother kept staring at her, in an effort to see what effect the quarrel had had on her. She had whipped her when she announced her first pregnancy and put her out of the house when her belly started to swell.

As soon as Mabel's mother began to talk Ben knew she had it in for him. She was more bitter towards him than he had ever been towards her, he reflected. He had not forgotten how she had come when Bamford was born and begged him not to turn Mabel against her because she was a fragile child and needed her.

"She not ordinary. She not a ordinary child," she now said, while Mabel sat down on a chair and whispered something to Bamford, who went behind the screen. "She uses to sit an' play alone when she was a lil' girl. All by sheself she uses to play, like a solitary tree from the savannah. An' my heart did break to see she alone. Sometimes when I go in the room I see a shadow sliding under the door an' she with she eyes wide open as if she been talkin' to somebody. An' sometimes she father go out to talk to her and she would tell him what he did come to say before he say it. 'Is how you know?' he'd ask. And she'd say, 'You tell me so jus' now!' And that happen so much times she father get frighten and say something wrong with she and he never did have no truck with spirits. But is when she start healing animals an' people that he get really vex an' threaten to send she away to she uncle, who is a earth-man and know all 'bout bringing up children. And is he that cure she; she uncle. But something in Mabel change since she go away from home. And when she come back she so change-up and secret-secret, she change us too. But at least the spirits stop pestering her. You got to be thankful for small mercies. An' instead of you appreciating she an' caring for she like a father. . . . "

Bamford appeared from behind the screen, dressed in the old cast-off shirt of Ben's he wore in bed. Mabel sent Laly over to Ben and he hugged her ostentatiously, while he informed her that he was coming soon to live with them. Bamford stared at his father but said nothing. They followed their mother, who was carrying Iris over her

168

shoulder. The little one's mouth was open and her eyes were closed tight in a sleep that a noisy adult quarrel did not succeed in disturbing. Her head wobbled slightly over Mabel's shoulder, the sight of which made Ben think of the young man who had left with Seetram and Claris. Was he a friend of Seetram's and Claris's? He must have been.

Someone was walking in the yard with a heavy step, the step of a stranger not familiar with its layout. For a moment Ben thought the stranger had stopped outside the room, but the footfalls were soon heard again, only to die away beyond the room, deep in the yard. The voices of Mabel and the two eldest children rose and fell. Finally Mabel came out again and sat down on the same chair. Her mother must have been waiting for her to reappear, because she promptly carried on where she had stopped before Mabel put the children to bed. This time she addressed Ben directly, with a bold tone.

"I got to bother about she 'cause she come out of me."

"That's why you put her out when she was expecting a child?" he asked maliciously.

She looked at him with her bloodshot eye. "You don' get on with nobody," she told him, "exceptin' for Tina."

"I don't want to quarrel," Ben said. "Why we're quarrelling? You wanted me to come and live with Mabel and now I'm going to do what you wanted you and your cock-eyed son are against it."

From her silence it was clear she no longer wanted him to live with Mabel, and this discovery annoyed him intensely. It had never entered his head that she could want anything else, despite his words.

"Who was the young man?" Ben asked Mabel.

But she sat staring at her mother and did not bother to answer.

"I want to know who he was!" Ben insisted.

"Is my brother bring him," she said at last. "He say he sweet on me and offer me money to move in with me. He offer me two five-dollar notes an' Seetram put another five-dollar note on top and say the boy had good prospects. They was trying to make him stay tonight."

"You don't have shame?" Ben asked her mother, feeling the old hatred well up in him. "Your own daughter!"

"You say you want fo' see her happy," the old woman said to him. "You always saying so. 'All I want is to see Mabel happy.' Suppose this boy did make her happy? But you say one thing an' mean something else."

"Don't preach to me, old woman!" Ben said, raising his voice.

169

"You wan' know who bring the boy here?" the mother asked. "You wan' know? Ask she, ne? Ask she who bring him here."

Ben turned to look at Mabel, who sat with her head bowed.

"Tell him, ne? Tell him is not . . . " the old woman persisted.

"Is me," Mabel said softly. And the sound of one of the children coughing brought a temporary end to the conversation.

Mabel got up and lit one of the two lamps fixed to the wall by a bracket, moving as if she wanted the ritual to last all night. She only continued what she was saying when she had taken her seat once more.

"I meet him in the road," Mabel continued, "an' he ask me if it wasn' for me they had the drum-healing in Ma yard. I say yes, but I din' know him. He say yes, that he was there an' he's Seetram friend. Then I look at him good an' thought I remember I did see him before. An' he ask if he could come with Seetram when he come with Claris to see me. An' I say, 'Suit youself.' "

"So what you blaming other peoople for?" Mabel's mother said triumphantly.

"But you saw him offer her money," Ben said, "and you did nothing."

"Is none of my business," her mother said in return. "Is my business who she go with and who she get child with? All I know is she not goin' be happy with you, 'cause you like a ship without a compass."

"What the ass you know about me, you old hag?" Ben demanded angrily.

Her knobbly hands were pressed into each other.

"I done with you," she declared, raising and lowering her hands above each other and slapping them together as she did so, in a gesture often used by Edna as a substitute for saying: "Never again!"

"I done with you long ago," she repeated.

"I'm not going to start abusing you," Ben said, "but you know my opinion of you and your interfering ways."

The apparently innocuous words stung her into action.

"She tell you 'bout the uncle who did *cure* she of she healing ways? You din' know that, eh?"

"I did!" Ben rejoined. "Mabel told me, you mischief-maker! All these things you're doing in her interest, eh? But all the time what you want is to see another man supplant me so you can go to church on Sunday with a triumphant heart. No matter if the

170

man is nothing but a boy."

"You're years older than Mabel," she reminded him.

"Isn't that what she likes?" Ben retorted. "Isn't that what she liked about her uncle?"

"You damned . . . !" she exclaimed, unable to control herself.

"Now it's you who must ask Mabel," Ben told her.

"I not answering no more questions," Mabel said quietly. "What's done is done. When I did go away as a lil' girl I couldn' ask no questions. Now I got children I not answering none. You an' Seetram leave me alone. Ben comin' back to live here an' if you quarrel I goin' take his side."

"An' when he beat you an' bruise you don' come runnin' to me neither," her mother said.

"If I don't beat her," Ben put in, "you're going to be glad? Knowing you, you won't be glad. You'd still hurry round here sniffing for sin. Well, I don't mind, as long as you don't cause trouble."

The last few words apprently pacified her, for she sat down and said nothing more. Mabel, too, settled in her chair with the appearance of an old woman carrying the burden of decades of experience.

In the flickering of the lamplight there was no difference between these two women sitting on opposite sides of the room. There were other resemblances as well, their stubbornness, the quality of dissembling which in the mother seemed hideous, while in Mabel it was a pardonable fault, to be laughed at sometimes; and a certain slackness in the face of distress, which in Mabel's case attracted sympathy from others and disarmed him completely.

Ben recalled how he fought against making Mabel pregnant while harbouring a secret wish that he would. Her words about taking his side had touched him so deeply he caught a glimpse of a different kind of love, a selfless love devoted to the need for the survival of someone other than oneself. For a while the recollection of the young man standing in his room was no longer painful, but rather proof of Mabel's need for protection and a masculine presence. He got up, kissed her and then put his hand on her mother's shoulder.

Ben did not go back to Mr Schwartz's house right away, for he could not face being alone. Besides, he was afraid that at that time of the night — about nine o'clock — some of the women might be at the window of the house opposite.

As soon as he turned into Rosemary Lane he saw the tables from

171

afar. Encouraged by the fine weather, the owner had put out tables which almost touched the edge of the gutter, in which vegetation was thriving like the grass on the verge. He caught the sound of guitars when he reached the crossroads, about thirty yards from the place of forbidden drinking. There were more customers than he had ever seen before; and on entering he got the impression that he was in an altogether different place, with younger people who were less solemn. In fact one group standing near the musicians was downright boisterous, and, from their manner, Ben imagined they must have been drinking for some time. No one greeted him, as used to be the custom; and the owner, when he touched him on the shoulder, gave him a quick nod with a "Hi, Ben," before hurrying over to a table to serve his customers.

Things had changed and he did not like it, the gaiety or the youth, the loss of intimacy. The crowd had discovered a favourite haunt, and his spoor had been trampled out of all recognition. Women were there as well, vulgar creatures whom you would not lay for the gift of a horse.

He bought a Tennent's beer and stood against the wall to conjure up the days when every minute carried the threat of the sergeant next door irrupting in the doorway as if he had fallen from the sky. Secretly Ben hoped Carl would walk in, even with one of his powdered friends, and found himself watching the door through which customers came and went in a ceaseless movement like a turbulent sea. It was astonishing that the character of a place could change so rapidly, only because the owner had a police officer in his hands.

Where did the poverty-stricken find money to buy so much liquor? he wondered. He took the ice into his mouth with the first sip of the cold, translucent, imported beer and rolled it round and round his tongue to banish the dryness and the heat which had settled on the night and the mad thoughts whirling inside his head and the longing for the fragrance of Mabel's fresh sweat bubbling under her armpits.

Bamford came to mind. Earlier Ben had watched him and the child had given him not a sign of recognition and Ben thought one day he would cut out the boy's tongue, for no reason, save that he was ugly and loved him only a little. Mabel would say he resented the boy's ugliness, that was all. But it amounted to the same thing, for children should love their parents. *Let him look to women for affection, as the girls sought mine and never failed to rifle my pockets when I went there during daytime.* Ben could never forget that day when they went on a picnic and his son was absent; because he would have hated lying prostrate under the palms with him a few yards away. Truth was, Ben loved him, but was ashamed of his ugliness and his own. In Skeldon there was a row of almond trees, and the iguanas came to sun themselves under them early in the morning, only to scatter at the sound of his grandmother's steps on the stairs on her way to the latrine with a po full of shit. He remembered the morning when she cornered one of them in the wood-room under the house and shouted for him to bring a cutlass. She locked the door behind her and he could hear her screams as the huge lizard went for her. When she came out bleeding at the ankles she was holding the beast by its tail and saying in a shaken voice, "I did break its back." Perhaps that was why he despised cowardly men and expected a lot of his two women and saw in Bamford the ruin of a mother's boy.

Smoke rose imperceptibly towards the pitched roof, far above the heads of the crowd who, though they might occasionally look at their feet, never lifted their heads higher than the plane of their eyes. Did they exist as individuals? Did he exist as an individual or was he just a bit broken off from a mass to whose purpose he was tuned? Only his aberrations fed the illusion of difference. Over there was the woman who haunted the public dance halls; beyond her in the corner was the man in the hat, who was always singing or humming like a field canary in the morning. And just next to him was Silver Fish who went from barber-shop to barber-shop offering to give a blow-by-blow description of the latest professional fight for a collection from the waiting clients. Yet they all lived in the same kind of room, died in a bed or on a heap of rags and were buried in a box. It was Carl who first got him thinking along those lines with his face that resembled all other Indian faces, which a Georgetonian would have found great difficulty in distinguishing from that of another Macusi; the way he walked or the way he looked through you; his passion for planting and watching things grow marked him out as an aboriginal Indian and not as Carl, the individual who deserted him when he was not looking and took refuge with a gang of women.

Resisting the urge to smash his glass on the floor, Ben made his way to the door where there was the smell of rain on the night breeze; and the bush at the entrance moved restlessly, like a sleeper at night time.

Ben could tell that the master and mistress were in bed by the silence and absence of shadows at the windows. On the nights he did not

173

bother to do his duty the master would creep down at one or two in the morning and lock up quietly, so as not to display his shame at being unable to control his cabman. Recalling what he had to do the following day Ben made up his mind to carry out his duties conscientiously. When he had secured the jalousies, the casement windows and the Demerara windows at the two ends of the gallery he raised the chimney of the lamp and blew it out. He repeated the operation with the other wall lamp and the lamp in the drawing-room, always left in semi-darkness except when visitors came. He then went and stood on the porch overlooking the empty street. There was a faint light opposite, but the windows were all closed, and he concluded that at least one of the women was working late. He yielded to the urge to go over only so far as to descend to the landing where the stairs turned away from the street. That single lamp burning steadily near the window, fainter than a night light, was hardly bearable.

Ben was drunk and his thoughts simply went their own way, now seeking out the beggar in the vicinity of the barber shop, now directing his eyes towards the rain clouds or considering the next day or wondering why the horse had taken to neighing lately as if a mare were in the vicinity.

Then he saw Violet turn into the yard in the company of another woman. Driven by an impulse he leapt up and ran across the road, but on catching sight of him Violet slipped into the doorway of the covered staircase. On arriving before the door he heard the bolts being drawn. The other woman, seeing that Violet had fled, looked at Ben suspiciously.

"Is who you?" she asked.

"I'm a vain dog," Ben told her. "And I know who you are."

"Me?" she said, taking a step backwards.

"Yes. You're a parrot dressed to kill."

"You touch me an' I goin' holler!" she warned.

"You remember the red people riots after the last war?" Ben asked her, "When blood was clotting in the gutters under the midday sun?"

She turned tail and bolted up the street, running as fast as a man.

His head began to spin and he realized that he was even more drunk than a half-hour ago, on arriving back from the shop of forbidden drinking.

"This woman dressed in taffeta and organdie," he reflected, as he crossed the empty street, "appearing out of the black smoke and laughing . . . and I knew that I had to dispose of something before she

174

would come near me . . . some kind of waste. I've seen those tiny eggs cocks lay . . . with my own eyes. Ah, the children playing while their parents are out buying things on account. Did we like to go visiting on Sundays? Not relations, but superior people who might be useful to us later on in life."

He must have fallen because there was grit in his mouth. Less than half an hour before he was putting out the lamps and closing the windows carefully enough not to wake up the master and his wife, while now he was struggling to cross the road and end up before the gate. He could see the painted paling staves broken only by the passage between the yards and numberless windows below the metal gutters running along the cornices; and above the single skylight on every house. Even the stray dogs ferreting in the passages were silent. He looked back, and seeing light in Violet's house made a last effort to make the crossing. Then an extraordinary thing occurred: catching sight of the woman in organdie and taffeta standing in the grass beside the master's gate he went towards her effortlessly, walking as straight as if he were sober. And on approaching her she walked ahead of him, through the passage, and vanished only when he stood before the door of his room. Then, with the same difficulty he experienced when he first tried crossing the road, he managed to find his bed, on to which he threw himself face down.

24

MRS SCHWARTZ had sent a message to her best friend, asking her to drop in when she had the chance. The friend, anxious to know if she had learnt about Mr Schwartz's misconduct, came within the hour to find the mistress wrapped in a shawl and complaining of how ill she was. The two women came down to the gallery and took seats by the windows.

"Whenever I come back from the States there's talk of my being my sister. Haven't they got anything to do? They talk, talk. In New York I could go out without being recognized, do as I pleased without feeling I was being watched."

"Would you remain there if you had the chance?" her friend asked.

"No," Mrs Schwartz answered promptly. "My sister wants to

come back because she's afraid of growing lonely. She doesn't want to be old and alone in a country where she has no dignity."

"You can't blame people if they think you're your sister, you know. Every time you come back you look different. Your hair is styled, you have a new set of clothes and even a slight accent. A foreign country does something to you without you realizing it."

"Yes, my sister is completely different, yet she believes she hasn't changed. Her gestures are different, her skin has a different texture, she speaks with a drawl. She isn't my sister."

The two friends continued talking and drinking green tea and eating corn pone. The mistress's best friend was trembling inwardly, thinking that she must have been summoned for a specific reason. She got the impression that they were sparring and that each was unwilling to come too close to the other lest she be hurt by an unexpected blow. They had been good friends for so long that each was attuned to the other's moods, and Elise thought she could detect a slight irritation in her friend's voice.

"I don't know," the mistress said wearily. "I've always trusted you."

"Don't you still?" Elise asked, her voice faltering.

"There're so many things I want to say . . . but there's so much suspicion in the air. When I came back, on the wharf a man and a woman were quarelling over a child. He was trying to pull the child from her and she kept shouting, 'You not taking him, 'cause you going go away with him to the Essequibo and I does sell in the Berbice.' He had the child by the left foot while she was holding on to his shoulders. And the poor child wasn't even crying. It kept looking past them as if its eyes were fixed on something in the distance. I was no longer interested in the quarrel although by this time people had gathered round the two. I can't explain how my attention was riveted on that child. I kept waiting for it to say something, or to start bawling. You'd think I was mad if I said that for a while I was convinced I was the child and they were tugging me in two different directions. . . . "

"But —"

"Don't interrupt! Please, don't interrupt me because I'm not myself; I've not been myself since I came back. I'll never go again. It . . . it's not safe to go away. My poor sister! She doesn't want to stay and she can't come back, because this small town would crush her."

"Why crush her?"

"Don't tell me you don't know about the intrigues, its anonymous

176

letters . . . and all."

"What anonymous letters?" Elise asked, now thoroughly in a panic.

"What letters indeed? Well, Thomas receives several anonymous letters when I go away . . . and after I come back." Then her voice changed completely, as though she had suddenly made a resolution to calm herself. She began to speak in a low studied tone. "And *I* received an anonymous letter too. Well, what do you expect from women who stay home and have servants to look after their children?"

Elise did not dare ask the question that was on the tip of her tongue.

"I'm sick, Elise, I'm sick of a disease for which there are doctors, but no cure." She gathered her shawl around her and turned to fix her friend with a stare. "I've got malaria, my yearly dose. It's nothing."

"Malaria!" exclaimed her friend, relieved that that was all and that the mistress was not talking about her grief. "You must take care of yourself, my dear."

Edna came in to ask if a place was to be set at table for the mistress's friend, at which the mistress turned towards her guest. It was only half-past nine and the midday meal was not served for another hour and a half.

"I don't know," the guest said.

"Set another place in any case, Edna."

Edna left, and the mistress's friend, unable to resist the temptation, asked her question.

"What was in the anonymous letters?"

"Oh, Elise, I don't want to talk about it."

"After dropping hints you have no right to say you don't want to talk about it."

And so began one of their freqent quarrels. Then when the quarrel seemed to be getting serious the mistress relented.

"Those Tom got said the same thing. I was going to America because I had a man there. Because Clarence is there."

Clarence was the small-islander she would have married had her parents approved of him.

"Because I go to America," she continued "I must meet him. The country's so vast. New York alone has twenty times the population of this country. How absurd! Trust, everything depends on trust. How can I go to see a man who's married? I'm a Christian!! But these Christians who write their anonymous letters would hate nothing

177

more than to find out I haven't met him."

"But you never defend yourself," her friend said.

"How can I defend myself against shadows who won't come out into the open? Is it any wonder I like going away?"

"Is that the only reason why you go?" asked her friend.

"Ha, Elise! You and I are chalk and cheese. You are full of hints, full of deceptions, full of things I find distasteful, yet we've been friends for years, as though we're defying some law. You do me things and I keep forgiving for no reason. I am sick with loyalty. . . . Yes, Elise, I've seen Clarence twice."

The two women stared at each other, and while the mistress's friend felt as if she had made a wonderful discovery, Mrs Schwartz was regretting her disclosure of two innocent meetings which her friend would not fail to remember, to her detriment.

"The first time he was brought to my sister's apartment in New York by some officious woman," the mistress continued, "who thought I might want to meet him. The second time I met him by accident at a Guyanese party and left as soon as I saw him. Sometimes I wish I were like you, seizing whatever takes my fancy, saying whatever I please. . . . I'm not well."

She had pulled the shawl round her completely and was now shivering uncontrollably.

"Come, come," her friend said.

The two women got up at the same time and while the friend went to tell Edna to make soup the mistress climbed the stairs to her bedroom. Her teeth were chattering with the chill. Not once had she escaped an attack when she came back from abroad, as if the disease was exacting a kind of vengeance on her. Holding on ponderously to the banisters she reproached herself for quarrelling with the friend. Since childhood she had attracted trouble to those round her in spite of her sweet nature, like those innocent children in stories whose appearance is the harbinger of disaster. Her parents had suffered on account of her association with the small-islander; her husband continued to suffer because he knew she could not care for him in the way he desired. Even her best friend continually complained, and although she saw herself as the innocent party in their quarrels, the fact remained that the unhappiness she brought others had afflicted their friendship as well.

If only I could tell her everything, Mrs Schwartz reflected, as she undid her corset. She would have liked to confess that each time she went to

178

the States she had hoped to meet the man with whom she had once been in love, although when she did meet him she turned away. She desired to see him simply because of the emptiness in her life, the limitless emptiness that, like a vast savannah under the shimmering heat of March, penetrated even her dreams. She had never loved any other man before or since and she desperately clung to the memory of those few months for which she paid with a guilt that could have been alleviated had she been able to share the secret with her friend.

Mrs Schwartz lay down and covered herself with the blanket. She did not put it beyond her friend to come up and try to drag from her the contents of the anonymous letter *she* had received. Elise was like that. But what did it matter, since she believed not a word of it?

Elise eventually came up, bearing a tray on which was a bowl of soup.

"Come on. Up!"

She stayed until Mrs Schwartz fell asleep with two blankets covering her.

25

BEN WENT to see Tina the following night, to tell her of his intention of moving in with Mabel. She was taking her midwifery examinations soon, and a large volume lay open on the oilcloth that covered the dining-table. Her recently washed secret cloths were hung up to dry on a line stretching over her bed; but otherwise the large room they were in was as tidy as a woman's hands could make it. The blind on the unshuttered window billowed gently in a breeze that came through the wide-open door. One of her two lamps hissed and whined while it burned brightly. The second one, which she used for reading, appeared superfluous. Now and then, a white moth would flutter in through the door, eventually to join the others circling the lamp ceaselessly.

Tina made him a cup of bird-vine tea, sweetened with thick condensed milk, then came and sat down at the table as well. She was unwilling to discuss what he had come to tell her, and they talked of the rise in the price of bread instead, and the disturbances that followed it. According to her there had been an increase in the

179

number of patients admitted to hospital suffering from malnutrition, malaria and related complaints.

Something in her manner made him feel uncomfortable. Perhaps it was the way she was sitting, or the offhand way she took the news Ben had brought, or the way she threw the condensed milk into the tea. Tina was not herself. And she had not been herself from the moment he arrived, before he announced the news.

Two of his shirts were folded one on top of the other at the edge of the table next to a pile of her own underwear. Ben was just about to ask her to remind him to take the shirts away when she spoke.

"She was here."

"Who?"

"Mabel."

"Mabel came here?" Ben asked incredulously.

"Yes. She been here with the two girls."

"What for?"

Tina smiled bitterly. "Why you think she did come?" she said challengingly.

"I don't know."

"The children had on new clothes. They did drive up in a cab and she make so much noise I had to come out and look. She pretend she come to pay a social visit, but she couldn' keep it for long. 'Ben comin' to live with us. In four weeks he comin'.' And the children sit there without a word. I tell her you free to do what you like. . . . When last you give me anything, Ben? When last you spend the night here? It's not common enough here, I suppose; not enough people traipsing in and out lashing their friends with their tongues or screaming and shouting and dancing to drums as if they still back in Africa. Well, this is not that kind of house, and it never will be. I does read my Bible every night and live by God's word."

"I don't. . . . "

"It's only because I'm barren you treat this house like a convenience. Admit it! I never know another man excepting you. I don' look left, I don' look right when I leave this house. Nobody can point a finger at me. Yet I had to hear about you going to live with her from her herself. But I tell you now, the day you walk into that house to live, your life goin' to be a misery. She goin' turn her mother 'gainst you and her brother too. And the children goin' learn to despise you like if you was a leper, mark my word. I see in that big girl face the same eye-pass the mother got, who never did respect nothing."

180

Ben did not reply, confounded by her outburst and the unjustifiable attack on Mabel. Besides, it was the first time he had ever heard Tina talk like that. When he put his arms round her she shuddered and burst into tears, touched by the proof of his caring. She wore neither jewellery nor make-up, and her only concession to vanity was the sleeveless frock she invariably put on when she was out of uniform.

"No, I not as strong as I look," she confessed. "The sight of your two girl children so big was too much. . . .But you got a hard way with people. You don' see it yourself. Carl did know it from the start."

"I give Carl everything," Ben protested.

"Yes," she said simply, meaning "No".

They were silent for a long time and their own words were replaced by the muffled sound of conversation from the yard.

"Why're you so blind?" she asked at length. "Don't you see what Mabel's like? To men she look so frail, but a woman only got to look at her expression to know right away what she like."

"Don't carry on about Mabel," he begged, aware of a mounting irritability in himself. "It's good for the children that I'm moving in."

"You goin' to live there because of the children? Or is it 'cause her people taking over the place?"

"Ah," he said, not knowing what to answer.

Ben had complained to her once about Mabel's family; but he had never spoken about his neglect of the children, so he resented the sarcastic tone in her voice. Her manner and words were in complete contrast to her temperament and it seemed to him she was not responsible for her actions.

"I remember her from school," she continued, while his irritation grew. "She was common and couldn't even add two rows of figures. I know her longer than you, but you still wouldn't listen."

"Shut up!" Ben shouted.

Then, defiantly but in a softer voice, he said: "You don't like her. She doesn't like you. That's the truth. Neither of you's got any good word to say about one another. But I tell you, you mean a lot to me, the two of you, and I'm not going to listen to lies from you about her or from her about you. Sometimes she makes me wild when she talks about you, imagining that I spend half of my nights in your company. Now I've got to listen about what she did at school! I've never heard you talk like that before. What the hell it matters if I live with her?"

"Can I come and see you at her place?" she asked.

"I don't see why not," he lied.

181

Tina looked at him with such contempt he was ashamed of speaking to her as he was in the habit of doing to Mabel, whose intelligence was of a different sort. In fact, he was so ashamed he felt a need to humiliate her, to do some sort of violence to her. It was on the tip of his tongue to remind her that she was barren and had no greater hold on him than the attractions of her flesh would allow. For it was not through her that he could achieve immortality, but through Mabel, who had created his three children in the secret of her womb.

The room was bright, almost garish, in contrast to Mabel's, which was always full of shadows. Even the voices that intruded through the open door and the window were different from the noises penetrating into that shadowed room where, at times, more than a dozen persons congregated, as if it was full of wonders. Here he was always at peace, was forever nodding off into an uninterrupted sleep; while at Mabel's there was never far away some vague threat that kept him alert, like a sentry on a dark, rainy night when trees twisted and the wind howled through their branches.

Sometimes he believed he was viewing life through a telescope, and at other times he felt as though he were the observed, not the observer. An Aztec god was said to have looked at the events of the world in a polished mirror of obsidian. How strange, that story. For this was just the way he appeared to himself, at times, as a man of apocalyptic insight, able to stand aside and regard, without grief or pity, things that were and were going to be. But these brief, intense experiences only gave way to hours of such foreboding and distress, he often believed his sanity would vanish in a crackling of malignant explosions.

Ben watched Tina again, anxious to make up. If she had disclosed for the first time a side of her character that was new to him, Heaven knew what else might lie hidden.

"What were you like when you were at school?" he asked.

She saw that he was trying to make amends and looked at him kindly. "Me? I was as I am now."

"Why you became a nurse?"

"There was nothing else I would've been allowed to do, except teaching."

Their conversation petered out. Things were not the same. He had hurt her and she would not be herself until the next time.

"You want to go for a walk?" he offered.

She shook her head.

"Visiting?"

"No."

"You want me to go?"

"No!" she said, almost springing up.

Ben stayed, seated at the table, listening to the lamps, watching the dead moths on the floor and the living ones in their fatal circling of the hissing lamp. He heard the noises from the street, thought of the horse missing Carl and his understanding hands and his visits to the stable even after his charge was put away. He reflected on the plants in the back yard withering from lack of water, on the months of contentment when Carl lay suspended above him, on his downy cotton hammock with its iron rings. In Georgetown he had moved from refuge to refuge. And one day he would put his hammock over his shoulder and set out on the long journey back to Orealla, Ben thought.

"You want to carry on studying?" he asked Tina, pointing to the open textbook.

She nodded, and he was hurt that she did not add: "You stay."

"I'll see you, then," Ben said, placing himself in the doorway. He believed she would cry when he left, although it was not her way, and she had already cried. But what else was there to say, when he had offered to stay and made a show of humility? He was what he was and was obliged to make decisions according to the way he saw things, and not on the advice of women with an axe to grind. Oh, these women with their buckets of tears and their wrong-headed ways. . . .

He stepped down into the yard and looked skywards, drawn by the salt-smell and the mewing of gulls over the river. Dark clouds were rolling inland, pressing the air down in a muggy, humid mass. Everyone he met seemed to be in a hurry, head bent down and shoulders hunched. Ben thought he heard his name, but went on his way without turning to the right or the left. He laughed softly, without any reason, shaking his head, so that a passer-by would have come to the conclusion that he was mad. Then he remembered how his grandmother used to talk to herself, unashamedly, ignoring anyone who came into the room and caught her at it. Odd observations: "So you not coming? Don' come, ne. I not forcing you. . . . "

He laughed to be alive and to feel the night air on his neck and hear the mewing gulls and know that the rain would fall as it did the year before, reviving the parched grass and the wild daisies at the roadside and filling the long trenches to the brim.

183

26

HE WAS awakened by a sound he could not identify. The full moon showed itself only now and then as gaps appeared in the thick clouds. Then a soft but distinct noise came through the floorboards above. He was certain that a burglar was in the house and jumped out of bed to go and investigate. Leaping the back stairs two at a time, he opened the door as quietly as he could and entered the kitchen which, for a few seconds, was half-lit by a shaft of moonlight shining through the door he had left ajar. While he stood at the entrance to the dining-room, scanning the drawing-room and the gallery, a match flared by the wall to his left, but fizzled out almost at once. He grabbed the long broom handle that stood by the window overlooking the yard next door, and, keeping to the wall, edged forward cautiously. Suddenly another match lit up the drawing-room and, to his astonishment, Ben saw the outline of a woman's dress. The lamp was lit and the chimney turned down; and the figure, which he now unmistakably recognized as the mistress, turned now to the right, now to the left. She must have seen him, yet, despite her scant attire and her dishevelled hair, she behaved as though she were alone.

Unsure what to do he stood watching her. Then when she came towards him and, ignoring him completely, opened the glass cabinet, he realized that she was sleep-walking. She was thin and drawn and unsmiling. She walked back to the drawing-room with the key to the gramophone in her hand. Opening it, she placed the record lying on top of a pile nearby on the instrument, which she proceeded to wind laboriously. The sound of the gramophone in the quiet night would not fail to bring the master rolling down the stairs, Ben knew, so he withdrew into the shadows of the dining-room, ready to slip back into the kitchen when her husband appeared. He could not leave her alone, in case she did something foolish.

At last the master came, the cord of his dressing-gown dangling from his waist and his arms outspread as if towards someone he had not met in years.

"Pet," he said in such a loud voice that she stood stock still. "It's me, Tom."

"No!" she exclaimed, stepping back from him.

Ben felt like rushing forward to tell him that she had been sleep-walking and must have had a shock on being awakened; but what

184

would the master have thought, with her dressed for bed and her usually well-groomed head looking like Tina's when she woke in the morning?

"Calm down! It's me — Tom."

"What're you doing here? I came alone."

"Pet," he said, embracing her as they must have done in their younger days.

"Oh, no," she said. "What have I done?"

"Why did you come back then?" he askd angrily. "If you go on like this I'll fill the house with whores."

The needle reached the end of the record and all that remained of the music was the sound of the machine wheezing like an old engine.

"Come upstairs," the master said, his manner changing abruptly.

She was now docile, and allowed herself to be led up the steps by her husband, while the gramophone wheezed and huffed away below the pale lamp.

Ben went downstairs, strangely moved by what he had witnessed.

At seven that morning Edna informed him that the mistress was ill. She had Bright's disease as a result of a bout of malaria. Her appearance the last time he had seen her before she took to sleepwalking came to mind, the swollen face and puffed-up look. As long as it was not blackwater fever, he thought.

"Any special instructions?" he enquired.

"No. The master didn't say anything 'bout you. But you better don' go far. I wouldn' be surprise if he send for the doctor again today. You know he and sickness."

After sharing bread and butter and a bowl of boiling coffee with Edna he took down the harness, intending to get the horse and carriage for the drive to the Public Buildings. Loud screaming and shouting broke out in the Frankers' room downstairs. *So early,* he thought, coming to the conclusion that he parents were either fighting or holding a prayer meeting. He would not give them the satisfaction of looking in, he decided.

It had rained the night before, and the leaves of some shrubs still carried blobs of water that trembled in the breeze like drops of quicksilver.

Suddenly Ben stopped, arrested by a terrible thought. Suppose the mistress went and died, where would he be with his blackmail of the master? He would no longer be able to threaten him with telling her of

185

the escapade with her best friend. Disconsolately he made his way back and set about performing his stable duties. A moment earlier he had been in high spirits, but now he would never be at peace until the mistress recovered.

Ben resolved to have his hair cut that morning. Whenever things were going badly his head began to itch and in the end he had to pay the barber a visit and get him to put him out of his misery by clipping off the excess hair and bathing his scalp in all sorts of herbs and lotions.

In the stables and on his perch he could think of nothing save the mistress's sickness and his admiration for her. . . . God, had he not promised Mabel to come and live with her within four weeks? The master would never allow it if the mistress went and embraced Death. Mabel would lose her respect for him and even Jesus Christ and all the obeah men in the country would not be able to save him.

He spotted his employer descending the stairs like a prince, with an unusually severe expression Ben would have despised the previous day and even punished him by driving off before he had taken his seat. He reflected on how one was capable of being diminished by an idea, a simple thought that occurred in a flash between the back stairs and the shit-house in the yard.

"Good morning, sir," Ben said, doffing his hat and bowing slightly. He waited until the master had been sitting for a good half-minute before he drove off at a respectable pace.

Wandering birds were gathering in flocks, flying out to sea, making arrow-head patterns against the black sky. Ben was distraught and attempted to banish every reflection. He felt as if he were in a garden full of scorpions. Once again that terror of the burglar, the belief that you were in a street which went narrowing towards the forest. Suppose she died! How often he had dreamt of finding himself naked or half-dressed in some public place with long avenues between him and his room, and the sun rising majestically over the houses, to expose him to every gaze. Such imagined fears were a thousand times preferable to his position if the mistress did succumb to her sickness. He knew his employer, the master, who, in his opinion, was mothered by the whore of pretence. Ben could not help feeling that all that love for his wife and concern for her brother covered an indifference that even she had only glimpsed. *Well*, thought Ben, *neither he nor I are going to decide. Life for me and Death for him. Winged spirits flying out to sea and not a single one would fall out of the sky. God!* However could one stop thinking?

186

This excrement, these droplets of indignity! He shuddered beneath the morning sun as the mistress must have been shivering under her blankets.

On arriving at their destination the master asked him, quite politely, to come down from his perch; he wanted to have a word with him. Ben stepped down carefully, pretending that he suspected nothing. But to his relief the master began telling him about horses. As dray-carts and carriages trundled along the busy grit-covered road he launched into a talk about horses and his friend Dr Bruce, the municipal veterinary surgeon.

"Dr Bruce will have it ready for you at ten o'clock," he said.

"A horse?" Ben asked.

"Yes. It's a frisky two-year-old and it's never had anyone on its back. It'll take a good three months before you can risk hitching his to the carriage."

"Of course," Ben said. "Ten o'clock. Very well, sir. Anything else?"

"Ah, one more thing, Ben. The mistress isn't too well. Offer to help Edna if she seems to be doing too much. She thinks the world of you, you know. And no doubt you admire her."

"You can rely on me," Ben said, all but leaping for joy at the news that the mistress was not seriously ill.

He wiped the sweat from his forehead and flicked the whip at the horse's flank.

"Soon you'll have relief, you old molasses drinker."

Then he realized there was something else to bother about. Another horse meant more work for him.

After stabling the horse, Ben went straight to the barber-shop. Taking a seat on the left — one had to be careful not ot offend the barber by waiting opposite the site of operations of his colleague — he looked around for the newspaper, which had evidently not arrived. The floor was clean, free of the hair that would be scattered about by midday. The other barber had not yet had a customer and was standing, hands in his pockets, staring over the frosted section of glass into the street. From time to time he made a disparaging remark about the state of the pavement or the conduct of a passer-by, hoping to draw Ben or his colleague or the latter's customer into conversation. Tired of being ignored he continued to express his displeasure by a series of suck-teeth delivered at fairly regular intervals, and intended by their degrees of intensity to convey the gravity of what he was witnessing or the extent of his disapproval. "Tchoops!" "Tchoooooooops!" "Tchoooooooooooops!" Carried away by the parade of decadence in front of the shop, he failed to notice the arrival of his first customer, who sat down opposite his swivel chair.

"You got business, Pawn-Fly," his colleague informed him.

"Look at these chil'ren today, eh? He rolling hoop 'pon the road itself, an' when he get lick down he mother goin' blame the cart-man. Six lash with a wild cane an' he would know wha' pavement make for!"

"You comin', man?" the waiting customer asked.

"Eh-eh, is wha' wrong with you?" Pawn-Fly asked in turn. "If you in a hurry why you don' cut it yourself? The scissors an' the shears there 'pon the shelf. Go 'long, ne?" He turned away to devote his attention to the street once more.

"You cuttin' me hair or you not cuttin' me hair?" demanded the client impatiently.

"You in' got manners? I old enough to be you grandfather. If you give me any mo' lip I goin' swipe you with that razor-strap 'cross you back. You not even in long pants yet an you using you tongue like big man."

But the working barber gave his cantankerous colleague a severe look and the latter slowly ambled up to the swivel-chair, which he turned with a violent motion of his arm before launching into his preparations for an assault on the youth's head. At the same time the client whose hair had just been cut stood up after his napkin was taken off and shaken out on to the floor, and laid his penny on the glass shelf while the barber brushed off the tiny loose hairs from his head with a soft-bristled brush.

Ben sat down in the idle barber's chair in turn, closed his eyes and took no interest in what was happening to his crown, knowing from experience that the result would be unsatisfactory. From time to time passers-by looked in over the swing doors or pushed one leaf to see if an acquaintance was there, each time attracting a disapproving "Tchooooops" from the phlegmatic barber.

When Ben's napkin was taken off he paid without bothering to look in the mirror, and left the shop to the sound of another long suck-teeth from Pawn-Fly, an expression of his view of Ben's reticence and unwillingness to acknowledge the weight of his remarks.

Ben called up to Edna, who shouted out that it was five minutes past nine and that she wanted to see him before he went out again. He then went and lay down, laughing softly when it occurred to him that he need not have had his hair cut at all, since the anticipated itch was unlikely, now he knew that the mistress was not seriously ill.

On the kitchen table were laid out a comb and brush, two cylinders of lipstick and a cloth bag containing — from its delicate scent — Edna's pretties. Not being one to ask questions he waited for her to explain.

"You got to get three prescriptions from the doctor shop," she told him, whilst blowing into a steaming cup.

"So the doctor been!"

"Two doctors been!"

"O God!" he could not help exclaiming.

"Wha' happen to you?"

"She's sick bad, then?"

"She mus' be, if two doctors been," Edna answered.

"But according to the master she's not bad."

"That's what he did think. But when the doctor come he send for another doctor . . . . You should see your face! She take so much quinine she can't even hear good. The doctor say she musn' take more. By this afternoon the house goin' full up with people. I don' even know what to cook, 'cause —"

"You've been in her room?" Ben asked.

"Yes, I tell you. The master ask me to come and sleep the night 'cause the doctor was coming. It would only be for one night. Now I got to go back home this afternoon and get more things and tell my mother I staying a few days."

"How you think she looks?" Ben demanded.

"Is what happen to you? She not goin' dead."

"You don' think so?"

"No," came her puzzled reply.

"One day she looked all bloated; the next day she looked like a corpse. Last night she was walking in her sleep."

"The mistress?"

"Yes," Ben answered.

"How you did know?"

"I heard the noise and came up here. She put on the gramophone and you should've seen her face: it was all haggard. And when the music started up it was lit up . . . her face, as if she was standing in front of a gas lamp. And her nightdress was hanging down on one

189

side. I didn't dare go and wake her. That record, I could swear I never heard it before; yet it was in the pile. But she's got so many. It must've been one she brought back from the States. So many shoes and so many records!"

"You see all that?" Edna said, staring open-mouthed.

"And the master came down. He rushed down the stairs so fast you could've thought she was trying to jump through the window, and he arrived just in time."

"What happened?"

"He grabbed hold of her," Ben said, recalling the scene with the utmost clarity, "and she was beside herself."

"Poor woman," Edna said. "You don' know what went on in this house before you come. Is when is full moon that people does walk in they sleep."

"Nonsense!" he declared, angry for no reason.

"I telling you! In Cane Grove when I was a girl —"

"You think she'll die?" Ben asked, interrupting her.

"I say no, Ben. I din' know you like her so much."

"She's a wonderful woman," he said feelingly. "She's a lady. You can't go around saying who deserves who, but I could put my head on a block that he doesn't deserve her."

"You remember that little girl I tell you about, who use to live here," Edna said, drawing a deep breath as though uncertain whether to say what she was about to say. "It was mistress brother daughter. He had this outside child. The master did want to bring the child up openly, an' let it come and go openly. But not the mistress! She keep the girl upstairs when people come visiting, an' only let her use the back stairs; only 'cause she was shame. The master's a good man."

"Well," Ben said, put out that his employer had to his credit something that could not be contradicted. "You know, Edna, you're one of those people who go through life as an observer. You observe, and nothing ever happens to you. And even in your observing you see nothing. That kind master of yours, so famous at the Treasury for his honesty, is going to break up a family and draw so much satisfaction from it you'd think he's worked all his life to do just that. He'll come with his magnifying glass and gloat over his handiwork, look at it from all angles. And when this family's house is full of strangers and he knows it's his doing he'll smile and say, 'Good! Good!' Yes, Edna. And you, observer with a bundle of pretty things and your dainty little comb with the broken teeth, you'll work here for thirty years; and

190

during all this time they'll be interested in one single thing: 'You've got a boy-friend, Edna? A young man, Edna? Is he jealous? Does he object to your working here?' And they'll never come straight out and say, 'Don't get involved with a man, because we won't be able to call on you at any time.' And as for me, something else interests them: where and how I spend my money. Because, you see, I earn a lot more than you. And if there was someone else higher than me they'd be other questions. . . . Poor Edna, with her sweet-smelling bundle and her kitchen of herbs and cooking-pots. . . . "

"Ben, how you talk!"

"No, I don't know as much as you about this house, but I've seen more than you. And I see they'll be a death soon, followed by a terrible storm that will sweep someone away and transform two households. One night I'll take you out, Edna, drive you along a dusty road to the sea and a kingdom beneath the sea, where good people like you live, who're palmed off with a piece of silver after thirty or forty years' unstinting service, and go into retirement without a pension or a visit from those you served, and the knowledge that a visit to the house that still smells of your sweat would be an embarrassment. But me, before that happens to me I'll choose the pit of snakes. I'll walk to the edge; but I won't throw myself in, like a common suicide. I'll lie down on the edge and fall asleep. Yes, Edna! Either that or begging with dignity, or prison, the house of sacrifice. . . . This morning I humbled myself and called him 'Sir'. But never again! This chest must be as straight as a greenheart trunk!"

Ben threw out his chest and put his right foot forward and stood there while Edna stared at him open-mouthed, her eyes moist, although she understood little of what he had said. He turned and faced her, intoxicated with the declaration of his independence and the response it had aroused in her.

Ben was suddenly aware of her admiration for him, which must have been building up over the past two years, fermenting like watered-down honey sprinkled with yeast, producing tiny bubbles without his even noticing until now, at the sight of her sitting down with a finger through the handle of her bush-tea cup.

He pushed the other chair round the table and sat down beside her.

"When I was a little boy," he said, disposed to tell her what he had never told anyone before, "I thought my parents were trying to poison me and wanted to escape back to my grandmother's house in Skeldon. Do little children and old people think a lot about death? It wouldn't

191

be unnatural, would it?"

Putting his right arm round her he drew her close to himself until her left breast was touching his shirt.

"Sometimes when I sit down to write," he continued, "ideas come to me with such intensity I feel someone's dictating them. The other day when I came up here I saw someone standing behind you. . . . "

"Me? When?" she asked, evidently disturbed.

"But the person vanished like that! Don't be frightened. That's why you dream. You sleep and *it* wakes."

Ben undid her blouse while she looked down at his hands help-lessly. He opened it down to her waist, and her full, virginal breasts hung like black fruit from her chest.

"Tonight," he said, "knock on the floor if you can't sleep; only if you can't sleep. Because, if you can sleep there's no point, is there?"

He got up and left her staring down at her chest.

The low clouds were almost touching the branches of the trees next door. There was no birdsong, nor was there the usual sound of voices from the yards around or from the street.

He set off to the municipal stables to fetch the new horse, his hands in his pockets and with that same feeling of intense satisfaction that overcame him when he wrung a higher wage from the master.

All morning he had not thought of Carl. All morning in that heavy atmosphere that presaged rain and all types of decay and the sound of conversations to come. A column of smoke was rising from a yard where the construction of a large house was in progress. The big-market clock started striking ten, and he thought how well he had timed his conversation with Edna.

A woman with her head through an upstairs window was quarrel-ling with a man in the street and, as Ben went past, she slammed the window shut. He turned into High Street and walked until he reached the yard where donkeys were standing around with their owners waiting beside them. Most of the animals had sores on at least one leg and must have been brought in for examination by the vet prior to a summons being taken out against their owners for neglect.

The door of the office was open and Ben stepped inside.

"You want something?" the young man asked.

"Yes. Why you think I came in? I came for a horse."

In less than a minute the young cock was taking him behind the office, where healthy asses and a horse were tethered.

"That's him," the young man said, nodding towards the stallion.

192

"You've got to sign this. If you're satisfied with it come and sign the receipt now."

Ben followed him back into this office and signed the receipt with a pen which was sticking out of an ink-well.

27

BEN DID all the jobs that had to be done around the house and in the stables and, after he had brought back an anxious Mr Schwartz from work, put away the horse and carriage for good. In his state he would not be going anywhere. When he came home at midday and heard that two doctors had been he began pacing up and down the gallery. The house was filling up with the master's and mistress's friends, all asking the same futile questions about the mistress, then sitting down with a suitably doleful expression.

Against his better judgement Ben decided to go over and see Carl in the house opposite, above the barber-shop. Only he could break in the new horse in a short time, so Ben would have to ask him outright, "Would you help me break in the horse?" And like that neither Carl nor the women could accuse him of begging for his friendship. What could be more straightforward than that? "Could you help me to break in this young stallion? You don't think I bought him just to get me to see you again, you olive-skinned Macusi? The animal doesn't even belong to me! Where would I get the money from to buy a frisky stallion who doesn't even know he's destined to spend the rest of his life pulling people a few hundred yards to one place and then a few hundred yards back, although they've got two good bow-legs? It's either yes or no. Do you intend to help me break him in? You lodged in my room for months and months; do you know me as a begging man? I hope living among these *decent* women hasn't ruined your sense of proportion. . . . "

Ben waited until nightfall, when the lamps were lit and the barber-shop was closed. The hammers of the carpenters had long ceased disturbing the afternoon peace and now, under the cover of darkness, clouds were gathering in a threatened downpour that had not yet materialized. He was standing at the gate like a loiterer, watching the shadows of people go by, hardly aware of the stifled, persistent

193

flute-calls of frogs. The beggar who frequented the women's house waved at him. Night was his time. He was one of those lovers of dirt and darkness for whom sunlight and starched clothes were a curse. Ben nodded in response, which surprised the beggar so much he waved again, violently. He seized the excuse to cross the road and bring himself nearer to his goal.

"You not visiting tonight, Mr Ben?"

"No."

"I see the new horse. Solid stock, he look like. I work in the Rupununi when I was a young man, near the Brazilian border. Horses and cattle, and anteaters when you could catch sight of them. You did live in the saddle. Jaguars use to kill the cattle in the dry season and rattle-snakes in the rainy season. In those days there was nothing in town. That's a stallion of solid stock, I can tell. How you goin' break him in?"

"That's what I'm going to ask Carl about."

"Good idea. They in' got nobody that know 'bout horses better than Macusi. Funny chap, though. Different, these bucks. In the Rupununi they'd work for a couple o' months then disappear. One o' them wake up one morning an' tell the boss his brother calling him. 'How you mean? Your brother living thirty miles from here.' But he go away. They like that: funny people. They does hear voices across the savannah."

"You know if Carl in?" Ben asked him.

"He does hardly got out. He there, yes, lookin' out the window in the back yard, where they in' got nothing 'xcept latrines and the backs of shops."

Ben left him propped up against the barber-shop and went to the door that opened into the covered staircase.

"They not goin' let you in," the beggar called out.

He got up and knocked once on the door, then three times in rapid succession.

"When it open I goin' go in an' you come in quick after me."

The woman coming down the stairs was singing. On opening she turned her back at once and began climbing the stairs. Then, when she looked round and caught sight of Ben, she gave an exclamation in a high-pitched voice and ran upstairs, for she was wearing the thinnest of apparel and believed the old man to be alone.

"She don' know you," he said to Ben. "She new here."

Carl, who was alone in the large room, smiled when he saw Ben and

194

got up from his window on the back yard.

"Si' down, man," he said.

Overjoyed at the naturalness of his welcome, Ben offered to go and buy a bottle of rum, but seeing that Carl appeared anxious at the suggestion he dismissed it with: "Later, later."

"I hear you got a new horse," Carl said.

"Who told you?"

"The whole neighbourhood know," the beggar declared.

"That's what I come to ask you about," Ben told him. "I want you to break him in for me. Not right away; whenever you're ready. Not even this week if you don't feel like it."

The same anxious expression appeared on Carl's face.

"Anyway," Ben assured him, "when you're ready."

He was just as worried about his reluctance to commit himself as he was anxious about his presence in his hostess's house.

"He's king of the bush!" the old beggar announced fatuously, showing an almost empty mouth in a grotesque smile. "He's king of the bush and I'm king of the pavement. Ha ha ha!"

Then, addressing Ben, he said, "You're king of the cab-drivers, a king in black hat and black clothes. When I was a boy I say to my mother, 'When was yesterday?' And everybody laugh. So I go about saying the same thing, but they din' laugh no more, and I couldn' understand why. Then another day I say to my father, 'Pa, what's the word in the book?' And he say, 'Boy, you ask too much question.' And I take up the book and read, 'Boo goo boo goo boo.' And everybody roll over laughing. And I say again, 'Boo goo boo goo boo.' But they din' laugh no more. So I stop. I was not a wise child, but I'm a wise man."

Carl was listening to him intently. He liked him, and Ben was jealous that never once had he been able to command his attention in the same way.

"I don't see you at the front window," Ben said to Carl. "Why you don't look out of the front like everybody else?"

Carl shrugged his shoulders to cover an expression of the utmost sadness, as if he had enquired about someone close to him who had died or gone away.

"He does look through the back windows," said the beggar, airing his smile, "so as not to have to look out at front. He does wear rags so he don' have to wear clean clothes. Everybody does laugh so they don' have to cry. Small children does laugh an' cry without thinking. An' old people? They don' laugh, they don' cry. There use to be a old woman living round here. She use to laugh a lot and people thought she was mad. They wipe the smile from she face when they threaten to put her in the Alms House for she laughing."

"And what about you?" Ben asked maliciously.

"What they goin' put me in the Alms House for? I living 'pon the pavement as it is." And then, after a moment's reflection, he answered Ben in kind: "Tobesides, I laughin' at you, how you go about riding 'pon you mattee back."

Ben took this to be a reference to his relations with the master.

"You know everything, don't you?" Ben remarked.

Carl seemed distressed at the turn the conversation was taking and Ben at once searched for something pleasant to say to the old man.

"It's this weather," he said. "You don't know if it's coming or going. Look how I'm sweating. I just had a shower and I already feel like another one."

The old man responded at once with his broad grin.

"Is time," he said. "Is high time the rain come and fall in style. You know people does cut they hair less often in the rainy weather? That's when the rattle-snakes in the Rupununi does worry the cattle 'cause they don' got enough dry land to hide in. You see, when this house get build — it was in . . . let me see. . . . It was around 1900. Marabuntas build they nests just over the windows and the people living here burn them out and nearly set fire to the place. And the marabuntas come back and build they clay nests again like dish turn upside down. And the people had to move out. Was years before they get rid of the marabuntas. An' you know how they do it? They smear the window tops with a paste mix with perfume. I telling you!"

"You're going to break the horse in for me?" Ben prompted Carl.

"I goin' see," he replied.

"We could take him down to the sea," Ben suggested.

"I goin' see," he repeated. "Is a mare or a stallion?"

"A stallion."

"A strong stallion," the beggar put in.

"You goin' do it? In the sea?" Ben asked.

"I goin' see," Carl said, less anxiously now.

"When you go," said the beggar, "take me with you." His jaunty manner had changed at the mention of the horse being broken in in the ocean.

"You goin' take him?" Carl asked.

196

"I don't know," Ben answered.

"I remember to this day," the beggar said, "the Macusi almost naked on those Rupununi horses. They could do anything on a horse, and use to gallop across the savannah with the women staring after them. When Carl go back home. . . . "

"You're going home?"

"I don' know yet," Carl said.

"Don' bother with him," the beggar declared. "He does think 'bout it all the time, specially when the women telling one another stories at night-time and all the windows open to let in the fresh air. Deny it! He can't deny it. He goin' go back an' pick a flower an' hold it in his hand an' blow the petals away, 'cause he sick of this place and all the people who want to make friends with him but can't even get him a job in this rat-hole of a town. He goin' leave this cage for good. Tell him, Carl! Don' frighten! Tell — him — man! All you love him up too much and feed him up, and now he got more pussy than he can salt an' dry an' put away for bambye. He goin' leave the town he did always dream of coming to. I been in the bush and come back to town. He come to town and goin' back to the bush. It all comes back to you, said the monkey, as he pissed against the breeze. And is only one thing Carl going miss. Your horse!"

He broke out into a peal of laughter, which rose so high he nearly had Carl laughing as well. Then they all turned to a man towards the doorway, where Violet was standing in the company of two other young women, one of whom was the woman who ran away from Ben the night when he was drunk.

Carl turned to look out of the window as though he were unconcerned at the consequences of the unexpected meeting.

"Who let you in?" Violet asked at length.

"I let him in," came Carl's reply.

If looks could kill, Ben would have been a corpse. Violet's friend must have felt the implications of Carl's prompt answer, for she gave Ben the same baleful look.

"He's the one I been telling you 'bout," Violet said to the companion whom he had not seen before.

"I know him," she replied.

"No," Ben said, full of malice at having these creatures point a finger at him. "You and I don't keep the same company."

Violet crossed the drawing-room with hurried steps, followed by her two friends. No sooner had they disappeared inside than the

197

sound of whispered voices was heard over the low partition. Ben knew she dared not put him out for fear of offending Carl; but he knew as well that he had to be vigilant. In his opinion she was capable of anything.

"You want to eat now, Carl? I bring some food from work." The voice was Violet's and had spoken in carefully articulated syllables.

"Yes," Carl answered.

"Man, you so cool," the beggar said to Carl. "You so cool you make me stop sweating. You see?" He passed his hand over his forehead to show how dry it was.

"You hold you tongue!" Violet shouted at him from the kitchen.

The beggar at once put out his tongue and held it firmly with the tips of two fingers.

"All you don' quarrel," Carl said, turning to them. "Rain goin' fall and it in' good to quarrel when rain falling."

"Rain in' falling yet," the beggar said, having let go of his tongue. "All you better start quarrelling quick before rain start fallin'. To-besides, you not goin' hear what anybody saying when the rain beatin' down 'pon this zinc roof."

Then all conversation ceased and Ben called to mind the day Carl and he went to his mother's house. It was so hot the concrete culverts were encased in a haze, and work was laborious. All seemed well on that unutterably serene day. Till then he had thought that life, to all intents and purposes, was at an end, because he was trapped in a strange household and marriage had devoured his ambition; but with Carl sitting beside him on his perch he was happier than ever.

"What happen to that man who was living in the room near you?" the beggar asked, apparently in an effort to keep the conversation going.

"He went to live with his sister and her husband," Ben answered.

"Funny how people go and come," he continued. "Not so long ago I was a young man leapin' about the dance halls. Now I got one foot in the grave. Once this town was full of marabuntas and bats. . . . "

"Marabuntas and bats aren't people," Ben took him up, growing more irritated at his complete indifference to what was happening around him.

"You catch me out," he said, pretending to be ashamed. "I hang me head in shame." He hung his head for several seconds, maintaining his chin theatrically against his chest. Then, springing to life suddenly, he almost shouted, "But Carl won't agree with you!

198

Accordin' to Carl the people in his clan believe that if a man go with his mother-in-law he goin' turn into a bat. Hi hi hi! Ask he, ne, if you don' believe me. Hi hi hi!"

Then he belched loudly, as if he had just eaten.

"The smell of food," he said. "O my godfathers! I does always do things upside down. You does belch after you eat. Me, I got to upside-down the thing. . . . "

"Shut up, ne," Ben told him, disgusted by his behaviour which, he knew, was intended for the women who let him into the house from time to time and were just within earshot.

"She tell me to hold my tongue," the beggar said, feigning annoyance. "Now you tell me to shut up. O my godfathers! Good, I goin' shut up."

He closed his mouth so completely that his lips disappeared inside his mouth, giving him a grotesque appearance.

Just then one of the young women came out carrying plates piled high with food, which she gave to the beggar and Carl in turn. Carl got up and followed her inside with his plate, coming out soon afterwards with two plates, having divided his own share into two. He offered Ben one.

The beggar, who was now eating voraciously, had evidently noticed nothing, and by the look of things, had no intention of entertaining them with his stories or remarks while eating. He finished first and took his plate into the kitchen, only to come out on the run when one of the women did him some violence.

"For God sake," he delcared, "don' go in there! Violet in a temper!"

He made a rapid gesture with his right hand to illustrate her mood. Then, rubbing his full stomach, he sat by a front window and declared, "Ow, man! When food good you can take anything. The las' time I eat like this was when my mother get married. That was in . . . le' me see . . . in 18 . . . 1874. I was twenty. She an' my sister had baby nearly the same day. She call she baby Ann-Marie an' my sister call she baby Marie-Ann."

Ben was praying that one of the women would come out and hand the beggar another plate of food and so save them from his reflections, when Violet and the two women appeared, carrying their own food, which they proceeded to eat, sitting on chairs by the window.

No one spoke and the tension was so palpable even the beggar dared say nothing. The sound of scraping spoons and of food being

199

chewed prevailed over the street noises, and in the gathering darkness Ben stole looks at the women without being noticed.

Then the rain broke on the heels of a wind that whipped through the kitchen window and disturbed the single decoration on the partition, a soiled calendar with a picture of the Kaiteur Falls.

"Go and shut the kitchen window and back door fo' me," Violet ordered the beggar gruffly. "And the windows in the bedrooms too. An' don' poke you nose in the drawers, understand? Rain falling, but I can hear you."

He complied, disappearing inside with a walk assumed for the occasion, a kind of tiptoe on eggs.

A few minutes ago it was light and now darkness filled the room like a wad of black cotton wool. Despite the women's hostility Ben began to feel at ease. He ate with deliberate slowness, simply because he was not sure what he would do with his plate when he finished. It was only after Carl placed his plate on the window-sill that Ben began to hurry through the last few spoonfuls. Carl closed his own window and took his plate away into the kitchen.

The master's house opposite appeared in vague outlines through the window-panes and the flickering raindrops. A pale light shone in the bedroom at the front, where the mistress lay a-bed, attended to by the master and Edna, and in all likelihood by her best friend, whose carriage was standing in front of the gate with several other visiting carriages behind and in front of it.

Now that the weather had broken they seemed to be inhabiting a different plane of existence. Their voices came from far away; insects would disappear, animals would hang their heads lower, as if they were the bearers of man's sorrows.

"You know the story of the Red Man?" the beggar asked.

No one paid him any mind.

"The Divine say loud," continued the beggar, "loud, loud: 'Is why I got so many boring people round me? Jesus! I want somebody wicked to bring things to life.' An' a woman dwarf who couldn' keep she mouth shut say, 'I goin' get you somebody really wicked. Jus' give me a year.' So she look look look, till she find a pale stranger who she thought had the strength to bounce she. It take three months for him to get a erection; an' when it come she say, 'Quick, quick!' And it happen. An' nine months later she had a mulatto baby. She take it to the Divine and say, 'Now this is a bundle of wickedness.' The Divine din' believe she; but is when the child grow up and become a man that he see what the woman mean. . . . "

"You like talkin' nonsense, ne?" Violet asked him.

"I prefer it to silence," the beggar said.

"And you cabman friend?" Violet's friend who had run away from Ben asked.

"Beryl, he got a name," Violet said mockingly.

She leaned forward andd whispered something into Beryl's ear, and the two women burst out laughing. Beryl in turn whispered to the third friend, who looked at him and laughed aloud.

"Leave me friend alone," Carl said, taking the women by surprise.

"Eh, eh," Violet retorted, trying to hide her shame at being put in her place by Carl, who would normally go a whole night without saying a word. "Eh-eh! I kian' even laugh in my own house!"

Ben could not suppress a smile, at which Violet gave him a poisonous look.

"I don' care," she said. "You think I care? He say he goin' back to Orealla in any case. I hear you got sickness opposite, that's why all them rich people cabs line up in front the house. An' that when you go back over you got to empty the shit-pails!"

Ben had never hit a woman, except out of love, but for the first time in his life he came close to knocking this Violet down as if she was a man. It annoyed him to see the hold she had over her friends, especially as he had such a low opinion of her. It annoyed him to see her arrive at the door ahead of the two women, to see her send out food to Carl, as a sign that she owned him, and ignore him in such a way that people would say, "She wouldn' even give him a grain of rice!" He remembered Carl lying drunk on the floor like a wounded cow-deer and her doing everything except trample all over him. And the news that Carl was going away, coming from her own mouth, over-joyed Ben, although it was as much his loss as hers. But she was the sort to have the last word.

"Edna empties the shit-pails if you want to know," Ben declared. "But from the smell that came across this room when you arrived the thought occurred to me that you not only empty yours, but that you live in them."

Pandemonium broke loose. Violet sprang at Ben and, taking advantage of her inviolability as a woman, kept coming at him, though he pushed her off each time. For a while he lost control as he felt a blow on his head. When, a moment later, he turned round, he found Beryl standing with a shoe in her hand. But before he could deal with

201

this danger from the back he staggered under another blow and sank to the ground. All he could recall after this was the sound of voices, and dull, painless blows in his face. Suddenly everything ceased, as must happen at death.

When he came to he could barely make out outlines floating about the room, until, gradually, he saw clearly the flickering lamp, lit since he lost consciousness. Oddly enough, the first person who came to mind was Bamford. Ben sought him out among the numerous chairs. It was the sound of the beggar's voice that reminded him of his whereabouts. Looking around, he saw the three women in turn, sitting calmly on their chairs. Violet was passing a cigarette to Beryl, who took what seemed an interminable puff before she passed it on to the third friend. Carl was nowhere to be seen, while the beggar stood behind Violet, a look of terror in his eyes.

"He comin' round," he said, craning his neck forward.

None of the women replied. Ben heard the rain on the panes lashed by the wind, which had not abated. He kept his eyes half-closed, uncertain as to what his position was. Where was Carl? Had he gone inside? Or out in the street?

Then he heard one of the women say, "You think we goin' have trouble?"

Violet answered, "If we get trouble I goin' fix him for good. Don' worry."

The room smelt of something sweet, which Ben could not identify. They must have eaten again while he was out on the floor; and it was the realization of this callousness that made him fearful of his position. Then he reflected that if Violet had intended anything worse than she had already perpetrated she would have done it already. There was no pain in his testicles, thank God. When these women took to knocking you about they went for your balls as if that was the home of all man's insults to women.

He longed to put his hands to his head. Where was Carl?

"Where's Carl?" he heard his own voice say.

Ben saw the faces of the three women and the beggar looking down at him and he thought that that was the way fish saw things, with twisted faces and inordinately large eyes. When he saw Violet's teeth he instinctively put out his hands, then imagined that she must be smiling when she realized that nothing happened to him. Then he saw her put something into her mouth and exhale a mass of white smoke.

"Where's Carl?" he asked again, thinking of the smile.

202

"He gone out," Violet said. "An' he better come back soon."

"Did he take his hammock?" he said.

"Oh, yes, his hammock," Beryl said, slapping her hand to her head and laughing with relief. "He kian' go far if he din' take his hammock. You see! Is all right."

Violet's two friends went and sat down, while Violet herself remained by him.

"Bring a glass of water," she ordered the beggar, who almost ran into the kitchen.

Ben drank the cup of water only with difficulty on account of the pain in his mouth. He then got up and moved towards the door.

"The door lock," Violet remarked drily. "You in' goin' nowhere till you tell me why you won't leave Carl alone. You not his father."

"I came to ask him to break in a horse for me," Ben managed to say.

"Don' talk stupidness! You got a horse."

He wound himself up to deliver an answer, which was barely audible: "We've got a new horse."

"Oh, yes. I hear Carl talkin' 'bout it," she said. "Why you kian' break in you own horse? You in' got two foot an' two hand?"

The pain prevented him from answering, and he closed his eyes again.

"Well, he in' comin'!" Violet exclaimed with violence.

In the long silence that followed he listened to the rain and the other sounds around him. He could hear the rustle of clothing, Violet's breathing, gusts of wind, a carriage moving off ponderously in the rain, noises not usually perceived.

"You know what Carl wanted me to do?" Violet said. "Your friend from Orealla who kian' stand living in town? He did want me to go an' pick up men. Ask she!"

She pointed theatrically to Beryl, who confirmed what she had said with a nod.

"He did want me to pick fair," Violet continued, "an' bring him the money. When he firs' come to town he wasn' interested in money. He tell me so himself. The firs' time I did feel sorry for him after the party, and I give him two dollars; but he refuse to take it an' make me look like a fool in front of the girls, as if he was my man and I was giving him money. I did get so vex I take the two dollar notes an' I throw them out in the rain. Now he vex 'cause I don' want to sell my body for him."

She laughed her grotesque laugh and Ben opened his eyes wide, because for a moment the thought occurred to him that her mouth was a vagina with teeth in it.

"Look this man, eh," she said to her friends. "He got two woman an' want to huff my man from me. Some people never satisfied." Then, with a sudden outburst, she shrieked, "I not selling my body!"

She kept staring at the partition, breathing heavily and shifting about on her chair as if she were on the point of getting up.

"Where is the beggar?" Ben wondered, afraid of being left alone with this mad woman and her friends.

"You want to know where Carl is?" Violet asked.

"He wan' know where Carl is," Beryl echoed. "Tell him where he is, ne? Else he goin'. . . . ."

"Is Carl that stop us from kickin' you to death," Violet declared calmly. "He right inside there, listening over the partition, to make sure we don' finish you off."

At the news that Carl was in the house, Ben was no longer afraid that the women might attack him with some weapon. He sat up and passed his hand over his face, wondering all the while why Carl had gone inside, and why one of the women spoke of his hammock, knowing he was still in the house.

"Yes," continued Violet, "your clean Carl, who never even hear 'bout the Devil, want to send me 'pon the road. But you got to hand it to him, he never pretend to love me. When I say, 'You love me?' he say, 'Yes.' Yet one day he say the Macusi language don' got the word 'love'."

She laughed a humourless laugh, like the cackling of a hen after laying an egg.

"Why?" pursued Violet, now in a state of great excitement. "Why would a woman love a man who's useless to her? You understand that?"

Violet's second friend spoke for the first time. "Love is love. I did read in a magazine 'bout a woman who did love a dwarf."

Beryl, no doubt encouraged by her friend's contribution to the conversation, said, "You kian' believe what you read in them magazines. It's jus' stories. My uncle say so."

"Carl!" Ben shouted, wrenching his mouth open for the effort.

He heard Carl's footsteps and the hush of stilled voices as the women stopped talking.

Ben gestured as best he could to get him to cover his retreat as he was about to go out by the back way, which was unlikely to have a lock on it. But he whispered. "Sit down, ne?"

Telling himself that his tone was a request for help, and fascinated by the danger he was in, Ben sat down one on of the chairs. The very circumstance that repels most people is attractive to a few, he reflected, recalling his love of heights, of travelling in a small boat on the ocean, and his passion for entering the houses of strangers to steal. Simply to walk out under Carl's protection was too simple, a kind of capitulation. It was evident that everything Violet had said until then had been meant for Carl's ears, and perhaps for the women, who treated her with excessive respect.

"I see you distributing money to East Indian beggars," Violet told Ben. "Just like a Catholic priest. I see how you order them to the back of the line, when they push in front. Yet is not your money. If it was your money what you would do? God! Carl, is what you see in this scarecrow? Between him and Edna I don' know who worse."

Carl sat down once more by the window that looked out on the partly concreted back yard. Since he came out he seemed to be continually on the point of speaking, but he said nothing. Ben saw that he was liked in the house, as he was liked in everyone else's house except Mabel's.

There was something odd in Violet's vicious attack on Ben; it could not be explained alone by her jealousy of his friendship for Carl. Besides, she was always harping on Ben's arrogance and on Edna, whom she hated as ardently as she did him. Edna this and Edna that, although they had never once engaged in conversation.

"We all at peace now," came the beggar's voice.

He stepped into the middle of the drawing-room like a vaudeville player making an appearance.

"War can't last for ever," he continued. "You know any war that go on for ever? It got to stop some time. And we only had a little war here, without guns an' fire. That kind of war don' destroy the body. Mind you . . . mind you! Some of them kicks you give Ben could've destroy his body, when you come to think of it. Of course you din' use guns an' fire like them barbarians in Europe, did you? No, we're peaceful folk. A lil' kick in the balls now and then never kill nobody. An' women are known for their peaceful intentions. They does reserve all they energy for giving birth, as everybody does know. If I did believe in rebirth like them East Indian beggars I would want to come back as a hermaphrodite, so I could be a woman for a week an' a man for another. . . ."

205

Beryl was looking at Violet, surprised that she tolerated the beggar's impertinence; but Violet was turning something over in her mind, from her expression, and from the way she puffed on her Lighthouse cigarette.

"Come to think of it," continued the beggar, "I'd be a man for three weeks an' a woman for one. I don' know why. I mean, you don' have to have a reason for why you want to do something. I don' explain why I do anything 'cause I'd be only telling lie. I mean, when all you start kicking Mr Ben you din' say, 'I goin' kick Mr Ben 'cause my foot itchin' to kick somebody, or 'cause he do so and so.' If you stop to think why you goin' kick him you'd spend such a long time tracking down the reason you'd fall asleep. Come to think of it I'd rather be a man for twenty-nine days and a woman for one. Kick! kick! Bam!"

The beggar started kicking an imaginary person.

"Bam! Tek that! An' that! . . . But suppose, jus' suppose the person you thought you was kicking wasn' that person at al! Ah! Scratch these white people who does run this country an' you'd find a corpse. 'Strue! But that don' stop them from thinkin' they're alive, eh? Jus' suppose you was kicking a corpse an' you thought it was a person! No, you don' understand. As soon as people start talkin' 'bout corpses, people does get worried. Well, what you think you shadow is? You think it alive? When my brother dead in the village the road was flooded an' the cart couldn' take the coffin. They had was to take it by boat to the burial ground. All that water! Who'd think the clouds could hold all that water? Is another ocean up there, you know. Truly! It wouldn' surprise me if they got boat. . . . "

"Shut up!" Beryl said vehemently, stopping up her ears.

Violet turned to her and smiled, so that the beggar, believing this to be a licence for him to continue, dragged a chair to the spot where he had been carrying on. Showing his gums in a caricature of his normal smile, he put a finger into his mouth, lifted it above his head to test the wind, then said:

"North-east fair, light winds. Well, as I been saying when a certain muffadite tell me 'Shut up!' they got boat up there an' people an' beggars an' people who don't 'fraid to act stupid like me. And the place full of hermaphrodites! They swarming all over the place like mosquitoes in the bush. One o' them — down here I mean — come up to me an' say, 'Good mawnin', I'm a muffadite.' Jus' like that. They're very courteous! People does laugh at them 'cause they does walk sideways, like a crab; but they wrong. Most courteous are they!

206

And I say to him, 'Does I know you, Mr Muffadite?' 'Cause I'm very particular who I does speak to in public . . . at least in those days, before I become a solicitor of alms. 'Does I know you, Mr Muffadite?' I say. He 'pologize and say No. But we get talkin' and he tell me he feel sorry for me, being only a masculine gender, 'cause I din' know what I missing. That's how I know so much 'bout kicking. It was the first time in my life I feel like kickin' somebody. Mind you, not like you ladies. Not so professional. I did feel like giving him a tap in his shin. Casting aspersions on my masculinity like that an' calling me a gender. But I jus' turn my back an' walk away. Well, they got a lot of them people up there where there's so much water."

Even Carl seemed to getting impatient with him.

"Tell me something," Violet said to the beggar, "you ever been married?"

The beggar pursed his lips, considered for a few seconds, then gave his answer: "You know, I don' remember. I know my parents was married, which was a very unusual thing in the village. I did feel like a outsider, an' one day I go home and say, 'Why all-you can't be like everybody else?' My father give me one slap an' send me to kneel down 'pon the grater in the kitchen as punishment. No, I don' know if I was ever married. But I been engaged. I remember that good; but whether I actually did get married I don' remember. I say to she, 'I breakin' it off 'cause you too good to me.' . . . I don' know. I talk so much nonsense I don' know how to talk sense no more. . . . You ever get married, Violet?"

"You want me to set the girls 'pon you?" Violet asked threateningly.

"No, Miss Violet. I don' mean it personal. You see when I try to say something sensible what does happen?"

Violet smiled bitterly.

"You jus' call," she turned and said to Ben, "an' Carl come. 'Carl!' you shout, an' he come. When I call him he does wait a good minute before he come. And me, I does call him gentle, 'Carl, Carl.' But he always keep me waiting."

"But," said the beggar, "I don' see why Carl should come when you or Mr Ben call him."

This remark seemed to please Carl, who once more began paying attention to what the beggar was saying.

"He only does come," continued the beggar, "'cause all you does feed him an' give him money. An' the day he don' come! Me, now, I does hold out my Capstan cigarette tin an' when somebody drop something in it I don' lose nothing. What I lose? The person who drop a coin in it can't come back to me an' say, 'Do this. Do that!' I prefer to be a beggar than be dependent on all-you."

Then, out of the blue, like rain falling from a clear sky, Violet got up and went over to Carl.

"Please don' go away,' she said. "You can go an' break in his horse if you like; you see him whenever you want. An'. . . . I goin' pick fair if you still want me to. . . . "

The two girls looked at her as if she had let them down, especially Beryl, who, with her viciousness, could have been her twin sister. But Violet, who had allowed the beggar to say and do as he liked, had all the while been preparing to make her declaration.

Carl was touched. He would never understand townspeople. As for Ben, he wanted nothing better than to see Violet rolling in filth and giving Carl his independence that way. In Carl's place he would not have hesitated to humiliate her. He was dying to shout out, "Accept her offer!" but controlled himself, not wanting to cross those three witches. He sat there pretending to be uninterested, while his gloating heart was on the point of leaping out of his chest. Carl, too confused to give her more than a quick glance, said nothing.

"You goin' stay?" she asked again.

He nodded, then turned to look out of his window. The rain was falling gently, now that the wind had dropped. The window on Carl's side was spattered with fragments that appeared to be a quality of the glass, while on the south wall, where Nora's friends and Ben were sitting, threads of rain sparkled in the flaring light of the street lamp.

The beggar himself sat down, speechless at the turn events had taken.

All the carriages in front of the master's house had left, though the drawing-room was still bright and the night-light in the room on the top storey below the tower burned with a ghostly green paleness.

28

BEN THOUGHT he heard the Stabroek Market clock strike. He lay down, fighting sleep, which had already overtaken him in Violet's house. And that persistent rain, nudging them towards the edge of despair, how long would it last? How ill was the mistress? Would the old woman who sucked the blood of children and the sick come visiting that night? In that weather you could believe anything. He recalled that Violet and her friends were more pleasant when their faces were masked in thick layers of powder and when there was music. They danced as if they were normal women, making men forget the miseries of this life, when their bodies swayed like gardens shimmering in the rain.

He was awakened by a gentle tapping on the floorboards above him. When it began again he remembered his promise to Edna to come upstairs when she tapped. But, overwhelmed by sleep, he promptly dozed off again, vaguely aware of the tapping, which was kept up for a while.

A woman whose face was hidden from him came down the stairs and crossed to the corner where the funnel of the gramophone rose from the small table. She picked up a record which she placed on the turntable before winding up the machine slowly, almost deliberately, in the way reluctant servants turn an ice-cream can. Then, as the music filled the room, the beggar appeared out of the shadows dancing with Beryl, who was looking down at him imperiously. And as they turned Ben saw that he was no longer dancing with her, but with the mistress, now in the prime of her health, as she must have been in the days of her youth. Unlike Beryl, she was smiling at the beggar. He turned away shyly at first, but as she swayed in his arms he thrust forward his head and kissed her on the mouth. Instead of pushing him away she laughed, her head thrown backwards and the swell of her bosom showing under her nightdress. When he kissed her again she responded with a violence that would have done justice to Violet. But Beryl appeared and dragged him away from the mistress, who stood watching them with a forlorn expression, an expression of such anguish, such desperate longing, that Ben thought of those shuttered mansions abandoned by their owners, who had no intention of coming back.

"You not gettin' up?" Ben heard someone say. "Is what wrong to you? The master at table."

Edna was shaking him by the shoulder. He was ashamed to look at her.

"They got a nurse for the mistress, and the master say I mus' introduce you to her before you go. You got to stay home all day in case they want you."

"All right," Ben answered. "I'll get up in a minute."

He waited until she was out of the room before taking stock of his position. Once more he would have to postpone his shower until after he got back from the Public Buildings.

Under the stand-pipe Ben's head felt refreshed, despite the buffeting it had received the night before.

He heard the horse neighing and snorting. When he went to see what was wrong he found Carl stroking the young stallion, which must have caused his old charge to feel jealous.

"I taking it down to the ocean later," he said.

"I don' know if I can come. Edna said the mistress's low and I have to stay in case they need me."

"I'll take him alone," he protested, not realizing how much Ben wanted to accompany him.

"I going come back later," Ben told him.

He went over to the adjoining stable, where the old horse made a song and dance as if a mare were in the vicinity.

Carl did not leave right away, as he inteded. When he had the carriage ready he began cleaning out the stables in a way which meant, "This is not work, just sheer pleasure."

Driving off, Ben cast a swift glance at the house opposite. And who could tell by looking at its exterior that a drama had been enacted there the night before, involving a beggar who slept under the stairs at the back, three women working in a low eating-house, a Macusi from the bush and himself, with a reputation for talking to no one outside the house. All those people jostling one another on the pavement, women with umbrellas, school children, workers going about their business, what might they have been up to in the privacy of their rooms and houses? Their bland expressions and identical gestures were undramatic, masks activated by the impulse to earn their bread. But what of the night, the egoism of love after sunset? They say the sloth sleeps sixteen hours a day because it only needs to feed eight; that cattle sleep less because they need to feed more. But what of man? What of that gap between earning and sleeping, that dangerous

210

lacuna? *Mark my words*, Ben thought, *the town will be our downfall*.

And in his preoccupation the horse allowed him to drive across High Street, towards the square where the molasses sellers sat in all weathers. He turned down Lombard Street and came back down Brickdam.

He thought he saw in the master's face an odd expression as he got out. Had he been reflecting on the consequences of the mistress's death? Anyway, it was a very peculiar expression, neither sweet nor sour, just odd, like the twist of a mouth that was neither a scowl nor a smile.

"Edna will give you your instructions," he said, pulling himself up to his full height, something he had not done for a while.

He knows, Ben decided.

Ben watched him go up the short flight of steps, walk along the open gallery a few steps and then turn into a doorway on the left. He had waited patiently for more than a year, Ben reflected, made concessions, suffered hints and insults at his hands; and now, from the way he put each foot on the steps, from his whole carriage, he knew that he knew. Think of it, there was nothing to prevent him from saying, "You swine! What can you say to the mistress now that she's on her sick bed? Can you very well say, 'You know what I saw on the ladder when you were in New York?' Even if she were to recover it would not be in his interest to tell her, Ben thought, provided he kept his part of the bargain. But no. He preferred to wait, like a jaguar that had cornered its prey. For the first time since Ben knew him he admired him for his cunning and ruthlessness.

On the way back his body began to itch because he had not had his morning shower.

There was a break in the weather and the sun had brought out the road-surfacing workers with their iron-wheeled machine. Surrounded by a thin vapour that spread out evenly before fragmenting and disappearing upwards, it stood, immobile at the roadside, dispensing pitch and sulphurous odours around it. The horse, which usually reacted to any change in the air, trotted through the pitch-smoke, its head lifted in an unusual pose of contentment, as if sensing that it might soon be sharing its duties between the shafts with the newcomer.

After dragging the carriage half-way up the yard — the mistress could not know, and in any case was not in a position to protest — he went upstairs with the cloth he used as a towel and the bit of carbolic

211

soap he had left. Edna barely acknowledged his greeting, but in the middle of his shower she spoke over the partition to him.

"The master write down instructions 'pon a piece of paper. I forget to tell you. I got it here."

"How's the mistress?" Ben called back.

"Bad. They say her sister from New York coming. They send a cable yesterday."

"Foolishness," he said. "She'll arrive too late."

Then he realized the meaning of his words, that he was convinced the mistress would die. But Edna said nothing.

How could he be convinced? Because she had a nurse in attendance and two doctors visiting? How many people over thirty had not been seriously ill at least once and recovered? The sick-room was a part of their lives, with its smell of camphorated oil and bread poultice and the closed door acting as a barrier against the wet eye of a malignant spirit.

"You're vexed with me about last night, but I can explain," Ben called out.

"What you talkin' about?" Edna asked.

"You know what I mean. I couldn't come."

"Come where?"

He ignored her and began covering himself with lather, as much as the inferior soap would permit, taking particular care to smother the whiffy places, the unmentionable parts of the body banned from conversation since the colony was showered with the blessings of Christianity. He scrubbed and caressed, dug, rubbed, polished, massaged, stroked, excavated; and when his body was tingling from his attentions and the water lashing the surface of his skin he felt he could not be less interested in his future than he was at that moment. Then, in the midst of a popular song he was singing, he realized that it was not the water splashing him that made him happy, but the knowledge that Carl was going to take the horse out.

Edna put his coffee and buttered bread in front of him and said, You don' want the list?"

"Well, give me, ne?" Ben said.

The instructions preceding the list of things he was to do confirmed his supicion that the master believed that he might recover the power that had drained from him as a result of his blackmail threat. "The following must be done before you come for me at the Public Buildings . . ." was written in thick letters. He must have kept dipping his

212

pen into the ink-well to maintain the vivid black of those characters. *Well, if he thinks I'm going to relinquish my grip on my new rights he'll have to learn the hard way*, Ben thought. Apart from getting prescriptions filled he would do nothing else; at least not that day. There was no need to buy greenheart or purple-heart planking for the new horse, which was too young to do much damage with his kicking. And why did the carriage need painting so soon after he had done it? And those other petty jobs that were only included on the list to cause him to lose his temper and do something foolish.

"I come back!" he heard Carl call from the yard.

"Come up!" Ben called.

"Naw, man."

"He doesn't want to face a bad-tempered woman like you," Ben said to Edna with a malicious tone. And with that he swallowed the rest of his coffee and left the table.

"You not finishing the bread, then?" Edna asked.

"No."

Carl was waiting at the foot of the stairs with the new horse.

"I put him away," he said, referring to the old one.

Carl never used the word "it" when speaking of animals, whether reptiles, birds or mammals, while Ben called the horse "it" or "him" indifferently.

"I put away the carriage too," Carl declared, smiling as Ben never saw him smile before.

"I'm coming after all," Ben told him. "We should take the old horse too. If this one sees him go in the water he'd follow."

And so he went back to the stable to bring out the other horse again. When Carl had put the saddle on him and equipped him with the reins which he had left on the floor of his room they took the road to the sea.

The young horse became restless when it smelt the salt-laden wind; but Carl patted its neck and waited for Ben to overtake him.

At the approach of one of the new motor-cars Carl turned off the road on to the path that led to the Parade Ground, only leading the animal back to the highway when the vehicle had passed.

A flock of blackbirds had descended on a field adjoining the road. Beyond the barracks from which the music of the Militia brass band was coming, the fan-like crowns of coconut trees were strung up in a row. Ben recalled the night before, the sky covered with clouds like a web of matted hair, and below the slime from long rains. But already

213

the mud had caked under the pale sun and the birds were foraging before the rains returned.

While Ben walked ahead of Carl he imagined he had gone to see Mabel, but could only prowl around the yard, for fear of being obliged to confess that he was unable to keep his promise if the mistress died. Many lamps were lit in the room and there were the voices of company. He was certain that she had boasted to her mother and boxer brother and the neighbours that he was coming back for good, as she had done to Tina. The neighbours, who could not have failed to embarrass her with questions about her absent husband, must have been more than a little interested. He imagined an outcry, followed by prolonged laughter, and looked through the window to see her brother taking off his shirt. Then, posing in the manner of a weight-lifter about to be photographed, he flexed his muscles for the benefit of the company. At that point Ben stormed out of the yard, wishing for the day when Mabel's brother would lie flat on the canvas on a warm night in front of a crowd who would howl him down with delight. He prayed for his humiliation and his death.

"Turn left," Carl said, as they reached the Sea-Wall road.

The horse's head thrust forward with every step, and its wrinkled neck was half-covered by its mane, which now parted under the force of the sea breeze.

Once they were over the wall Ben mounted the old horse and ambled along on the wet sand where, from time to time, the waves came dying at its hooves. He looked round and saw that Carl was leading the foal towards the left to get its hooves accustomed to the water.

"Go out more," he called out in his calm voice.

Ben's horse was to be an example to the foal.

Ben veered left and was soon splashing the water underfoot. Behind him he could hear the sharp sound of displaced water and wondered whether the foal was alarmed.

"A'right, go straight out," Carl said.

Soon Ben's horse was walking in about nine inches of water. Suddenly there was a crash, and looking round, he saw that Carl had mounted the foal, which reared upwards in its attempt to throw him; but he kept it on course for the deeper water, where it headed despite itself, making spectacular evolutions on its hind legs.

"Keep going!" Carl shouted to him.

Ben's horse liked nothing better, and in a couple of minutes he was

214

waist-high in water. Carl was nearly abreast of him, urging the foal out to sea until it ceased to struggle. He changed course and came swimming eastwards, and the young horse, with nostrils flaring and protruding eyes, was filled with terror. But it came by, bearing a triumphant Carl on its back. Ben watched them drawing away in the swell where there was no boat, no other man or animal save the gulls floating on their sea above, under a wan morning sky. Suddenly Ben was in the throes of a boundless joy and glimpsed the futility of trying to judge Carl's personality from his conversation or his behaviour in the company of people so different from himself.

He headed for the sand once more, wondering how the young horse would react when he was out of the water. Carl was evidently trying to tire him out, for he kept him in the swell; and when at last they turned towards the shore Ben goaded the horse into a trot to meet them. The young horse was so exhausted that it hung its head as it freed itself from the salt water and only continued walking because Carl was determined to show it that he was its master.

The two horses walked at a dead-slow pace, the old one behind the foal. Carl was erect on his mount, his wet clothes sticking to his brown body. The dun-coloured sand stretched as far as the eye could see, broken here and there by mangrove and courida bushes whose shadows trailed behind them in the mid-morning. Ben was calm.

29

HE WAS late. The master was already home and had told Edna that he wanted to see Ben as soon as he returned.

Jumping the stairs ahead of Edna, Ben found him eating at table.

"You did not get the prescription," he said in the careful, sharp voice he used when he wanted to smother Ben with his authority.

Then, as Ben was about to defend himself, he declared, "In fact none of the things I asked you to do were done, by the look of things. Were you drinking, visiting your numerous family, or simply whiling the time away?"

"I'm sorry about the prescription," Ben answered. "It completely slipped my mind. I've been breaking the foal in with Carl."

"Are you aware that the mistress is dangerously ill? That the house will be full by sunset? Can you once in your life show a sense of responsibility which seems to be foreign to your nature? Had it not been for Edna the mistress would not have had the medicine and you might have faced a serious charge if she had taken a turn for the worse. . . . "

"If—"

"Don't interrupt! Do the jobs I have listed on the note, in your own interest. That's all. I think we understand one another very well. I'm sure you're praying for the mistress's recovery as I am."

Ben was not even angry. Had it not been for Carl he would have been overcome by the oppression of shame and tempted into some hasty action. But he left the dining-room with a humility that must have surprised his employer.

The midday meal — a bowl of split-peas soup with cow-heel in it — was already on the table, and Ben guessed that Edna wanted to make amends for her behaviour earlier in the day.

"Carl and I broke in the horse," he told her.

"Where?" she asked promptly.

"In the sea."

She was scrubbing an iron pot in the aluminium-lined sink, which jutted out beyond the kitchen wall into the open.

"I din' know you could break a horse in there."

And they got into a deep conversation, to his relief and hers as well. Her white teeth smiled as she turned away, half-cocking her ear to listen to what he was saying.

"The doctor came again this morning?" Ben asked.

"Yes," she answered. "But he so quiet the nurse don' even dare ask him how she is. She never come in this kitchen once and does examine the edge of the plates as if I just start working. Is 'cause of the mistress we all eating split-peas soup. The master say he eating what she eating."

"You've never asked about Carl and Violet?" Ben said, "the woman opposite. Those things don't interest you?"

"They're bad women," she answered. "My brother get cut up by a woman like that. When they get you in they clutches they don' let go. I prefer them to say I playin' great than to got anything to do with them. You ever been over there to see Carl?"

"Yes, more than once."

"I don' want to hear. I don' know 'bout them and I don' want to know 'bout them."

216

"I understand," he said. "You're so careful about everything, yet last night . . . eh?"

"Well, it won't happen again. I did pray afterwards. You don' understand. God was keeping watch over me. That's why you din' come."

"You'll come for the drive, though," he said.

"Yes! I did buy a new hat for it and I know just what I goin' wear. When we goin' go?"

"As soon as the mistress gets better," he promised. "You're the simplest and most beautiful woman I've ever met, Edna."

"Yes? So you say . . . ."

"When I say things like that to a woman I mean it."

"All them newspaper articles you write make you know exactly what to say to women. You don' talk like nobody I ever meet before. You know that in the beginning the master did like you a lot? And you-all fall out so suddenly."

"You should've told me that before," Ben said to her. "It's no use my knowing now."

To think I would've spoiled her life if I had gone upstairs when she knocked! Ben reflected. *Because once a woman has had the visitation between her legs she'll get sick if she doesn't have it at regular intervals. And with her living for her mother it would've been a life of torture and longing.* How little she needed to be content. Her life consisted of a string of obligations. He had already observed that many people could be classed as givers or takers, strongly one or the other. He had met people who had never worked, others who had never married, yet others who had stayed on in their parents' homes as a child, without responsibility, well into their forties. He knew a few takers whom he avoided as if they were stricken with some terrible disease. But it was the first time he had been able to study a giver at close quarters over a length of time; and what disturbed him was the lack of concern she showed for her own position, a lack that had something animal-like about it. Even the speed with which she had forgiven him was animal-like. Perhaps it was this instinctive behaviour that made her recognize Carl as a kindred soul and not worthy of any particular interest, the very quality that took Tina, Violet and himself. Were there not many planes of existence, with their own logic? Planes with their own landscapes of fascination? He felt sorry for Edna, who in turn felt sorry for him on account of his violent reactions to behaviour that left her indifferent. Perhaps Edna was not being devoured by her

217

mother's possessiveness at all, but was playing out a role more profoundly significant than the individual destiny.

Ben had sent in nothing to the papers for more than a month. He knew that if Fatpork were still living there, spreading his diseased body on the back stairs in the twilight, he would not have neglected his journalistic work. His disappearance had changed him. Fatpork, Edna, Violet, even the Frankers had all operated their influences on him, which had not prevented him from clinging to his fancied independence. Yet, without it what was he? He clung to it as desperately as Edna clung to her virginity.

"I'll be busy all day," Ben said to Edna. "If Carl comes I'll be around somewhere. Don't make him go away. If I'm out tell him to wait. I won't be gone for long."

He stepped out on to the landing, where spare bits of harness were hanging over the balustrade stained with bat droppings. The grass in the yard next door had begun to flourish again and was pushing up between the parched stubble, where the servant was hanging out shirts all of one size, hopefully exploiting the gap in the rain. Having been put down so often by Edna she no longer looked over the fence for the chance to practise her servile smile. Ben deliberately waited to catch her eye, and when at last he did he bowed, to which she replied with an open-mouthed, dumb howdyedo and was obliged to wrestle with the arms of a shirt half-hanging on the cord.

There was so much to do he did not know where to begin. In descending the stairs a sudden chill gripped him at the thought that he was not in control of his fate and that some day he might need the support of friends, as old people needed their relations.

People began to arrive from about four-thirty, soon after Mr Schwartz and Ben came back from the Public Buildings. The first were their daughter and her weeping husband. She went up at once to see her mother while he remained to chat with his father-in-law. They spoke in whispers, an unnecessary precaution, considering their distance from the patient. Ben had lit all the lamps, after trimming the wicks for the long vigil.

Edna prayed that it would not rain, so that the polished floor would not be soiled with mud from the guests' shoes. Ben ignored her remark, unable to keep his eyes off the son-in-law, who had broached one of the rum bottles Ben had set out for the men. He and the master made faces as they swallowed the schnapps. Although the master

218

always drank his liquor mixed with ginger-ale, soft drinks were not appropriate on an occasion like this.

Their conversation was soon interrupted by the arrival of a man whose manner marked him out as a Civil Servant. The master gripped his hand, shaking his head dolefully at the same time, and even after being introduced to the liquor table and while examining the different rum labels he kept looking up and shaking his head.

And so they arrived, in the afternoon, more men than women; but in the evening the women made up for it by coming in far greater numbers than the men, until the house was full of relations and friends. The mistress's best friend was the centre of one group of women — the women were in the drawing-room, separated from the men in the gallery by an invisible but distinct barrier. Edna came and went among them carrying sandwiches Ben had helped to make and chocolate she had thinned down out of consideration for her employers. Silently, dutifully, she came and went, with that patient, indefatigable expression that had no parallel in nature.

The hum of voices sounded like a nest of marabuntas about to erupt; and bits of conversation covered every conceivable subject, from the approaching sewage works to the possibility of the banning of masks on the nights of the Christmas season. The men had to help themselves at the rum table and the constant stream of jackets heading for the liquor was an offence to the solemn cocasion.

Then the mistress's brother arrived. Mr Schwartz pretended not to notice, which was not difficult in the press. The sweat had penetrated his jacket, which bore a dark patch at the back. He had come from another function where there had been a lot of people, only setting out for this house when he knew it would be full and he could slip in without attracting attention. Apart from the resemblance, he had nothing else in common with the mistress. Furtive, bat-eared and lanky, he looked the part of a man protected by a sister. Her death would be a blow to him as well.

Ben got to thinking of the gulf separating him from those people. He spoke as well as they did. He came from people who went to church as assiduously as they; but the yawning gap between his way of life and theirs was unbridgeable. When his grandmother was dying her relations wailed so loudly and persistently that the fowls started flapping their wings in the trees and the cocks started crowing as at morning time, and the little birds flew away to the wild courida bushes. That was mourning for you, a deep resonant celebration of relationships, in

219

memory of one once young and green like a ginnip leaf, now come to her lone resting place beyond the terrors of this world. Her coffin was made under her house by a family friend, dedicated with a bottle of rum by her neighbours and lowered into the grave by her relations. Watching the mistress's friends broach bottle after bottle, he saw that they respected nothing except outward appearances and the fetish of skin-tone.

At ten sharp the mistress's best friend came into the kitchen, strands of her hair out of place.

"Edna, kindly take up the spirit stove and a kettle of water," she said. "They've sent for the doctor."

Edna did as she was told

"Is she bad?" Ben asked her.

"I. . . . She can't die," came the answer. "Did you tell her what you saw that day?"

"I did not," he declared, confused at the question, the last thing he expected to be asked.

"She knew," she continued. "She's never been the same since she came back from abroad. O my God!"

She went out on to the back porch, into the damp night air without her shawl. Even on a night like that she was showing the top of her bosom. Small wonder she tumbled into adultery as a fly falls into a bowl of guava stew, Ben thought, with a sort of relish. Sin must have been invented to counter this longing for pleasure. Ben experienced a terrible urge to approach her, as she wept softly on the porch, and rip the scanty blouse from her shoulders and drag her to the stables among the piles of horse dung. She would not have dared talk of what happened, because of the penalty of ostracism. With all his principles, despite his hatred of her for what she had done to the mistress, he was ready to worship her. He could hear her sobbing and imagined the blue shirts billowing on the line next door and the mango blossoms giving off an imperceptible scent for the bees and marauding wasps, and the watery moon of December with its edge gnawed off. *In February when the stars come back to haunt the sky,* Ben thought, *the mistress will probably be dead and this she-dog weeping on the porch will be different, as will all of us, except the horses, which might well be sold off since the need to keep up appearances won't be so pressing. Death's like an explosion, which changes everything within the radius of its force. Certain it is that the mistress is not yet dying. The ghosts know their own and never fail to turn up when a spirit is about to be released from the body. Even in town with all its buildings and other*

220

impediments they come and wait. And those who follow the signs know when someone is about to die and a child is about to be born.

"You'd better come out of the night air, Mistress," Ben told her, wondering as he said so why he had never liked her.

She brushed past him and he wondered why women were not raped more often and at the extraordinary restraint of men. If he had been unable to interest women he was certain he would have become an enthusiastic rapist; he would have dressed for the occasion, in his pumps and gloves and serge suit, like those men who decorated the dance halls and displayed their punctilious behaviour to women they were not even permitted to take home. *How we scatter like million-fish at the slightest noise! Only a vague threat is preventing me from doing violence to her decency and procuring a life-long satisfaction to carry with me to the Georgetown jail with its twin staircases and deep window ledges.*

By dint of thinking about it he had almost come to accept his inevitable fate in case the mistress died.

Edna came downstairs and looked at him as though he were a stranger. "She's dying. And the doctor in' even come yet."

A chill ran through Ben's body and even had he wanted to speak he could not. It was as if a screen separating one side of his life from another had been drawn back to reveal a company of grinning dwarfs.

"Can you make some more chocolate?" the mistress's friend called out from the edge of the dining-room.

"Yes, ma'am," Edna said dutifully.

Before Ben could arrange his thoughts in some order the doctor arrived, carrying his black leather bag. He hurried up the stairs with Mr Schwartz in pursuit, while the line at the rum table dispersed and the company of sympathizers dropped their voices to a whisper. Ben followed Edna among the guests, bearing the spare tray with eight cups of thinned-down chocolate, which he shared out among the men in the gallery. Through the windows he saw the line of carriages which must have spread over and round the corners.

" . . . I'll tell you later," one woman was saying. "She didn't even have the satisfaction of being given a grandchild. I don't know what young people are up to these days. . . . " "I have a horror of funerals," said another woman. And yet another declared, "His six months' leave is coming up and he wants to spend it in Venezuela. The authorities will never permit it."

And so their lives went, reflected Ben, in snatches of futile conversation, never suspecting the despair around them, believing that the

221

islands on which they lived were the extent of the world.

"Look here," one of the men said to him, "can you put some more sugar in this chocolate?"

"You're speaking to me?" Ben asked, fury in his eye.

"Yes. Who else?"

"Somebody's dying and you want sugar in your chocolate?"

"That's what I said."

"The bowl's in the kitchen," Ben told him, pointing in its direction.

"Look here . . . !"

Ben walked away from the man and shared out the rest of the chocolate; and the silence that followed his refusal to comply was greater than the silence that fell on the company on the arrival of the doctor.

Back in the kitchen Ben realized that he was in a sort of daze and he sat down to review the consequences of the news. He was overcome by sleep and put his head down on the table to rest. His thoughts kept pounding his temples.

His grandmother, he recalled, lay ill on a bed in a cluttered room in Skeldon. A teapot was on the floor, its spout broken off. Garments were strewn about the room, among which he saw a frying-pan and unwashed crockery. Then he was on his way to the roadside booth set up by a man who bought meat from the butcher in the afternoon at half-price. The sun was low across the river.

"You still got that bad liver you sell me yesterday?" Ben asked the meat-seller. "Since I eat it I can't walk straight."

"Is what you want today?"

"A pound of mutton."

Back home he found that the room had been mysteriously tidied; and on the floor beside the bed were spilled the yolks of nine eggs.

"Why not go downstairs?" someone asked.

Edna sat down at the table next to him.

"Nearly everyone gone," she said.

"Little ants," he told her. "You know that originally insects were underground animals, that's why they're obsessed with light? Edna, that's one of the great secrets of the world."

"What's wrong with you?" she asked. "Poor woman."

"If I told you about a broken teapot, mutton and yellow. . . . What did I say was the secret of life just now? Can you remember?"

"Ants," she answered, a little frightened of him.

"That's it, ants. Do you know Dutch Guiana owns the whole of the

222

Courantyne river? Not just up to the middle. . . . "

"Well, why. . . . "

"Nobody wears yellow," Ben said. "But they wear black and white and other colours."

"Ben, the mistress dead!"

He stared at her. "When?"

"A hour ago. Her best friend and the master upstairs with her."

"Why you didn't wake me?" he asked.

"I only just come down," she told him. "When I wanted to come down the master ask me to stay. And when I drop to sleep he tell me I could go."

Now that it came to it he was unable to believe what had happened. The croaking of the crapauds from the gutters was the same as yesterday; the gramophone was still in its corner; the staircase turned at the same place and went up to the bedrooms. Her lamp glowed at the foot of the stairs and could not be blown out except by her own breath. She probably did not like him at all, but was too much of a lady to show it. In fact it was a matter of principle with her to protect him from her husband. They would bury her tomorrow, before her body started to reek, probably removing one of the coffins from the ancestral tomb to accommodate her corpse. And in the seventies or eighties her bones would be collected in an urn and stored in a corner to make room for her daughter and weeping son-in-law. Meanwhile her spirit would wander about the house and take up position at one of the front windows after the sun went down. Broken teapots, a pile of garments, just the language of dreams to torment you, and the comfort of red exora shaking in the wind. Would these obsessive pictures pursue him in the wake of an irreparable loss? Would they grow like mosses on the heart? He knew he was unable to face up to the significance of what had happened upstairs because it was not morning, and until she failed to come downstairs and leave the scent of her womanly perfume trailing among the tangle of possessions that made the entrails of a house he would not understand. Now he could only bend his head at the majesty of Death, who treated all women as if they were prostitutes and men like convicts, who walked among them, now disguised as a horse, now as a dog.

They would not be the same after that night. But how he would be different he had no idea, thought Ben. Yet, were they not changed by everything around them, by the rains and the debilitating sun, by little children with their deadly sweet faces, by people to whom you

223

whisper destructive secrets, by the phases of the moon raising tides in the blood, by the beds you lie in, by the judgement of one's children? All those women who received their shattering religious visitations, did they not do so in their late thirties or early forties, in the season of change?

When the time came and he understood what his position in the household was to be he would take advice from his dead grand-mother. But in that night when Death scattered all the guests it was enough to guard the house with Edna, the mistress's best friend and her brother.

30

COCONUTS GROW in clusters. A house with one child is an offence to Death. It was not enough to wake up with the memory of the mistress's death. The timid knocking on the door sounded like Edna's or one of the Franker children; but on Ben's invitation to come in it was the beggar who stepped into the room.

"Good morning, Benjamin," he said. "You remember what Job wife say to her long-suffering husband? 'Curse God and die!' I come with bad news and you got to promise not to hit me if you wan' hear it. You promise? Good, so you promise. Carl gone. He take his hammock an' gone back to Orealla. . . . You in' vex? You see me here poised for flight in case you jump 'pon me, an' you just lie there like comoodie when he swallow bush pig. I wish Violet did take it like you. She did want to go with him down to the train station; and, according to one of the girls, when he refuse she boil hot water and he leave when the water start sizzlin' and she throw it at him, but it wasn' very hot. I don' think she could've burn him, though. She say she goin' play dance music this afternoon when the hearse and the procession move off with you master dead wife, 'cause that's how she feel 'bout you and the people that live in this house. She keep callin' out, 'Beggar man! I want you run some errands for me.' And she vex bad 'cause I wouldn't go up. You see these women? You eat they food one time an' they think they own you. They start being familiar and all that first time respect they did show you gone down the sink like water when you pull the plug out. I'm no beggar-man. You ever see me go up to

224

people house an' beg like them East Indian beggars with they ass hanging out from they dhoti? 'Cause Carl gone back to the Courantyne. . . . But she's always like that. She don' respect men. Them sort o' women does resent whatever you do. If you say 'Howdye' they does answer: 'Is what you want?' If you say nothing they say, 'You in' got manners?' "

Ben let him talk, unwilling to disturb the illusion that he was not yet wide awake.

It was the season of migrating hawks, of the autumn planting of rice, of ghosts crowding the shore for a glimpse of Africa, which loomed on the horizon on certain propitious days, people said. What saddens the heart more than an empty shop or a lamp burning low? wondered Ben. Is the artist, the gambler not infected with the idea of status? Do we not all die unfulfilled? *I used to watch the boats of the shrimp fishermen and torture myself with the thought that if I saw one close up I would die. . . . Before we entered the church my grandmother attended we took off our shoes and laid them on the beaten mud floor of the forecourt. Thoughts, even while we sleep, never leave us in peace.*

"You not listenin', Mr Ben. You in' care that Carl gone? I thought you would've jump out your skin when you hear the news. But they say you never can tell with children an' cab-drivers."

"Take out the capstan tin under my bed and give it to me," Ben told him.

The beggar reached for the tin, which Ben opened. He lifted off the silver paper on the top of the contents and handed him the tin.

"You want them?"

"Is what in the tinin?" the beggar asked.

"Tram-car tickets."

"I can't travel in a tram-car with these clothes, Mr Ben," he protested. "Beggar-man don' ride 'pon trams. . . . "

"I'll lend you a jacket and my old serge trousers."

"I . . . my brother use to borrow clothes," he said, "to go an' dance; an' I use to laugh at him. Well, I din' know you so generous, Mr Ben. I thought you was a man who would see his own mother starve. I know what you do for Carl, but seein' you dress only in black an' with no men friends and with what Violet and the other women say 'bout you I did think. . . . "

"What do they say about me?"

"How I can tell you that when you give me a handful o' tickets, Mr Ben? They say you in' had no mother and that you'd screw anything

225

in sight. Woman or. . . . You better take back you tickets, Mr Ben."

"No. Keep them," Ben told him. "What else they say?"

He scratched his head and made a face. "I been to Brazil one time, you know, Mr Ben. A *flim* company was makin' a flim an' they hire me as cook. We been to the Rupununi an' then we come back to town an' then go by boat to Belem. I thought the Catholics in this country was serious people. But in Brazil! An' the number of black people over there! You know I see them wading into the sea with flowers an' candles because it was the time of the year when they give offering to Eimanja, Goddess of the Sea. Serious people, Mr Ben. One woman fall into a trance and did want to swim to Yoruba-land, and a man give her a cuff in she face. . . . "

"Do they say anything else about me?"

"You want back the tickets?" he asked.

"Keep them. Answer me. What else they say?"

He shook his head.

"You-all think I a bit tetched," said the beggar, "but I'm a sane man. You know that the truth destroy my father house, Mr Ben? He was a man who did believe in tellin' the truth. He cause one disaster after the other until my mother tell him if he din' start telling lies like everybody else she'd leave him. . . . "

"You're going to tell me or not?"

"All right, Mr Ben, but only if you promise not to hit me."

"Yes."

"They say only you son Bamford is your own."

Ben leapt up and grabbed him by the arm as he tried to flee. The beggar collapsed and embraced Ben's feet, in one single action.

"Please, Mr Ben. Please. You did ask me —"

Ben gave him a blow full in the face and he fell back on to the floor. When the cabman came back to throw water over him he found him sitting on the bed, fumbling in his pocket with his left hand while holding his mouth with his right. Then he stretched out a five-dollar bill towards Ben.

"Is Violet give me this to tell you that. She do it out of revenge 'cause Carl gone away. You're not a wise man, Mr Ben. After all, anybody can say anything 'bout anyone. Is the firs' thing you enemies does say 'bout you, even if you in' got children. I jus' tell you something I don' believe an' you buffet my face. You see how dangerous that Violet is? And I tell you! This afternoon she goin' embarrass all o' you when the funeral procession set out. She goin' stand at

226

the door wearin' a black see-through dress. I see it already, all ready an' ironed lying 'pon she bed. . . . Now why you hit me, Mr Ben? I hardly got teeth to lose, that's why I still sitting here. I got the same old teeth-brush from 1909, make out o' real ivory. Why you hit me, Mr Ben? I din' know you was a violent man. . . . Anyway take back your tram-car tickets; I gone off you. An' I don' want your serge trousers neither."

He got up and left, apparently no longer afraid of Ben.

It was a grey, ugly day, as if the world had grown old. Upstairs there was coming and going, yet, in spite of the large number of people assembled for the funeral, more noise penetrated Ben's room from the Frankers' room. He had cleaned out the stables and let the horses out to roam the yard, but, pursued by a feeling of foreboding, he was unable to do any work. Although he knew that the master would not need his own carriage that day he was bothered about the pointed way his services were ignored.

After Ben had taken tea that morning and had a shower following his work in the stables he lingered upstairs, but only Edna spoke to him between her trips to the upper storey and the hundred and one errands that are part of the preparation for a funeral.

The uncertainty of his situation tortured him more than any quarrel he had had with the master in the past. If Carl had not gone away he knew he was capable of facing anything. He was like a man who had lost a limb and stood apart helpless, while others settled his future. He was tempted to do something violent, something sensational, rather than be beset by the waiting. Soon after Carl left Mr Franker came to ask him where their wreath was to be taken and Ben dismissed him with the gruffest of answers. Now he regretted his conduct and would have gladly gone over and spoken to him, but for his pride. He felt like buying sweets for the children and showering his wife with compliments. If only Tina would come! His independence, so important to his way of life, suddenly appeared like a burden he was not permitted to lay down.

A bleak day, windless beneath a scarred sky. True it was: he was friendless, except for his women. He was at war with a man who had begun to toy with him as a cat with a bird fallen from its perch. The thoughts that kept coursing through his mind were far from normal, and the urge to rush upstairs and kiss the hands of the mourners and beg them to help him, to plead for his children, was so pwerful he

227

could have cried out. Then his thoughts were interrupted by a terrible crash from upstairs. Having overcome the shock he realized that the pall-bearers must have just performed the ritual of kicking down the supports on which the coffin rested.

Ben hurried outside to witness the departure, but drew back on catching sight of the whole Franker family assembled beneath the overhanging gallery. He stood back and listened to the ponderous steps of the bearers, followed by the echo of mourners' feet, the downward march of the living dressed in black, white and mauve. When at last it stopped there was a short silence, broken by the sound of harness and the neighing of a horse. At last the procession of carriages and motor-cars moved off in the fading light; and when the last one went by Ben realized that Violet had not made her threatened demonstration. Instead the windows of the house opposite were closed in deference to custom.

Ben, like the Frankers, stood gazing at the street in expectation of some remarkable occurrence.

Back in his room he was overcome by such a desolate aloneness, he lay on the edge of the bed staring at the yard, the grazing horses, the weeds that throttled the plants, so carefully tended by Carl not so long ago.

Ben had the curious feeling that if he fell asleep he would never wake up and he fought to keep his senses. Later he recalled being overwhelmed by images from his childhood, a half-alive bird being devoured by sweat bees under the afternoon sun, skirts billowing on a line and the mysterious flight of Canje pheasants above a stretch of riverside vegetation.

After the funeral Mr Schwartz went back home to receive the condolences of his close friends who came in carriages. There were no women. His son-in-law, who looked after the drinks, left only when the last guest had gone. Now Mr Schwartz sat alone in the gallery. He could not help thinking of all the money he had spent on the funeral and on entertaining his guests, who, for two days, had been coming and going throughout the afternoon and evening. At first there was no grief, only a feeling of bewilderment; now he would have to face the day-to-day problems which until then he had considered to be his wife's province. While she was away in New York the knowledge that she would be back caused him to see all these wifely duties as irritants to be delegated to Edna and his wife's best friend. Now he could hardly believe that he was to be permanently responsible for dispensing money to Edna, or for enquiring into the quality of laundry.

It was only at the thought of going upstairs and not finding his wife lying in the bed they had shared for more than twenty years that he was afflicted by the first pang of grief. He reflected that if she had lived until the following year the possibility of her dying young would have been much smaller, since by then the sewage system would have been laid throughout the town. According to the doctors the death rate was bound to fall dramatically. Suddenly he was overwhelmed by an intense hatred for everyone alive. What was Edna, except a servant? Yet she was bursting with health. His wife's fingernails were always very well groomed, for she abhorred dirt; but Edna, from the very nature of her work, could only wash her hands before she ate. And that beggar opposite, who lived partly on the pavement and partly under a staircase, was set fair to live to be a hundred if appearances were anything to go by. Something was not right with the world when beggars and the poor in general could throng Regent Street on Saturday night in pursuit of pleasure, and his wife, one of the most elegant women in Georgetown, should lie down and stop breathing. When they became seriously ill they were obliged to stay in the paupers' ward of the General Hospital. She on the other hand could pick and choose her hospital and ward. He detested all those in good health, all those who dressed well, the children who would be going to buy sweets the next day or nuts at the nut-seller stalls, and all the cripples who dragged themselves from relation to relation in quest of sustenance. How could he go to church and kneel alone, when his secret thoughts turned to the slaughter of whole congregations? He had accepted his parents' death — he was in his thirties when they were both carried away at an interval of three years — with fortitude, having told himself that death was inevitable. In his wife's case death seemed infinitely stupid and wasteful. It was true that their only child had grown up and that, from Nature's standpoint, his wife had outlived her usefulness — so he would have agreed had he been reflecting on someone else's bereavement; but his stoicism had deserted him and in its place were images he would not have cared to admit to anyone. Why should he be expected to display a morality that Nature disregarded?

His desire to avenge himself on humanity was so strong he refused to enter into contention with his conscience; and if he were not afraid of the string of East Indian beggars who came regularly for their alms

229

he would dismiss them summarily. The obvious target of the violent reaction to his bereavement was Ben. There was reason enough to detest Ben, but now he could attribute to him much more than ingratitude and insolence; he could actually lay at Ben's door his wife's death, by a quirk of projection Mr Schwarz would not even have cared to defend. Ben had reduced him in his wife's estimation, he was certain, and somehow her death must be connected with him!

All Mr Schwartz's confusion, his bewilderment and grief now flowed into one channel and would be directed to his cabman in an effort to overwhelm him. The poor *must* know their place and Ben's fate would serve as a lesson to all those who took charity for granted and regarded equality as a right.

Fortified by his resolution Mr Schwartz went upstairs, took away the mattress from the bed in the guest room and hoisted it up the stairs to the tower, where he went to bed for the night after changing into his long night-shirt.

As Ben expected, the master sent Edna down to say he wanted to see him upstairs next morning at nine o'clock. When he went up at five minutes to nine, as Edna had advised, he found her in the kitchen. She looked as fresh as she always did and appeared to feel no distress at the mistress's passing. She had just returned from market and the contents of her basket were spread out on the kitchen table: the meat, the coreilla, bolonjay, cassava, sweet potatoes and tania. Her home-made cotton frock was modestly buttoned up to the top, like her mind, secure from risks.

Ben was tempted to confess his unease at the imminent meeting with the master. But what was she? Just ears and eyes and hands. She would be the last to believe she was an individual, separate from her mother and her employer, whose death would make of her a swimmer without a shore.

He stepped into the dining-room and saw the master at once on the further side of the room.

"You're on time," he said. "So you are on time. Hmmmm! You must know how Edna stood by me. . . . Now, what of your threats, Ben?"

"I. . . ."

"Don't interrupt me!" he shrieked, his hands gripping the arms of the bent-wood rocking-chair. "You must know what your position is now. You're an intelligent man, who *writes* for papers, who creates

230

little puddles for small minds to wallow in. Who's ever heard of a Guyanese writer? And a lackey at that! You begin the day cleaning horse dung. . . . All these months of humiliation, obliged to endure my wife's disparaging remarks about you running this house. Even my friends knew . . . but I will rub your nose in the dirt for the rest of your life! You can always go and talk to her in the cemetery, tell her what you saw while you were on your ladder."

"Please allow me to say something, sir. My family didn't do you anything!"

"And you managed to feed them on a much smaller wage, the wage you'll get from now on. It's you who'll suffer in this house, not your family. Starting from tomorrow none of your lady friends is ever to cross the gate of this yard. That goes for your wife as well. You cannot perform your obligations in this house to my satisfaction if women visit you. Furthermore you are to attend evening service on Sundays for the good of your soul; and for the good of your body the drinking place in Rosemary Lane and every other house of vice is out of bounds. The only public place Edna ever visits is the church and her mother's always prevented her from mixing with so-called friends."

"So you think you own me," Ben said quietly.

"I don't bandy words with lackeys. You'll simply do as I tell you. From now on I intend to check all your work, control your every movement."

"You. . . . "

"Get out! . . . Edna!"

Edna came runnning into the gallery.

"This man is not to use the bathroom and his meals must be taken downstairs. When he comes up in the morning for the harness you're not to let him into the kitchen. You understand?"

"Yes. . ." she stammered, evidently frightened by the violent tone of a man she believed to be mild-mannered.

"Listen, Edna," Ben said, angry at her compliant manner. "When he's done with me he'll turn on you."

"Edna is loyal!" the master shouted.

"How much do you pay her?" Ben demanded.

He jumped up and screamed: "Get out!"

Ben grabbed him by his collar and pushed him against the wall, while Edna stood aside, aghast at what was happening before her eyes.

"How much do you pay her, eh? The humiliation *you* suffered.

231

What about me? And my family? What about Edna, who dare not have a man? Are *you* loyal to her? Tell me, you crook, d'you know what grows in your back yard? You tell me. I will drink where I like and bring anyone I like to my room. And as for attending service, what makes you think I'll obey a man who couldn't even control his wife?"

Ben let go of him and he stood, rooted to the spot, not certain what to do.

"Get your tail out of here, Edna. I've got something to say to this man."

Edna stood wringing her hands, not knowing whom to obey.

"Get out, Edna. He won't sack you."

Edna hurried off towards the kitchen. But just as Ben was about to speak he heard someone coming up the stairs. And before Mr Schwartz and he could assume a pose of some dignity the door opened. It was his son-in-law who, from his expression, had guessed that they had been quarrelling.

"I say, is everything all right, Dad?"

"More or less," Mr Schwartz replied, pulling himself together.

And Ben, disgusted at the way things had turned out, stormed out of the gallery down the front stairs.

He walked through the gate into the street where the kiskadees and bicycle bells and voices of children on holiday hung on the air. "What would I have told him?" he wondered. He calmed down, and realized that it must have been a good thing that the son-in-law had arrived when he had. What now? His employer would be ashamed to tell the young man what had transpired; at the same time he would not take the risk of seeing a recurrence of the incident. Ben felt he had to speak to someone he trusted. Tina was on day duty and the last person he wanted to see was the mother of his children, because he would have to admit that he could not come and live with them after all. A death from a chance sickness, a body gone cold and his whole life had changed. Sooner or later he would have to inform Mabel that he would be giving her the few dollars a week he used to, before he began blackmailing the master.

Ahead, streets instead of ploughed fields of his childhood. Without wanting to he found himself walking towards Mabel's street. What about that young man he saw standing in the background, was he the father of the girls, whom he would lie down in front of a train for? Sperm is sperm. Some aboriginal Indian tribes believed the whole living world drew on a single pool of sperm and that its indiscrimate

232

use would reduce the number of animals available for hunting. Sperm is sperm. Mine and thine. It would take him a hundred years to put into practice the beggar's doctrine of love. No wonder he was capable of dwelling under a staircase. Yet, even he could not exist in town without money. How many people had reached that last outpost of tenderness? There was a terrible secret in his failure to understand Carl, who had returned to Orealla, his clan-womb and a landscape of water and razor grass, to a vanishing horizon beyond the humiliation of wage labour and charitable deeds.

No, he could not go and see his children and their mother. He could only face Tina. Her love had never faltered. It suddenly occurred to him that he might drop in at his mother's friend's and talk of Carl, whom she had taken to from the start. But he gave up the idea at once, knowing full well that she would call over his mother, in the belief that flesh yearned for flesh.

He was less dangerous when he used to lie awake for hours dreaming up insults for the master. Now that he was afraid of him he was capable of wiping him from the face of the earth. His grandmother's last dream was of all the lamps of the world being put out by men with long poles curved at the tips like tendrils, as she lay shivering in a garment secured with press-studs and buttons like metal saucers. They were to have visited so many places: Lake Ituribisi, Morawhanna, where her buffianda relations lived. "All mixed-up," she said, "part Arawak, part Warrau and part African." His grandfather died there. For her, he never grew up, retaining his fondness for sweets to the day he died. *Why was I angry when all was said and done? I have played and lost. The beggar would no doubt say that I should not have played until I was a master of the game. I had studied my opponent and knew the ground thoroughly; but of the game itself I had an insufficient knowledge. Only women weep over their mistakes.*

This view of his plight made it much easier to bear. He turned back and made for the master's house. Somehow he would make his peace with him and try to salvage as much of his pride as possible. Ben passed the cloth stores with their cluttered windows, a group of men moving a piano out of a public dance hall, bare-footed children racing their hoops, judging the distance between vehicles to an inch, the old whose grey hair had turned yellow under the sun and the faceless who might have been dead, but for their gestures; a fruit seller with her mottled mangoes offered him one for tasting in an attempt to entice customers away from the more attractive display of her neighbours.

233

Ben came home, as distraught as when he went off to walk the streets and put some order into his thoughts. He sat down on his bed, his hands still thrust in his pockets. He felt utterly frustrated at the way his altercation with the master had been interrupted. *He'll certainly not remain in the house alone after that*, thought Ben, *and my own position will become intolerable*. He got up abruptly, having decided that there was nothing for it but to try and see the master once more. He could not stand the waiting.

Night had fallen, and to his surprise he found the back door unlocked, which struck him as a curious neglect on the master's part, since he expected him to go to great lengths to keep him out and prevent a repetition of the earlier scene.

The kitchen was in darkness, as were the dining-room, drawing-room and the gallery, whose windows were still open and through which a fresh night breeze was blowing. *So he's put out the lights and gone to bed*, reflected Ben. *And no doubt his fawfee-eyed son-in-law's keeping him company*.

Ben, already at the foot of the stairs, was about to go up, when someone said, "Don't turn round! Dee, put the light on."

While Ben was trying to place the voice, which he thought he recognized, he heard a match being struck. Not knowing how many people there were in the room he remained where he was, aware that having set a trap for him they would not let him get away. The lamp fixed at the foot of the stairs flared, and he saw the sergeant who lived next to the house of forbidden drinking standing before him.

"Sit down!" ordered the sergeant, nodding to two men who were behind him.

They approached Ben, who obeyed, taking his place in an easy chair which stood near the couch. No one spoke for a while until one of the sergeant's assistants asked when *he* was coming down.

"Don't you bother about that!" came the sharp rebuff.

The company remained as silent as before and the only noise penetrating from the outside came from the occasional passage of a vehicle.

The night was humid and Ben, becoming aware of the perspiration on his forehead and in his armpits, wondered whether he was in a cold sweat.

"Ah, here he is," the sergeant was heard to say, relieved that the waiting was at an end.

Mr Schwartz came down the stairs and, ignoring Ben completely,

234

went past him and into the gallery, where he stood looking out of a window into the darkness outside. The circumstances were identical to those in which Ben had met Mr Schwartz for the first time, except for the size of the room and the number of people in attendance. Then his employer ignored Ben completely, as he was doing now, and as then, he stood with his back to him in order to emphasize his authority and to make the cabman as nervous as possible.

Ben sized up the sergeant's assistants and judged them to be serious characters who would do as they were ordered. One was burly, the other slim and exceptionally tall. They were both young men and, from their dress, either unemployed or stevedores who did occasional work and cared little about their clothes. The taller one, who took exception to the way Ben was measuring him from head to foot, would have welcomed the opportunity to knock him about.

Then Mr Schwartz spoke, in the same high-pitched, affected voice he had used at the police station.

"Well, at last. Stand up!"

Ben did as he was told, but Mr Schwartz, angered at the leisurely way in which he had complied with the order shouted, "Sit down!"

The burly assistant, at a signal from his superior, cuffed Ben in the small of his back and the sergeant bellowed, "On the double! Stand! Sit! Stand! Sit! Stand! Sit!"

The speed with which Ben obeyed evidently satisfied the sergeant, who looked over in Mr Schwartz's direction.

"That is power, Ben," said the master quietly, leaving his window and coming over to him.

Ben looked away, but even this gesture was interpreted as insolence.

"Show him the things," the sergeant said to the taller of his assistants, who took a cardboard box from behind a chair and placed it on the ground in front of Ben.

"Is this yours?" asked the sergeant.

"Yes, it's mine."

"How d'you know?"

"From the print on it and holes in the side."

"Good, good," continued the sergeant.

He bent down and lifted the lid covering the contents of the box.

"Have you ever seen this before?" his interrogator continued, pointing to the contents of the box, in which was an assortment of jewellery, bangles, churials and necklaces, all in gold.

"No."

"Then how d'you account for the fact that they were found under your bed?"

Ben turned to look at the master with an unconcealed expression of hatred. He wanted to protest that there was no point defending himself since he was the victim of a conspiracy, but, recalling the blow he had received, said instead, "I have the right to be silent."

"Oh, yes, Ben," the master told him. "Be silent. It is preferable that you are silent. After all that's the sort of advice I've been giving you for some time, but which you prefer to take now it's no use to you."

There was much Mr Schwartz would have liked to say but could not, on account of those present. He wanted to speak of Ben's lecherousness, of his friendship with Edna, an association of which he disapproved; of his insolence, of the blackmail which had gone wrong, and of the hundred and one things that had fired his desire for revenge. Now he was obliged to choose his words carefully, knowing that they were liable to be repeated elsewhere and, in all likelihood, distorted.

When Ben appeared before him Mr Schwartz did not experience the satisfaction he had anticipated. It was not simply the presence of the sergeant and his two assistants that disquieted him. There was something else, something which escaped his discernment. Perhaps the blackmail had worked on his mind for such a long time he could not shrug off the dread of it, simply because it was no longer there. He had sat upstairs in the tower, quivering in anticipation at the thought that his cabman would be dragged before him, that he would have him struck at the slightest display of disrespect, that he would rain insults on him. But, unaccountably, his appetite for revenge had vanished, and in its place was something just as strong, but infinitely less satisfying. He felt like someone who had rushed to the door in the expectation of collecting a long-awaited parcel, only to find standing before him a stranger with threatening features.

In all his reflections Mr Schwartz refused to consider the enormity of the fact that he had framed Ben and that his unease on that account had grown by the hour and now cast a shadow on all he did and said.

"For someone who writes for a newspaper you ought to have learned to take advice by now," Mr Schwartz told Ben, marshalling all the scorn he was capable of in the circumstances. "Like all lackeys you should take advice."

236

He would have liked to say to the sergeant and his helpers that the words were meant for them as well and that he was revolted at the thought of having them as accomplices.

The men around Mr Schwartz were indeed an ill-assorted group. Ben, tall and severe in his black suit, looked like a demented forest ranger who had been deprived of contact with humans for years and was ill at ease in company. The sergeant's assistants, who relished their supervisory role, had their eyes fixed on the cabman, unaware of the contempt in which Mr Schwartz held them. The sergeant was as anxious to have Ben put away as Mr Schwartz was, never having forgiven him for flouting his authority in the house of forbidden drinking. Poised to order him to carry out another series of humiliating orders, he stood over him with clenched fists, the buttons of his well laundered uniform gleaming in the lamplight. Like Mr Schwartz, he was a believer in order at any cost, and in order's companion, sexual continence. But unlike Mr Schwartz he had never been guilty of offending his principles and he was convinced that Ben, with his two wives, with his tolerance of Carl who had consorted with notorious women while in town, was a dangerous example to the other young men of the lower classes. He could not understand what was holding Mr Schwartz back from delivering Ben into his hands. Once they were out of the house he would turn back while his two assistants thrashed the cabman in payment for all those times he had defied him.

Mr Schwartz was seeking an opportunity to dismiss the company, while Ben, unable to contain himself any longer, asked, "Can I say something?"

The burly assistant, who had no personal interest in attacking Ben, was about to throw himself on him when Mr Schwartz shouted:

"Enough! I want him charged, not maimed. Although God knows he deserves it." Then, to Ben he said, "I hope you rot in jail. And remember, if you behave they'll give you all the paper you want for writing. Take him away, Sergeant."

Ben was escorted out of the house by the sergeant and his helpers.

Mr Schwartz turned down the wick of the lamp and watched the flame abate and finally splutter out. While his wife was alive he would place his hand high over the chimney, lowering it gradually until, to feel any warmth from the heated glass, he had to put his fingers against the chimney itself; but now he made straight for the staircase, reflecting on the anticlimax in his meeting with Ben. He felt that in some way his *inferior* cabman had changed him. So many things were hard to admit, let alone to confess: that his wife's death had resurrected his self-esteem, that his protection of Ben from the sergeant's violence was nothing more than the expression of his fear of the wronged servant. Were not his utterances, his opinions and even his unwitting thoughts a core of lies enmeshed in a web of respectability?

31

BEN LAY in prison with two whole years before him. Many things that at one time had appeared to be of the greatest urgency now struck him as being trivial — Violet's boasting or the noisy eruptions from the Frankers' room, for instance — while others of little importance were added to his preoccupations, like the picture of his youngest daughter sleeping on her grandmother's lap. He kept thinking of ways to make Tina happy when he came out, of his health, of paying regular visits to his mother (in truth more of an aunt for the distance that grew between them while he was living with his grandmother in Skeldon). He also decided to give away most of his shoes to whoever would take them, for he was convinced of the futility of possessions he never used.

Nothing pleased him more than Tina's visits and he marked off the days to her coming on a notebook in which he had drawn an elaborate calendar, annotated with riddles written as an exercise while he was at secondary school.

Monday, 2 July: I am soft-pulped, yellow-brown,
With the odour of stale sweat.
I am shunned by adults
Yet children fight to possess me. (*Locust fruit.*)

Tuesday, 3 July: We cause confusion
Insubstantial as the shadows of leaves
We serve as weapons, cutting deep.
But we leave the skin unbroken. (*Lies.*)

Wednesday, 4 July: Speechless house,
Womb of desires,
I only talk when struck. (*A drum.*)

Tina had passed her midwifery exams and had been able to buy herself a bicycle, indispensable for emergency cases, especially late at night when the buses and carriages were no longer running. He listened avidly to her stories of midnight sorties to places such as Lodge and Houston when the streets were deserted and she set out dressed in her uniform to deliver some women whose husband was unprepared.

Once Mabel came to see Ben in the fullness of her beauty. He was so disturbed by her appearance that he could hardly speak. The children were well and would visit him at Tina's when he came out of prison. Ben looked at her steadily, wondering whether he knew her any better than he did her mother or her brother. He could never hate a woman with whom he had had a close association; he was no more capable of hating her than of hating Tina or Edna, for they had at some time contributed to his welfare, thereby leaving a debt at his door.

It never entered his head to enquire whether Violet's disclosure of her infidelity was true, believing that kind of self-torture to be designed for lesser men. And oddly enough he could not discover in himself any hatred for Violet, who had such an abiding dislike for men that she could only be aroused if she were spurned. Were they not all one, like the aboriginal Indian model carved from a cedar trunk and capable of appearing different at different times, as Mabel was different on each occasion he visited her?

"And suppose I came home to you?" Ben asked.

"If you want," she declared with no conviction in her voice.

He recalled what the beggar had once said about loving without the expectation of being loved in return, and as though speaking with his mouth he said:

"I'll be living at Tina's house, but I'll still give you enough money for yourself and the children."

She seemed surprised. "Two years is a long time, Ben. But I does always talk to the children 'bout you."

It was after that visit that he felt a terrible longing for the things he had lost. He began to watch the vultures circling beneath the afternoon sky and called to mind cobwebs and mice and bedsteads, and the fact that prisons were a fairly recent innovation. And he lay down at night, dwelling on these things until he fell asleep to the murmur of failing lamps.

Mabel came again several weeks later and announced that she was about to get married.

"You got to forget about supportin' me and the children. When you come out. . . . *He* won't like it."

"How's Bamford?" Ben asked, deliberately neglecting to ask after his adored girl-children.

"He all right. He look more an' more like you."

How much did my ugliness have to do with my character? Ben wondered, unable to take his eyes off her well-formed body. She was not made to go hungry or to worry about the future or to play a role in the shadow of another woman.

That night as he lay in bed he looked back on Mabel's visit, on the calm way he took the news of her impending marriage, almost certainly to the youth approved of by her brother and mother. He contemplated the featureless prison wall just as he used to stare at the partition of his grandmother's house as he lay abed, when the objects around him would come alive. He now listened to her voice as if she were in the same room, telling a visitor how she dreamed for a whole year that there were train lines running behind her house, on which nothing ever ran. Her mother took her to a healer, who attempted to *build-up* her self-esteem so that she could stand alone. But the dream persisted, so she was put in the care of another healer, who set out to *destroy* her self-esteem, to enable her to forget her separate existence in the interest of her family and others close to her. He recalled how he heard her confiding in a friend that she gave birth to her first child in the cane fields, where the birth pangs seized her during the harvest. She gave birth in a squatting position, surrounded by the lofty cane and the voices of harvesters unaware of her plight. And somehow he imagined that all this had happened to Mabel, that *she* was the object of his reflections, and not his grandmother.

Then he was certain that outside the door of his prison cell were assembled a group of weeping women, all with heads bowed in a gesture of despair. But, held down by a weight which prevented him from investigating, he could only listen to the implacable sobbing. It seemed – he must have been asleep by then – there was a knock on the door; but, hard as he tried, he could not prevail against the weight that held him down. Somehow they managed to enter, two women and a man, their faces hidden behind masks. Suddenly Ben found himself in the middle of the room.

"We've come," one of the women said.

240

"What for? Who're you?"

The man went by him; and Ben could hear him moving the furniture about.

"Come in," the other women said to Ben. "It won't take more than an hour or so."

Ben got up, thinking that what was happening must be natural, since the visitors were behaving as though they were entitled to his co-operation.

"You don't have to stand as in most courts," the same woman continued. "After all, you're not guilty until you're proven to be; not like in those foreign courts where you're guilty until you prove yourself innocent. At least that's what they tell us. Hi, hi, hi! And sit anywhere. I repeat: you're only charged, so you're not a prisoner."

"Charged with what?" Ben asked. "Now look. This is my room—"

The man, who had taken his place behind the table, interrupted: "You're charged with entertaining the belief that you're an individual."

The two women sat down on the chairs which he had drawn up on two sides of the table.

"That's not a crime," Ben protested. "Doesn't everybody believe the same thing?"

"Did you think you were an individual when you were a child?" the taller woman asked.

"I don't know. I wanted my own way. I would've had all the beef at table if I was allowed."

"So would the dog," the same woman said, "but he doesn't think he's an individual."

"He doesn't even think," the smaller woman said.

And they all laughed heartily.

"You see?" said the man. "If this had been the sort of court to call you a 'prisoner', to make you stand in handcuffs, you wouldn't hear laughter, would you? In fact if you want us to go away and come back another time we'll do so."

"No, no. I prefer to get it over with."

"Very well," the man continued. "When you were a child, did you used to stand in front of mirrors?"

"I don't think so," Ben answered.

"Were you vain? Embarrassed? Proud?"

"I don't think so," he said again, having little recollection of his attitude at that period of his life.

241

"I remember," declared the smaller of the two women, "how my brother began walking like my father."

"Is that relevant, sister?" the man asked. "He is charged with believing himself to be an individual, the most dangerous of all crimes. What does it matter if he copies his father or his mother, or even the canary? O my God!"

"I lost my head, Comrade Judge," the woman apologized.

"Were you vain?" he continued, now addressing Ben in a more kindly tone. "No, Ben: you were neither vain nor ambitious. Now from all accounts you spend half of your life reflecting on dangers to your pride. You abandon your lady friend and three children. . . ."

"May I interrupt?" Ben asked, putting his hand up and pretending not to be frightened to death by their presence.

"Interrupt whenever you like," the taller woman said, with a genial smile.

"I did not abandon my family. I was required to live in when I took the job."

'Then why when you began blackmailing your master did you not go and live with your family? He wouldn't have dared stop you."

"I didn't want to push him too far," Ben said.

"A good answer," the short woman put in enthusiastically, and laughed at the pleasure she took in Ben's reply.

The man glared at her.

"Why didn't you take the opportunity to leave his employment?" the man asked. "After all, he forced you to work for him in the beginning when he saved you from the police, and you detested it."

"When I was accustomed to the job," Ben answered, "I didn't want to go anywhere else. At my age it is difficult to find a job."

"What makes you think you're an individual, Ben?" he asked.

"It's so obvious. When I wash, I wash myself, not somebody else. When I eat, it's the same."

"Do you talk Hindi?" he asked.

"No."

"Do you pray to Krishna?"

"No."

"Do you wear a dhoti?"

"No."

"Do you like Chinese music?"

"No."

"Would you feel the same way that an Eskimo feels at the

242

sight of a polar bear?"

"How does he feel?" Ben asked.

"He all but swoons with excitement."

"I wouldn't, no."

"But you love listening to a certain kind of music. You like the taste of tanias and split-peas soup. You feel shame when you're unkind to Edna. The memory of your grandmother is more precious than other men's praise. You still say you're an individual, Ben? You're like the thousands around you. . . ."

And while he was talking Ben was desperately trying to call to mind traits that were unmistakably his.

"You heard about that boy they found living alone?" he pursued relentlessly. "He walked on all fours and grunted like an animal. He tore off the clothes that were put on him. He shit and pissed when he liked and touched whatever and whomever he wanted. That is the condition of the human who does not grow up in society, Ben. You are no individual! If some spark of individuality ever escapes you you have as much chance of catching it as I have of jumping over the Demerara river."

"Very well," Ben said. "But what's wrong with *believing* I'm an individual?"

"You've ever heard of Baku?" the judge continued, ignoring his question. "No? Baku is the little man in the bottle all country people know about. Only last month one destroyed a family in Den Amstel. If you acquire a Baku you have to feed him well and care for him; and in return he'll bring you gold and jewels on being let out at the right time. But if you neglect him, the day he gets out he'll take his revenge and might even dispose of your whole family."

"What's that got to do with the charge?" Ben asked, indignant at the judge's time-wasting.

"Everything, Ben. You see, you're not an individual: you have an individual *in* you; and that is completely different. That individual is Baku, the man in the bottle. It is Baku who introduced the second wave of evil into this world, when man believed he'd conquered the first wave. You're charged with believing you *are* an individual, which is the most dangerous nonsense imaginable. If you understood the difference between what you *are* and what you *have* you would appreciate the women you've trampled on all these years. If you knew how to take care of your Baku you would be invaded with such love that you wouldn't care to worry about the paternity of your children."

243

"Are all my children mine?" Ben asked eagerly.

"All three are yours, Ben. But one is more yours than the others."

The smaller woman burst out laughing, but stopped at once when the judge fixed his masked gaze on her.

"Is any one of them not mine?" Ben insisted.

"The one you don't like is your flesh. Your two girl children you love too much are children of the spirit. You see now how we're betrayed by *mine* and *thine*? Since you love them, they must be yours; and the ugly one, your flesh and blood, belongs to Mabel. No, no, Ben. Why are you so stricken? Baku can teach you a love that goes outwards, a love so complete it is like a garden of perpetual bloom, overrun with flowers of every kind, a love like the power of the moon and the stillness of trees. . . . I must condemn you now, Ben. Please stand."

"One more question," Ben asked.

"Go on."

"Should I have given up Tina and married Mabel?"

"Married? How little you understand! I spoke of treating her right. Which man wants to get married? The large male apes roam about alone, except for the young and the few that choose to set up with females. Why? Ah, that's a long story, Ben. But more crimes have been committed within marriage than without. One night I'll take you with us on our rounds and you'll see for yourself how men hate marriage. And women? They hate it even more, but with the silent fury of the dependent."

"But man isn't an ape," Ben protested timidly.

At this remark the three fell about themselves roaring with laughter. One of the women kept pointing at him while she danced and cavorted in in the most grotesque way.

"Poor Ben," she said at last. "We all dance to a secret drummer. . . . Tell us about your experiences as a burglar."

Ben answered, somehow consoled by her interest: "I used to draw chalk rings on the partition of the room I was burgling."

"Why?" she asked.

"I don't know. But no sooner I entered a room I would take out a piece of chalk I always carried with me and start drawing, drawing."

"Ben," said the man, "Ben, sing us the song your grandmother was fond of singing."

And like a child Ben complied. No sooner had he sung the first line, however, than the judge took a guitar out of his trouser pocket — as if it

244

were a small handkerchief — and handed it to him.

"Its strings are broken," Ben protested mildly.

"Play it, Ben."

No sound came from the instrument, but he sang, none the less:

"Some people likes the chocolate, some people likes the tea,
Some drinks the sugar-watah an' some the lemonade;
But I in' care for for none o' those, the only t'ing fo' me
Is me bowl o' b'iling cawfee in the marning.

I's an ole woman now an' does often punish hard,
But I's had me good days an' I mus' be satisfy;
I can still hold together an' still praise the Lard,
If I only gets me cawfee in the marning.

Sometimes I has it grand with me saltfish an' me fat,
An' the yellow plantain b'iled an' green pepper an' some rice;
But what me mind does give me for, more better than all that
Is me cawfee with a gill-bread in the marning.

With the gunfire I gets up every marning, dry or wet,
So as never to be lated for the work I has to do;
And I gen'lly says me prayers — unless I does fo'get,
But I always drinks me cawfee in the marning."

The women's clapping was interrupted by a peremptory "Silence!"
from the man.

"Do you see, Ben? I can make you mew like a cat, just as I can make
a woman roar like a tiger."

Thereupon he took off his mask with great difficulty and stood up,
flanked by the two masked women.

"You're only the beggar!" Ben shouted out. "Only a beggar!" But
he was powerless to move when he spoke.

"You are condemned to one woman for the rest of your life," the
beggar declared in a loud, resonant voice. Then, with dignity, he
bowed and started to leave.

"Wait!" Ben shouted after him. "What about Grunt-Hoo, the
master?"

"You're not yet up to him, Ben."

"Am I just to give in to him?"

"You gave in to him long ago. But the real enemy is the one with the
weeping eye. I must go now. I have to try a case in the house opposite.
A woman this time."

He bowed and left, accompanied by the women.

Ben was convinced that there was something left undone. Then suddenly he remembered Carl. He should have asked about Carl.

He rushed out and into the passage leading to the street, and was just in time to see one of the two women disappearing into the doorway of the covered staircase of the house opposite. What did it matter? He would only have answered him with riddles. All lies that came from within, Ben thought.

He knew one thing: he would never yield to the master.

32

IT DID did not take Ben long to come to the conclusion that the need for money and an implacable desire to revolt against their condition were the true reasons for his fellow prisoners' incarceration. And, dwelling on the fact that aboriginal Indians never went to jail except for crimes against those who intruded into their territory, that money was for them a useless commodity, and the absence of any régime of their own dispensing punishment made revolt unnecessary, he gained a deeper understanding of his attachment to Carl and the fascination Orealla held for him. Far from despising Violet and her friends he should have recognized them as kindred spirits. Their revolt had been assimilated into their way of life, finding expression in a society of women. If the *men* of the district dismissed them as viragos the only women thinking it proper to use that term were *decent* ones, who made a fetish of order, and the Ednas, who sought refuge in docility.

With all his book learning, Ben reflected, he had taken the path to prison as unconsciously as had the other inmates: his revolt had been directed against a man who was himself a servant and tarnished by a too great concern for his own welfare.

Henceforth, if his life was to be worthwhile, he must begin at the beginning. Orealla was doomed to be trodden into extinction by the horsemen of progress; and Carl, who had no stomach for life in town, was destined to drink from the same bitter cup as his father. The beginning was Georgetown itself with its inequalities, its prison, its avenues of jacaranda and flamboyant, its stretch of river and ocean, its fishing boats laid up in channels along stone jetties, its secret back

246

yards, its sugar wharves, ships sinking below the street at ebb-tide and floating out to sea on flood-tide, its hundred churches bearing the cross of an alien martyr who had taken root in their hearts, and administrative buildings conceived for permanence of an alien rule, its elegant houses inspired in the dream-time of slavery, its stray dogs, said to be descendants of a pair of mongrels escaped from a governor's yard; its beggars deformed by continual stooping and its drummers, who had never lost the art of summoning up the spirits of departed ancestors.

He spoke to Tina of such things and she, in turn, told him of the children she brought into the world from the security of a womb that resembled Carl's Orealla, to which there was no return from the terror and beauty of this world. She always came in her uniform because it reminded him of the one she wore as a girl of sixteen at school, where he remembered her gathering the small children together. Tina, Tina, Tina the barren, who had brought hundreds of children into the world.

So the days passed. And on cloudless nights when the sky flaunted its constellations, Ben sat at the single window of his cell and summoned up memories of horses in a foaming sea, of Carl immobilized in front of a fire, of Tina's mother, of her father who drank nothing without ice. And this life, apart from his work in the prison tailor shop, was like a clotting of hours, capable of destroying the strongest will, until the third month before his release arrived. Then he listened hungrily to everything Tina told him, displaying such a keen interest in life outside that she saved up every impression to share with him. And the day a band passed in the street below, its trombones blaring, he stood with his eyes fixed on the stone walls and knew that his life had changed beyond recognition.

33

IT WAS the third night in succession that Ben had passed in front of the house in Regent Street. The previous night Tina had told him of a dream she had had, which she found so funny she had laughed while relating it. But Ben was so perturbed by her dream that he demanded to hear it in every detail. She had dreamt that, seeing him leaving the house, she asked where he was going. He turned to answer

247

her and she saw that he was wearing lipstick and eye-shadow and that his nails were painted a vivid red. There was nothing more to tell, she insisted; and at once it seemed to her that she had opened a cage from with a serpent crawled, its divided tongue testing the air.

Two nights before that he had made his first excursion past his employer's house, drawn by an urge as vague as it was compelling. Now he had no doubt what had drawn him there: he had to attend to unfinished business on the master's house. He must see him soon! A resolution made in prison to rise above any irresistible urge had restrained him until three nights earlier. And now this dream, as disastrous as anything that had happened to him before then! Why did Tina, of all people, have it? Why not himself? He would have shrugged it off as being unworthy of a moment's reflection. But Tina, who admired his masculinity! He would have rejected a similar dream by Mabel, for she was riddled with jealousy and probably had always wished for his ruin.

The third night, the night following Tina's dream, he could hardly control the hatred for his former employer on setting out from Tina's house. Taking the shortest route to the master's house by way of a muddy alleyway strewn with rubbish, he walked towards the mansion in Regent Street with long quick steps. As he approached the house, he heard someone calling him from the other side of the road.

"Hoo! Hey, Mr Ben! Is me."

His first reaction was to ignore the greeting; but thinking it curious that anyone should address him so familiarly, he glanced across the road and saw the beggar waving vigorously at him. Ben stopped. He looked around him, as though he might be the object of some surveillance, before crossing the road to join the beggar.

"Mr Ben!" the beggar said demonstratively. "So you alive, man: is a long time. Eh, eh! I see you coming round here three nights. I know is Regent Street and if you stand here long enough you going to see everybody sooner and later; but three nights!"

"Your mouth is as strong as ever, beggar man."

"Ah, Mr Ben, you right. But you better let me drop me voice, *because* you friend Violet still living upstairs." The beggar whispered the last few words theatrically. "And, she worse than ever," he continued, "because she in' got nobody to oppose her. Carl gone, you gone. Who else going oppose her? Me? I got more sense than that. Tell me something, Mr Ben. Why if somebody stick a knife in you people does say he bad? And why if you give a beggar four cents people does

248

say you good? When you come to think of it, is funny. When your dog bite a thief-man you don't say he bad; or when . . . . I just don't understand. You understand? And why it make some people sick to hear that people in some countries eat cat?"

"Shut up!" Ben exclaimed.

The beggar said no more, but he got up and hurried behind the stairs under which he lived. Almost at once he came back out with a paper bag which, from its appearance, contained something hard.

"I want to show you something, Mr Ben."

The beggar took out a metal object from the bag and handed it to Ben, who involuntarily took it. It was a revolver, an old firearm which, from its appearance, had not been fired for a very long time.

"Why're you showing me this?" Ben demanded.

"But why you so violent, Mr Ben? I just showing you it. I show a lot of people this gun and they take it and fondle it and say, 'Eh, eh, a revolver! Just like in them Yankee *flims*.' You're the first person who vexed."

A little ashamed, Ben opened the revolver, and, to his surprise, found it was loaded. He spun the chamber to test that it would indeed move and then gave the firearm back to the beggar, who accepted it with a wide grin.

"Look at the tower," he said, nodding towards the mansion across the road.

There was light in the tower, but the rest of the house was in darkness.

"Funny sight, eh?" said the beggar, "A house in darkness, especially a big one like that. . . . You know what you want to do, Mr Ben, and I know what you want to do."

"What do I want to do?" asked Ben, almost mechanically, for a mist had come down on his thoughts, so that he was not even certain what the beggar had been talking about. "What do I want to do, beggar-man?"

"You want to kill him," the beggar answered, malice in his voice.

"Hm! So that's what I want to do," Ben said gravely. "And who is *him*? You?"

The beggar placed the revolver on the ground in front of him.

"Not me," the beggar said. "You know what I talking 'bout. You in' one of these people who you got to teach that one and one make two before you can argue with them. You're sparing with words, but not with logic. Me, I'm not sparing with words, but with logic. I'm instinctive, Mr Ben, like a monkey and snake and thing. I can read people. And I say you want to kill him. The mystery is why you din' do it when you come out o' prison. Two months you wait! And you got to admit you don' like waiting. I bet when you tell somebody you goin' meet them at such an' such a time you does walk off when they don' come. Well, you did wait, but now is time to act. Admit it ne? Teh! Logic? It in' worth my Aunt Sheila bubbies. An' my Aunt Sheila don' got none, she got cavities. Well, logic in' worth my Aunt Sheila cavities."

Ben did not say anything for a while. Then, as if he were acting in a play, he said, "My life is now starting, beggar-man. You are nothing but a lump of shit. You and all the men in this town, because you depend on wage-earning. . . ."

"I not a wage-earner!" the beggar protested.

"You're worse!" Ben put him down. "Infinitely worse. You've got to talk all the time to hide the stink that comes from you. I am free, beggar-man. Since they locked me up I'm free!"

"Let's talk 'bout you, Mr Ben," said the beggar, at last losing his temper. "You think you hate the master and his kind; but I know you admire him, just as you did admire his wife. Oh, I know, 'cause your Edna does talk. You understand Edna as little as you understand me. Let me tell you, Mr Ben, you admire the master. That's why you does talk like him and why you vex 'cause he don' say: 'Ben, you does talk like me, come let me clasp you to my bosom because we're brothers.' If he say so you would weep and fall 'pon him and say, 'I don't hate you, Mr Schwartz, I did never hate you. Forgive me for all them things I do to you, for my insolence and rudeness and thing.' I not telling you nothing you don't know, but just what you won't admit. To tell the truth I don' understand why you in' hit me yet, 'cause you're the most violent man I know. Funny, eh, I never hit nobody in my life, yet I keep this gun for years. Even as a rusty thing it's a beautiful piece of iron, eh? Look at the muzzle, and the butt. A beautiful, rusty thing."

"I'll buy it from you," Ben said abruptly.

The beggar recoiled, as if scandalized, "No, Mr Ben. It's a present. Because, well, because you'll be doing what you going to do for all the beggars in the world, the East Indian beggars who did uproot themselves from a great civilization and end up roaming the streets of a country ten thousand miles away, the beggars like me who not starving, but love guns and all manner of arms, and the others who

250

people expect to be grateful 'cause somebody drop money in they begging bowl."

"I'll give you ten dollars for it," Ben said.

But as the beggar began protesting Ben turned away from him and went off home to fetch the money.

The beggar followed him with a look of utter contempt; and then, when Ben rounded the corner out of sight, he involuntarily cast a glance up at the tower of the master's house which was still lit.

In due course Ben came with two five-dollar bills, but the beggar was no longer on the pavement. He delved into the murky yard and before he had taken three steps heard a rustling on his left. The beggar came out from under the staircase.

"You want to come in, Mr Ben?" he offered. "But you got to pay! Hi hi hi hi. Pay, yes."

"I'm not coming in," Ben answered testily. He gave the beggar the two five-dollar notes, which the latter took.

"I can't thank you enough, Mr Ben," he mocked. "You're a man of your word, honest, punctual and a model of the work force. Do accept my weapon in recognition of your services."

Ben snatched the revolver from him, checked that the bullets had not been taken out and then walked away.

"One thing before you go, Mr Ben. I can't guarantee it goin' work. Instead of 'bang, bang' it might be 'hik, hik', as if it laughing at you."

Ben was already across the road and making for Mr Schwartz's yard, which was in complete darkness. It was eleven o'clock and on that side of the road, where there were only houses, nearly every dwelling was unlit. Mr Schwartz's and the one next door — where the crying child had died — were the only two with a bright light burning. Ben penetrated into the familiar yard and made for the back where the ladder was kept. The horses were unusually quiet, he thought. He was obliged to put down the ladder more than once because of the difficulty of negotiating a way through the bushes which had sprung up since he left. There was no light in his room, nor in the other two at ground level, and he had the curious impression that everything had changed because he was no longer living there.

Ben had no difficulty in getting into the house by the same window through which he had seen Mr Schwartz fanning his lady friend on the bed. He crossed the empty room and opened the door, then, hesitating for a moment at the foot of the staircase leading to the tower, he began climbing it softly, two at a time. Unexpectedly, one of

251

the stairs creaked — he was not familiar with that part of the house.

"Who's it?" came the master's voice.

Ben stood still, expecting him to open the door. But the question was followed by a long silence, and from the undisturbed line of light at the base of the door it seemed to him that the master had not got up. Pulling back the trigger of the pistol he tested the two remaining steps before placing his weight firmly on them. Then, with a sudden resolution, Ben turned the door knob and pushed the door wide open, appearing before Mr Schwartz like a malicious ghost.

The master stared at his old cabman with a look of such bewilderment, all trace of authority vanished from his face. Then, catching sight of the revolver Ben was holding against his thigh, he tried to rise from his chair like an old man who had difficulty in getting up.

"O my God, no! F . . . f. . . ."

But, unable to bring out the words, he could only look at Ben helplessly. Eventually, the tension proved too much for him, for Ben did nothing, made no movement, and under his unflinching gaze Mr Schwartz broke down and started to weep, hunching his shoulders over his knees while he squeezed his head with his pudgy hand. His authority had vanished under the spell of the gun. He recalled how he had said that whatever happened he would feel superior to Ben, even if he were under threat of death. Now nothing was further from his mind. He had become convinced, as his wife lay dying, that following her into the other world would not only be easy but even desirable. Although with the passage of the months life had become more bearable and he envisaged a life of more intense social activity — more frequent visiting, bridge parties, lodge meetings, *bachelor* gatherings he had shunned while his wife was alive — he had convinced himself that he was prepared for death, simply because she was dead. But now that Death was standing before him its old terror had not diminished. He could not even sustain the cabman's gaze or open his mouth to bargain with him. Instead of thoughts senseless, unrelated images presented themselves to his mind: the sight of a washerwoman dissolving blue in water, mute cattle under a blazing sun, the indolent flight of vultures. If only he could open his mouth his life might be saved. *And the spirit and the bride said, "Come."* . . . If only he could repulse these thoughts that kept intruding like insects penetrating into a room through the louvres of closed shutters.

When finally Mr Schwartz was able to look he saw Ben aiming the gun at him, and before he could decide what words were least likely to

252

offend the cabman there was a click of the trigger being pulled. As it suddenly occurred to Mr Schwartz that Ben might have come to test him with an empty pistol the cabman fired again, hitting his former employer in the chest. The master slid off the chair, astonishment in his eye. The cabman fired again and again at point-blank range, and only once more did the pistol fail to go off. But after the first shot the body remained immobile, bleeding visibly from two wounds, in the back and in the chest, from which blood oozed to amplify a widening pool beside him.

Ben threw the weapon down on the floor beside the body and, as he went through the door, was surprised at the silence around him. He had foreseen a commotion, a raising of voices in general alarm.

He departed from the house the way he had come in and left the ladder leaning against the house. And for the first time it occurred to him that he could escape the consequences of a deed done with so much noise. The need to protect himself now dictating all his actions, he hurried out of the yard, head down and hands in his pockets. Then, something he had not foreseen happened. He had expected to be apprehended immediately after the killing, so had not taken the precaution of finding out what the beggar would do. Now the man was calling to him from across the road.

"Mr Ben! Don't run. What you frighten of?"

Ben hurried across the road and seized him by the collar.

"Listen, you beggar-man!" he said, dragging him to his shelter beneath the stairway. "I've just done what you said you knew I'd do. What do you want of me?"

"I want to talk, Mr Ben, only talk! Wanted to know if you still have them tram-car tickets . . . and to talk in general . . . 'bout things."

"What things?" Ben thundered.

"Little things; not big things."

"Well, I can't talk now, beggar-man. But when I've got time I'll come and have our last talk together. Meanwhile don't forget you gave me the gun."

"Mr Ben, it wasn't my gun," the beggar said sheepishly.

"But you said you had it a long time."

"Ah, Mr Ben. I should've say I had my eye on it a long time."

"So you stole it?"

"No . . . is the women upstairs give it to me to give it to you. I did warn you 'bout them."

"You slimy, rat-faced yowaree!"

Ben made as if to strike him, but kept his fist raised in the air. Then, as he was about to warn him to keep quiet, there was a scurrying of feet. Placing his hand on the beggar's mouth Ben whispered into his ear:

"Beggar-man, don't you say one word!"

The footfalls grew into a trampling and a general hue-and-cry.

A woman screamed, "I hear shooting!" from a nearby house and when, finally there were voices crying, "Murder!" Ben decided to try and escape through the back yards behind the beggar's lair.

He found an alleyway fenced with zinc sheets in his way and doubled back, intending to hide under the beggar's rags if the lair was searched. But two policemen and three men helping in the search were already in the yard and caught sight of him. Recalling the need for dignity in a situation from which there was no escape, he walked towards the five men and gave himself up.

Epilogue

BEN SAID nothing throughout his trial. He knew that there must be crowds standing in the streets that flanked the Law Courts because he himself had *attended* murder trials in the past. Not once had Tina appeared in court; but during a recess on the fifth day a policeman handed him a note from her in which she stated that the trial was too painful to endure, but that she was praying for him, since she knew that at heart he was a good man. The policeman took the note back from him, folded it and placed it in the pocket of his tunic.

From the third day on, he was incapable of concentrating on what was being said and he had to be nudged awake on several occasions. Then on the sixth day, when it was clear that the trial was coming to an end, his attentiveness was once more aroused.

When the verdict of guilty was pronounced, Ben experienced a curious indifference, as though his last stay in jail had irreparably damaged his instinct of self-preservation. At that time on leaving jail, the abiding impression had been of a profound change in his life. Now he knew the extent of the change and indeed its peculiar quality. He had become indifferent to death, that was all. What he had told the beggar in anger was true: prison had indeed made him free and all the

254

paraphernalia of human justice — the obscenity of the sentence "to hang by the neck until you are dead", the judges in their extravagantly absurd robes — had made not the slightest impression on him. Even the offer entitling him to say something before judgment was passed Ben being rejected as being an invitation to indulge his vanity.

As the police van made its last journey from the Law Courts to the jail, he imagined voices of children in the failing afternoon light, sunset on the Courantyne river, and Orealla, where Carl and his clan were holding out against the advance of an alien way of life, with the dead hand of its justice sanctifying a crime of appalling enormity.